Letters from the Crimea

LETTERS FROM THE CRIMEA

Writing Home, A Dundee Doctor

Edited by Douglas Hill

Introduction by Trevor Royle

Dundee University Press

First published in Great Britain in 2010 by
Dundee University Press
University of Dundee · Dundee DD1 4HN
http://www.dup.dundee.ac.uk/

ISBN: 978 1 84586 094 3

Dr David Greig's biography on pages VII–VIII
is by Dr Graham Lowe, Tayside Medical History Museum,
Ninewells Hospital and Medical School

British Library Cataloguing-in-Publication Data
A catalogue record for this book is available on request
from the British Library

Designed by Dalrymple
Typeset in Caslon and Sentinel
Printed and bound in Britain by
Bell & Bain Ltd, Glasgow

Contents

___

Preface

The following collection of letters was uncovered during a house clearance in the city of Dundee. The leather-bound volume, dated 1906, contained typed copies of letters from a young Dundee surgeon who had volunteered to serve with the British Army during the Crimean War 1854–1856. They were sent to his family (his mother, father and sister Anne), who lived in the centre of Dundee.

The main chapters of the book provide us with a first-hand account of life in the Crimea.

There is very little about the much-documented chaos of the campaign and the misery in the British Military Hospital in Constantinople. Instead we have this young doctor's first-hand, mostly cheerful, sometimes angry, sometimes sad, almost blasé, comments on events that took place around him.

Much has been written about Florence Nightingale's role in the Crimean War as the 'Lady with the Lamp', and Appendix 2 compares and contrasts Miss Nightingale's well-documented writings with Dr Greig's observations over the same period.

Douglas Hill

The Characters & Their Roles in the Story

DR DAVID GREIG

These letters are written by Dr David Greig (1832–1890), the son of a surgeon and chemist. As a boy David would assist his father in the preparation of medicines. Later, as a young house visitor to Dundee Royal Infirmary, he gave valuable help during the cholera epidemic of 1849. He graduated from Edinburgh in 1853, and subsequently held the post there of Demonstrator in Anatomy. In 1854 he was selected, with other distinguished Edinburgh graduates, by Professors James Syme and James Young Simpson to go to the British Military Hospital at Scutari in Constantinople (today's Istanbul) to look after soldiers serving in the Crimean War. He narrowly escaped the fate of two companions, who died of typhus. He was later sent to the front, and served as surgeon to the 17th Regiment of Foot until the end of the Crimean War, receiving the Turkish and Crimean medals.

On return to Dundee he established a large medical practice and was appointed Surgeon (and later Consulting Surgeon) at Dundee Royal Infirmary. He was a kindly doctor, noted for his common sense and being open and honest with his patients. In contrast to his early enthusiasm for mixing medicines, he was to use these sparingly in later years, believing in nature as the best restorer of health – the *vis medicatrix naturæ*. However, when it came to serious illness or emergency, there were few who were more skilled or resourceful.

Dr Greig was influential in movements concerning the welfare and honour of Dundee, and took a special interest in the management of the children's asylum. He was one of the first surgeons of the newly formed 1st Forfarshire Rifle Volunteers, and was instrumental in founding the Forfarshire Medical Association in 1859, for which he was the first Secretary.

Dr Greig returned to Scutari in 1890, where many of these letters were written, but developed typhoid fever, from which he died. The Crimea, which stole the life of so many of his friends in his youth, eventually took his too. He is buried in the Western Cemetery in Dundee.

His son, Dr David Middleton Greig, was a surgeon at Dundee Royal

Infirmary from 1892 to 1920. He became an internationally recognised authority on the pathology of bone and built up an extensive collection of specimens including more than 200 skulls, which had been left to bleach in the sun on the roof of his house. These were all destined for the Museum of the Royal College of Surgeons of Edinburgh, at which the third generation Dr Greig worked as Conservator for 15 years.

JAMES YOUNG SIMPSON

James Young Simpson (1811–1870) was one of the professors who originally selected and sponsored Dr Greig and two other doctors to go to the Crimean War. He was a pioneering Scottish doctor, famous for discovering the anaesthetic properties of chloroform on 16 November 1847. In his original sponsorship letter, Professor Simpson advised the young surgeons to contact him if they encountered any difficulties, which he could use his influence to remove.

FLORENCE NIGHTINGALE

Florence Nightingale (1820–1910) devoted her life to nursing and campaigning for better health care and sanitation. She helped to select and then led a team of nurses caring for thousands of soldiers during the Crimean War. She and her team of nurses worked at the Military Hospital in Scutari alongside Dr Greig. It was her work there that created the legend of the 'Lady with the Lamp' and motivated her to continue her work in later years as a health reformer, writer and campaigner.

Although she had her critics and even enemies, to the British public she was a legend. The *Illustrated London News* February 1855 stated:

> She is a ministering angel without any exaggeration in these hospitals, and as her slender form glides quietly along each corridor, every poor fellow's face softens with gratitude at the sight of her. When all the medical officers have retired for the night and silence and darkness have settled down upon the miles of prostrate sick she may be abroad alone, with a little lamp in her hand, making her solitary rounds.

DR ALEXANDER STRUTHERS

Dr Struthers was one of the three doctors (Greig, Struthers and Johnston) originally sponsored by Simpson; he travelled to Scutari with Dr Greig. A detailed report from Struthers to Simpson contained stinging criticism of

Florence Nightingale and her nursing methods. He criticised the nurses for 'spying' on the medical staff, noting times when patients' dressings were changed and complaining to the superintendent physician instead of going directly to the surgeon involved. All this, Struthers stated, was totally against the co-operation, mutual respect and the honour of the medical officers, and would, he suggested, lead to inevitable conflict unless the nurses were reduced to their true position of nurses only.

He complained of Miss Nightingale keeping a man waiting on the operating table for fifteen minutes because she had insisted on being present at all operations and could not be found. He mentioned other indiscretions by Miss Nightingale such as 'attending the dressings of a soldier whose person was exposed in such a way that must have caused embarrassment to the man'. He also highlighted the fact that, although there were three nurses in his ward, he was only allowed to speak to one of them: 'Could there be anything, or any malarrangement, more intensely ridiculous and absurd?' Unfortunately his letter was discussed with a colleague in London and, somehow, the details fell into the hands of Sydney Herbert (1810–1861), who was serving in the War Office during the Crimean War and was a confidante of Miss Nightingale. As the letter got around it was rumoured that it contained malicious remarks about Miss Nightingale's religious beliefs. As further rumours spread, Simpson decided to send Struthers' letter direct to Herbert.

Herbert's reply, dated 15 December 1854, is on record stating that:

> the allusions which it contain regarding Miss Nightingale differ considerably from those which had been shown to me previous. Her description and judgements in all these matters is well documented in correspondence from other eminent medical men and they say her exertions have been invaluable. But I must say that anyone who knows what the young surgeons or medical students are as a Body must allow that too great caution cannot be exercised when young men and young women are thrown together amid such scenes in a Male hospital. Struthers is hardly prepared for the kind of work in which he is engaged. His letter was a private one and except by his authority no one has a right to treat it as a public or official statement – and the sooner the matter is now forgotten, I think the better.

Struthers died on 20 January 1855. Official reports show that Struthers had contracted typhoid and developed a parotid abscess which developed into a fatal septicemia. He had been a house surgeon in the Edinburgh Royal Infirmary with the surgeon Joseph Lister (1827–1912) before volunteering for war service, and had been regarded as a gifted and accomplished student. Heron Watson, an Edinburgh contemporary, wrote of Struthers that he overworked himself trying to do justice to his patients, sitting up until three in the morning and rising whenever he was called for, as he thought it was what was expected.

Greig wrote to Struthers' brother John with details of Alexander's last days 'at his death bed were three of his greatest friends… and at his funeral there were many more who had learned to appreciate his worth since he came out here. Miss Nightingale I may state was exceedingly kind to him during his illness and latterly visited him often and did all she could for him.' Whether Miss Nightingale knew of the letters from Struthers, which had caused such a furore in medical circles back home, is unknown.

DR JOHNSTON

Dr Johnston was one of the three doctors originally sponsored by Simpson. Greig and Struthers later distanced themselves from Johnston as they found him difficult to get on with. In the letters there are very few references to Dr Johnston but it appears he was invalided home in 1856; he died later that year in Portsmouth.

DR MASON

Dr Mason cared for Struthers during his illness and was a close friend of Dr Greig. He sent for Greig when Struthers was in his last few days. However, Dr Mason died of 'the fever' on 8 February 1855.

MARY STANLEY

Mary Stanley assisted in the original selection process of Florence Nightingale's party of nurses who were sent to care for soldiers during the Crimean War. As the success and fame of Miss Nightingale spread there was a public demand for more nurses to be sent to Scutari. Mary Stanley organised a party of Irish nurses under the authority of their Mother Superior. However, they agreed to serve only on condition that they remained independent of the army and Miss Nightingale. Miss Nightingale felt her authority was being undermined. She was so incensed she even threatened to resign and return home. Miss Stanley's party arrived at Scutari to a cold reception and were informed that there was no accommodation for them. They were eventually stationed at Therapia for a few weeks before ending up at the hospital in Koulali (Kulalie). It was at Koulali that Dr Greig was treated for a bout of cholera by Miss Stanley, who kindly wrote to Greig's parents about his condition and progress.

DR HALL

Dr Hall was the Principal Medical Officer throughout the campaign in the Crimea.

He cautioned surgeons against the use of chloroform as an anaesthetic: '... better to hear a man bawl lustily, than to see him sink silently into his grave'. His directive was seen by many of the other doctors and surgeons as evidence that he was out of touch with contemporary developments. When his infamous quote was reported in the British press he was openly criticised by James Syme, Professor of Surgery in Edinburgh, among others. Hall had many detractors who seized upon his comment as evidence not only of his out-dated knowledge but more damagingly of his heartlessness.

RICHARD JAMES MACKENZIE

Richard James Mackenzie volunteered to be a surgeon in the Crimea before taking up the post of chair of Military Surgery in Edinburgh. Unfortunately he too died of cholera, and the vacancy in Edinburgh was taken by Joseph Lister, who was to embark on a remarkable career as a pioneer of anaesthesia and the antiseptic system that revolutionised surgery.

DR NICHOLAS O'CONNOR

Dr O'Connor was a Staff Surgeon at Scutari and the only recorded suicide by a doctor during the campaign of the Crimean War. He died in Balaclava on 7 June 1856. He served at the Barrack Hospital with Greig in 1854 and later became Principal Medical Officer of Koulali Hospital. It was reported that he was overworked and under stress, which is confirmed by Greig's observation in his letters.

Introduction

Of all the wars fought by the British during the Victorian period the Crimean War was the most singular, being neither a colonial policing action nor a 'little war' fought for territorial gain. While British diplomatic imperatives were at stake it would be fair to say that it was an unwanted war in that national interests played second fiddle to the need to curb threatened Russian expansionism in the Balkans and to prop up the Ottoman Empire in the Black Sea geo-strategic region. It was also a watershed in world history: it broke the long peace of 1815 when Napoleon Bonaparte was finally defeated and then it set in train the succession of European wars and power struggles which dominated the second half of the nineteenth century. One other factor makes the war pertinent: by failing to solve the Eastern Question – the consequences of the slow and chaotic decline of Ottoman influence – it paved the way for the greater conflagration of 1914. Basically, what happened was this: through a series of diplomatic blunders and compromises Britain, France and the Ottoman Empire drifted into war with Russia during the spring and summer of 1854 because they failed to take sufficient steps to halt a growing confrontation between Moscow and Constantinople (today Istanbul) in the Black Sea and the adjoining Balkans.

The immediate reasons for the outbreak of war were faintly absurd. For some years there had been a religious dispute between the monks of the Greek Orthodox Church and the Roman Catholic Church over possession of the Church of the Nativity and the Church of the Holy Sepulchre in Jerusalem. Russia supported the former and France the latter and although the argument was written off as 'a church wardens' quarrel' it escalated when the Ottoman Sultan Abd-el-Mejid adjudicated in favour of France and Tsar Nicholas I despatched a diplomatic mission to Constantinople. This failed, thanks mainly to the intervention of the British ambassador at the Porte, Lord Stratford de Redcliffe, and as a result Russia deployed its army in the Ottoman principalities of Moldavia and Wallachia. As tensions escalated, both Britain and France sent naval forces into the Black Sea while further attempts were made to find a diplomatic solution. When these failed, Russia forced the issue by destroying an Ottoman fleet at Sinope on 30 November 1853, and the stage was set for war. Russia refused to withdraw from the Principalities; Britain and France declared war and made preparations to send an expeditionary force into the region.

From an operational point of view the ensuing conflict was Janus-like. It was rooted in black powder warfare, its tactics were little different from those employed during the earlier Napoleonic Wars, the fronts were small and manageable and senior commanders fought in the same claustrophobic front lines as their men, just as the Duke of Wellington and his generals had done. And yet, as with every war, it produced and utilised technological innovations which would be further developed and which helped to change the shape of modern warfare. For the first time, thanks to the development of the telegraph, senior commanders could keep in contact with the politicians in London (this proved to be a mixed blessing), the killing power of infantry weapons such as the Minié rifle was increased, railways became part of the battlefield, war reporters appeared in the front lines and the trench systems outside Sevastopol looked forward to the battlefields of the Western Front. Although the war only last two years, and the main set-piece battles of the Alma, Balaklava, Inkerman and Sevastopol were relatively small-scale affairs, the casualty rates were high. Britain alone lost 19,584 men but of those only 10 per cent were killed during the actual fighting; the rest succumbed to illness and disease, largely because of the primitive sanitary and nursing conditions in the military hospitals.

Figures of that kind helped to give the Crimean War a ghastly reputation for incompetence, and in time the conflict became one of the bad jokes of British history. It encompassed maladministration on a grand scale and human suffering without parallel; disaster marched hand-in-hand with heroism, and to exacerbate those failings the entire conflict was witnessed by watching war correspondents who recorded the litany of disaster to their readerships at home. As a result the people of Britain and France were appalled by the suffering of the men who were dying in their name in the far-off Crimean peninsula and, for the first time, showed that they cared. Small wonder that in time the war was written off as a catalogue of blunders redeemed by basic human courage and a refusal of the respective armies to surrender to overwhelming odds. In no other country did that feeling put down deeper roots than in Britain where the war quickly became a shorthand for disasters such as the Charge of the Light Brigade or the redemption offered by Florence Nightingale, the Lady with the Lamp, and her gallant band of nurses. In the first instance muddled orders led to heroic deaths during the Battle of Balaklava, while in the second nurses intervened to save lives in the face of official indifference.

Neither the cavalry charge nor the nursing sisters account for the whole story but both episodes have stuck, especially the role played by the medical services, which is generally (but wrongly) represented as a succession of blunders eventually put right by the application of some sound common-sense through the intervention of Florence Nightingale. That oft-told tale has a curiously British ring, of an enterprise begun badly and ending tolerably; of initial bumbling, ineptitude and disavowal made good by the sacrifice of doctors and nurses who found themselves frequently out of their depth but rallied to introduce much needed improvements. Dr David Greig from Dundee was one of that number. An Edinburgh graduate, he volunteered for service on the Crimean front in October 1854 when it was clear that the war was going to take longer than expected and that more medical staff would be needed to succour the wounded. Greig does not say explicitly why he volunteered but it is not difficult to understand his reasoning. Not only was he a young and recently graduated surgeon who would have been seeking employment in any case, but exposure to casualties in an active military hospital would have given him the kind of experience that he could never have gained in civilian life. Other inducements included sponsorship of £50 from the Royal College of Surgeons in Edinburgh (worth £5,070 today) as well as a smart military-style uniform complete with sword, an outfit which Greig declared to be 'quite stunning'.

It was also an apposite moment to be travelling to the 'seat of war' (as the Crimean battlefront was invariably described). Having landed in Crimea in September the British and their French allies had fought the inconclusive Battle of the Alma as a preparatory move to seize the port of Balaklava and then to lay siege to the Russian garrison in the huge fortress of Sevastopol. As a result of those operations casualties began mounting, and concerns began to be expressed in the British press about the paucity of decent military equipment and the low standard of medical provision for the sick and the wounded. When the readers of *The Times* opened their copies on the morning of 12 October 1854 they received an unwelcome surprise. Following the euphoria of the victory on the Alama the newspaper's latest report made disturbing reading; here was the first stark evidence of the revolting conditions faced by the sick and wounded at the British Military Hospital at Scutari, which stood on the opposite side of the Bosphorus from Constantinople. While wounds and death are unavoidable in war, and while it is true that British soldiers were not immune to suffering and official indifference, in the past they had died like flies far from the public gaze. Now thanks to the presence of reporters such as Thomas Chenery, who wrote the original report in *The Times*, and, later, William Howard Russell, who pioneered war reporting from the front lines, the people of Britain could understand what was being done in their names.

Within days money started flowing in from the newspaper's anxious readers. One letter in particular stood out and helped to change the course of the war by forcing the government to take action. Written by Sir Robert Peel, a son of a former prime minister of the same name, it proposed the creation of a privately funded scheme to assist sick and injured soldiers and from there it was a short step to the well-known introduction of Florence Nightingale and her band of 38 nursing sisters. It helped that the Secretary at War, Sidney Herbert, was a family friend of the Nightingales and he was able to convince colleagues that the army sent to the Crimea lacked the medical services needed for a lengthy campaign against a major European power. Within days of intense activity Nightingale had accepted the post of Superintendent of the Female Nursing Establishment of the English General Hospitals in Turkey and, equipped with a preliminary budget of £1,000 (worth £101,000 today), Nightingale and her party left for Constantinople on board the steamer *Vectis* and arrived after a storm-ridden passage on 4 November. With them had gone Dr Greig who noted: 'What a cargo we have, it consists of 18 doctors, from Inspectors downwards to Assist. Surgeons, 48 nurses, – black and white nuns included, Protestants, Episcopalians, and Catholics, Sisters of Mercy, Nurses from the London hospital, etc.'

It did not take the new arrivals long to get the measure of the conditions within the hospital at Scutari. Nightingale's first letter home described in graphic detail the appalling state of the building with its blocked privies, filthy floors and overcrowded conditions in rooms and corridors in which, Nightingale noted, 'we have not an average of three limbs per man'. However, the main problem at Scutari was not so much the filth, squalor, vermin and lack of basic hygiene – these were commonplace in many civilian hospitals in Britain – it was the complete absence of any recognisable management.

The army's medical department was a law unto itself and composed of doctors who thought they knew best. Working ineffectually alongside them the Commissariat and Purveyor's departments were responsible for feeding and clothing the sick and wounded but so labyrinthine were the administrations and so timorous the civilian officials who manned them that their obsession with red tape and correct protocols produced an atmosphere of indecision and paralysis. Worse, they combined to hinder Nightingale and her nurses: the doctors because they resented their presence, and the administrators because the nurses were an unwanted intrusion in an already complicated world. Later, Nightingale would say of them: 'Their heads are so flattened between the boards of Army discipline that they remain old children all their lives.'

To be fair to the doctors who had accompanied the expeditionary force, the army's medical department was badly funded and it possessed little influence amongst the high command. While surgeons were considered socially superior to the personnel in the Commissariat and Purveyor's departments they were still not considered 'gentlemen'. This sounds anti-quated and wrong-headed but at the time it counted. For evidence, here are the words of the patrician Lord Palmerston, prime minister in 1855, who said of the situation that the greatest deficiencies in the Crimea had been caused not by people of his social standing but 'where there were persons belonging to other classes of the community – in the medical department, the Commissariat department, the transport service, which have not been filled by the aristocracy or gentry'.

The lack of respect meant that many doctors were touchily jealous of their positions and fearful of any outside interference which might put them in a bad light. Coming from a female colleague only made it worse. Their medical opinions were also typical of an age when a civilian doctor could happily admit that he almost died of blood poisoning after under-going an operation in a hospital whose walls were 'reeking with germs'. And in a notably heartless profession – mid-Victorian doctors were not noted for the delicacy of their sensibilities – military surgeons were reckoned to be a particularly callous bunch. Dr John Hall, the Inspector-General of the medical staff in the Crimea, warned his colleagues not to use anaesthetics while operating because 'however barbarous it might appear, the smart of the knife is a powerful stimulant; and it is better to hear a man bawl lustily, than to see him sink slowly into the grave'.

Much of that began to change with the arrival of the nurses, not just because they helped to introduce improvements in the regime but through *The Times* Nightingale had access to much-needed funds. With that money she was able to buy the scrubbing brushes and soap to clean up the wards, the food which aided recuperation and the boilers which introduced a hygienic laundry service. As she described herself in a letter to Herbert, she had become 'a kind of General Dealer in socks, shorts, knives and forks, wooden spoons, tine baths, table forms, cabbages and carrots, operating tables, towels and soap, small tooth combs, precipitate for destroying lice, scissors, bed pans and stump pillow'. It would take time and effort to right the wrongs at Scutari but despite all the best intentions the death rate continued to escalate. By January 1855, 10 per cent of the entire army had died from disease, mainly cholera, and in the following month the death rate was 52 per cent of all casualties. It was only after the intervention of a government-sponsored sanitary commission in March that it was discovered that Scutari was built on top of a cesspool which allowed sewage to spill into the drinking water.

It was against that background that Greig recorded his impressions of the war for his family back at home in Dundee. With him went two other doctors, Struthers and Johnson, and they all reported at regular intervals to their sponsor Dr James Young Simpson, the distinguished doctor who had already discovered the anaesthetic properties of chloroform. Inevitably Florence Nightingale and the work carried out by her nurses became a topic for discussion. The press reports from the battlefront generated a good deal of publicity and in his comments Dr Greig was remarkably prescient and even-handed about the growing fame of the nursing sisters and their indomitable leader. On the voyage to Constantinople, Nightingale's presence on the *Vectis* had meant nothing to him but he soon came into contact with her and his observations are instructive. While he admired her industry he was also aware of her failings, namely that she had a tendency to be something of a bossy-boots (witness the letter in which he describes a 'farce' in which a legless soldier asked for brandy and water to ease his thirst).

Unlike Struthers, who wrote official letters of complaint about Nightingale before he succumbed to typhoid in January 1855, Greig kept his thoughts largely to himself and, overall, the picture he paints of Scutari steers clear of the familiar descriptions of the fetid conditions. Instead he concentrated on his impressions of life in a remote and frequently exotic part of the world. He was after all a young man whose previous experiences had been confined to Dundee and Edinburgh yet here he was bearing witness to great events and he was determined that his family should share in them, at one point telling them: 'I suppose it is no use trying to escape giving you a full, true, particular account. I must just tax your patience and tell you all, at least I will try to do so.' As a result a later generation has been left with a plain yet fact-filled account of a war that impinged itself on the nation's conscience and in so doing excited many different emotions. Reading Greig's letters is also to be reminded that war is not just about battles, honour and glory but also about other less heroic things such as loyalty, comradeship, occasional boredom and the exhilaration of being alive.

Greig was one of the lucky veterans who survived the war and who returned to his native country to pick up again the strands of his life and career. In his case, following a long and protracted journey by sea, he made his way back to Dundee to work as a surgeon in the city's Royal Infirmary. Having received the queen's commission as an officer he retained his links with the army by joining the local rifle volunteers and seems to have led a happy enough life. Shortly before his death at the early age of 58 he made a return visit to the scenes of his youth and wrote a short epilogue in which he noted that, while so much had changed, it was also true that much remained the same. By then, 1890, the Crimean War had long ended and in the aftermath attempts had been made to count the cost, not just in financial outlay, but also in human terms.

Efforts were also made to learn from the experience although these were fairly desultory and the expected sweeping reforms of the army and its support services failed to materialise. That we know so much about the war and its manifold problems is due to many factors, the growing power of the press and also the huge number of personal accounts which appeared in the years that followed. From private soldier to general, the soldiers wrote down their memories or published letters and diaries, sometimes writing with a passion that surprised the Victorian reading public. Over a century and a half later, young Dr David Greig has fallen in beside them to join that honourable company of soldier-writers.

Trevor Royle
Edinburgh and Angus, Autumn 2010

CHAPTER I

Departure from Great Britain

David Greig was born in 1832 in Dundee, where he lived with his family in Union Street. Immediately after graduating from the Royal College of Surgeons in Edinburgh he volunteered to serve as an Assistant Surgeon in the Crimean War. Together with two of his Edinburgh colleagues, Dr Struthers and Dr Johnston, he made his way across land to Marseilles in the south of France to catch a ship, the *Vectis*, sailing to Constantinople on 27 November 1854. He was 22 years old. Each of the doctors received a small sum of money from the Edinburgh College of Surgeons in the way of sponsorship to cover their immediate expenses.

The first letter reproduced here was from Sir James Young Simpson (1811–1870), sent to the three doctors shortly before their departure. Simpson is best known for his work as the pioneer of anaesthesia (there is a statue of him in Princes Street, Edinburgh). His request that chloroform be taken out and used extensively as an anaesthetic was all but ignored and not mentioned again in any correspondence from Dr Greig. In the 1850s medical doctors were not noted for their gentle bedside manner or sensitivity towards their patients. Military surgeons were reckoned to be a particularly callous bunch. Dr John Hall, who commanded the army's medical staff on the Crimean front, warned his colleagues not to use anaesthetics while operating because 'however barbarous it might appear, the smart knife is a powerful stimulant; and it is better to hear a man bawl lustily, than to see him sink silently into the grave'.

My dear Doctors,

I do not know if this will reach you in time but I hope it will. Dr Storror will have already told you that Lord Blantyre has written about the money and I suppose you already have each received £50. The House Surgeon of the Aberdeen Hospital is to hand the remainder, but I do not know his address. I have telegraphed to Aberdeen for it. Be so kind as remember that Lord Blantyre's conditions simply are:

1st. That you write me now and again how matters go on with you and with the sick.

2nd. That if his brother The Hon. Mr Stuart, an officer in the Rifles, is wounded or ill you will be kind enough to pay him special attention.

3rd. Lord B's sister, Lady Seafield, has a brother-in-law an officer in the 42nd – Mr Grant – for whom he and his sister would lain claim on equal privilege. Further he wishes the chloroform taken out. They have not had nearly enough there and I hope you will be able to show them how to use it properly. Please let me ask of you as a personal favour to make any incidental enquiries you can about the existence of leprosy (Elephantiosis Graecorum) in Turkey or the Crimea. Have they anywhere hospitals for lepers and what symptoms does the disease principally exhibit? I have heard that one of the Greek Islands is used as a Lagar house or Leper House. Dr Storrar has £10 over, if you can lay it out on Heman's Mediterranean (a model military medical work) or Pringle's Campaigners, or Larrey's works, please be so kind as expend it on these or other books as a present from me. And if you take notes of the diseases – as well as the wounds etc., – I do not see why one of you or all of you, conjointly or separately, should not write an excellent essay (a Medico-chirurgical) on the campaign. I feel sure that three more energetic and more able medical officers will not be found in the East. One point more, pray do take care of your health and do not unnecessarily overwork or expose yourselves. If you meet with any difficulties that Lord Blantyre, Mr Lyme, or I can remove, write at once to me. May God Bless and prosper you and believe me that no one feels more deeply interested in your prosperity, success, and well-being, than Yours ever faithfully,

J Simpson

To Drs Greig, Johnston, and Struthers.

My dear Father,

We have at length got fairly appointed as Staff Assistant to the Army in the East. Yesterday we were examined at the War Offices, and today were told we had all passed 'an optinic examination', and to hold ourselves in readiness to start at twelve hours notice. We do not expect to be off before Wednesday however, but we cannot say, and whenever we do get notice I will write you immediately and also from on board the transport if possible. It is fairly settled we do not go overland so I must prepare for a few days of horrid sickness in the Bay of Biscay. The Director General told us we would in all likelihood be stationed at Scutari, but if Sebastopol was taken we would winter there with the troops, we cannot tell until we get out. I have got my uniform, sword etc., all right. We take as little uniform as we can and are to wear it as seldom as possible. We must have it however and it is quite stunning. If I am here on Sabbath I shall be at the meeting and hope to see some friends, at least I shall pay good attention to the sermon for it may be a while before I hear another.

The Director General seems to think a great deal of us and told us he would expect good things from us in Turkey. No fear of us when we have Argyle and Blantyre at our backs. Dr Struthers of Leith has got your address and may send you a read of his brother's letters when out and so may Johnston's friends, if so you may send them mine. Their addresses are Dr Struthers, 22 Charlotte Street, Leith, and Mr Johnston, Fish-curers, Montrose. If Anne will write immediately I will get the letters before starting, if I am off it will be sent back. Please address 21 Great James Street, Bedford Row.

PRESSING. ARMY AND ORDNANCE, MEDICAL DEPARTMENT
21ST OCTOBER 1854

Sir

I request you will immediately proceed overland to Marseilles, so as to arrive there on the 25th inst for the purpose of embarking for Turkey on board the 'Vectis'.
I have the honour to be, Sir,
You obnt servt., Andrew Smith
Director General, Dr Greig, Act. Asst. Surgeon.

My dear Father,

   We have at last been ordered off and have to be at Marseilles on
the 26th inst to embark on board the 'Vectis' for Turkey. We leave this
tomorrow evening and proceed to Paris, and thence to Marseilles. I do
not know if we will have troops on board, if we have any, they will in
all likelihood be French. I was very much obliged to Mother and Anne
for their kind letters, and also to Mr McIntosh for the introduction
to Farriday, but I am sorry it will be out of my power to present it. I
intended to have gone to the meeting today but cannot get the least idea
where it is.

   We have not got any money from Simpson yet but will get some
tomorrow. If I have more than I want I will give it to John Alexander
who will send it to you. I have left my diploma with him and I may
leave some of my things which he will get forwarded to you sometime
or other. Dr Struthers is much better but both he and I are disappointed
we are not sent by Gibraltar, however, that can't be helped, and I doubt
not we will be sick enough without having so long a voyage. I will try if I
have time to write you from Paris and Marseilles but I will not promise.
We have not got our outfit, complete uniform, and all. I am sorry I
cannot oblige Anne at present but if I get an opportunity in Turkey I
will have a likeness taken – I am sure she would not know me – I do not
think I have much more to tell you. I have seen very little of London,
not even St Paul's, but I will have a while in it when I come back. The
Agent who draws my pay and manages all my army business here is Mr
Grigor & Coy., 17 Charles Street, St James Square. You had better keep
his address as it may be useful afterwards. And now I may say 'Farewell
England for a while'.

My dear Father,

Here I am at last on the shores of the Mediterranean and propose
to give you a slight account of my journey from London to this place.
Before leaving London each of us was paid £50 besides a present of
£10 amongst us from Simpson himself with a great many good wishes
and good advice. The time spent in London was passed on the whole
very pleasantly, more especially as I stayed nearly the whole time with
John Alexander. I saw a good many sights and got an idea of the City
if nothing more. We left London on Monday evening in company
with 11 other surgeons all bound for Turkey: the most of them young
fellows – but three or four – of considerable standing in the Service.
From London we went direct to Dover, it was quite dark and nothing
was to be seen the whole way. When we reached Dover we found the
packet steamer waiting for us. Before starting the sailors said we were
very lucky in getting so calm a night and I of course began to flatter
myself I would keep up and enjoy the sail. The white hills of Dover were
faintly seen, and as they became fainter and fainter I of course thought
of home and when I would see England again. The ship began to pitch,
I soon got dead sick, and my last sight of the hills of 'Merry England'
was anything but a pleasant one. We reached Calais about two in the
morning and we immediately bundled into the Custom Houses and
had to show our passports. When this important ceremony was gone
through we got some coffee, which of course I being sick could not take,
and then started in the train for Paris. As officers in the army we always
travel first class and do so at a reduced rate. We were very comfortable,
more especially in the French carriages which are far better than the
English ones. As soon as I got fairly seated I fell asleep and never awoke
till 6 in the morning, it was broad daylight and I may say I then got
my first view of La Belle France. We were passing through a beautiful
country somewhat like England, richly wooded, irregular fields, and
every now and then a vineyard. What amused me most was the number
of windmills going at a great rate in all directions, as if the safety of
the country depended on them alone. We rattled on at a glorious rate
and entered Paris about 9 o'clock. Immediately on entering Paris one is
struck with the sight of so many soldiers. At the station when we landed,
soldiers took our tickets, soldiers took our luggage, soldiers told us where

to go, in fact you could not turn but a soldier met you. Our luggage was taken from us and when we saw it again there was a soldier mounted guard over every bundle, who demanded the key and proceeded to open it in the coolest manner possible. We objected and I explained to the fellow in broken French that if he emptied my trunk I would never get it packed again as it had taken me a week to get it into its present state. I told him I was going thro' France and not to stay in it, and that I was a British Officer. This latter had the desired effect and after a short conversation we got clear off without any examination. We drove to the Hotel de Normandie, washed ourselves, hired a guide and set off to see the sights of Paris. Some parts of Paris are very bad, but in general it is a beautiful city, fine buildings and gardens all open to the public. We visited the Galleries, Palais Royal, Louvre, Luxembourg, Notre Dame, St Sulpice, Boulevards, Champs Elysees, etc. etc. Of the first we only saw the exterior. The Luxembourg is full of paintings and statues the like I never saw before. Notre Dame is a splendid old Cathedral, which I suppose would hold all the churches in Dundee put together. Saint Sulpice is of smaller size but equally beautiful, and here we saw a Roman Catholic Service for the dead. When we entered the Church it was a while before we could make out what was the row, fourteen priests all chanting the Latin service, and two trombones going as hard as two good pair of lungs could make them, this continued for about half an hour, the body was carried out and we followed to see something else. The Boulevard and Champs Elysees are very beautiful and here we saw the large glass building erected for the exhibition of next year. Besides these we also visited the Hotel Dieu, the largest and oldest hospital in Paris – it can hold 900 patients. It is a curious old house, large wards and very close, and ill ventilated. It was very curious how well we got on with the language, talk about murdering the Queen's English, we certainly did so to the Emperor's French. However we got on very well, in fact, we were surprised at ourselves, we stammered, spluttered, laughed and often fairly broke down. The French, were not in the least put out, they laughed too, and then we generally came to an understanding some way or other. The food we have got in France is just so so, you never know what you are eating; the only good thing is the coffee and the bread. At dinner you get about six or eight courses, some good and others bad, and very suspicious looking, a plate of green stuff with a greasy taste will be set before you, you ask the name and you are just as wise as ever, if you are hungry you will try to eat it, if you are not you will of course refuse to have anything to do with it. A bottle of wine is set down always to every diet, but what beastly stuff it is, sour beer is a treat to it but nobody knows what that is here. We left Paris at 8 in the evening. I was very much fatigued, and falling asleep I never awoke until we were near Dijon, it was near 7 o'clock and we were running thro' a fine country covered with vines. We got to Lyons about 10 and getting on board a large punt-like steamer we had a sail of 120 miles down the Rhone. It was a beautiful day and the scenery was very fine, just like the Tay near Perth, the whole way, every now and then we passed a curious looking village, an old castle, bridges etc., etc. Anon we caught a glimpse of the mighty Alps covered with snow. Along the whole of the river the banks are steep and as usual covered with vines which seem to grow anyway in the country. We reached Vincennes at 3pm and got into the train reaching this place about 11pm. We were all as tired and sore as possible, and after getting some supper we were very glad to turn into bed, the first we have seen in since Sabbath night in London. It is awful work travelling especially at the rate we are going, the distance can be easily understood by reference to the map, but the fatigue can only be known by one who has gone over the ground. This town is one of the best we have seen in France it is somewhat like Dundee, but larger, has splendid docks, and of course strongly fortified. We hired a boat and went out to the 'Vectis' this forenoon. She is a splendid steamer belonging to the Peninsular and Oriental Co. and carries the mails from this to Malta, Constantinople and Egypt. We sail tomorrow at 2 o'clock, will call for about six hours at Malta, and then go direct to Constantinople. I am in good health and Dr Struthers is now quite well, we are as jolly as possible, so many of us together and besides we have about two dozen nurses, or rather Sisters of Mercy, from London, going out with us to Scutari. I will not write again until I am in Turkey. I might write from Malta but I suspect I will be busy getting a view of the Island and will not find time. I hope you got the money in safety from Mr Alexander and did with it as I requested you. I will not expect a letter from any of you until I write again and give you my address, where that may be I have not the slightest idea. I hope you are all well. Give my love to Mother, Aunt, and Anne, also cousins, Dr Crockett, Stuart Lithgow, etc., etc.

PS. When I write Mother's name it puts me in mind she told me to tell her about the ladies I saw. The French ladies are a curious looking set, very neat and clean, but not at all pretty, in fact I have not seen a good looking lady since I left London. They all wear caps and look very smart. At Lyons and the interior of France they wear straw hats with very broad brims, very like the celebrated seaside hats of Punch. It is more difficult to understand them talking than the men, for they talk so fast and look astonished when you do not understand them. It is very curious to hear the little children talking French, this strikes an Englishman more than anything else. What a beautiful climate we have here, today it was as hot as a day in June with you and yet there was a coolness I never felt before. If I am not sick I will enjoy the Mediterranean voyage very much. Everything seems so beautiful, soft, and ethereal. Farewell at present.

My dear Anne,

As we will be here for an hour I take the opportunity of sending you a few lines. We left Marseilles on the afternoon of the 27th inst, very glad I can assure you to escape from France, and especially glad to find a good English dinner ready when we came on board. When leaving we had a nice view of the south coast of France, and as the sun was setting at the time I can assure you it was most beautiful. I was quite sure I would get sick but was very fortunate in being disappointed. I kept up very well all that night and next day. We have had moonlight every night, and moonlight in the Mediterranean is what I can't describe. The evenings are quite pleasant and warm, while the day is uncomfortably hot. We sailed along the coast of France all evening and next morning when I awoke we were scudding along the West coast of Corsica. We had a distant view of Ujacia the birthplace of Napoleon – and Bonafacio. About midday we passed thro' the straits of Bonafacio, wilder and more beautiful scenery I never saw, it is very like the Kyles of Bute but far grander. I sat at the prow of the vessel, it was rough, I did not get sick, and I must say I enjoyed myself. The coasts of Sardinia and Corsica are very rough and rock bound like the east coast of Scotland. Every now and then we saw a small village on the coast but we were not near enough to see any of the people. Sleeping on board ship is very curious, you no sooner get into bed than you have the feeling of being thrown out. The ship is constantly creaking and you think she is going to pieces. It is not at all comfortable. You are glad to fall asleep and dream of home. When I rose yesterday morning there was as the sailors say 'a great swell on', and the result was I immediately got sick for the first time, I got on deck however and remained on all day better and worse. It was Sabbath but no bells to tell you so. I often looked at my watch and thought where you all would be at the time. No land was to be seen in the morning, during the afternoon we passed a rocky island, St Marguereta, and then the coast of Sicily looking smooth and beautifully white. As I was very sick all day I tumbled into bed soon and was very glad to fall asleep, for the ship was pitching and no mistake. I was awoke this morning with the idea the ship was blown to pieces but was very glad to find it was only a signal gun to announce our arrival to the Maltese. I dressed and six of us hiring a boat went on shore and saw the town of Valetta and church built by the Knights of St John. The interior of the church is the most beautiful piece of coloured ornamental architecture I ever saw. Service was going on but that did not matter, our guide took us close to the priest and told us about the things in the church, and the priest going on with his service. The town of Valetta is strongly fortified, the fortification having been built by the Knights of old. It is a pretty but irregular place. The men are an ugly blackguard looking set, and the women far worse. Every person seems to be a beggar and we were followed by a crowd of women and children through the whole town. I was only about an hour on shore, and we all felt so giddy we were glad to get on board again. We are now taking in coal and will proceed straight to Constantinople, which we expect to reach on the 4th November. I hope you are all very well. I am very anxious to hear from you, please write me a long letter, give me all the news, and nonsense going, and address to Dr Greig, Asst. Surgeon, British Army in Turkey. That I believe will find me out wherever I am, and when I reach Turkey will write you again and give you my correct address. Mother was asking about the watch, I have been so confused myself and everybody seems to keep their own time here, that I cannot tell how it has been going. I hope Father is quite well, also Mother, Aunt and cousins. Remember me to Mrs Hill, Mr and Mrs Sandeman, Mr McIntosh, Don, Crichton, Baxter, and all enquiring friends. I am in first rate health, and if the sickness keeps off I will enjoy my sail among the 'Isles of Greece'. We are now about to start, excuse this awful letter, I am sure I do not know what I have written but I know anything is better than nothing and I hope you will think so too.

Tell Dr Pirie how sorry I was, having to go off without seeing him, it would have pleased me so much. I will not promise to write him from Turkey but he must write to me. Dr Struthers is much better. He and I stick together. Johnston is not such a good fellow. We take our way and let him take his. Adieu…

My dear Father,

As we are all anxious to get our letters posted immediately on our arrival at Constantinople I write you from this place. I wrote Anne from Malta and I hope she received the letter, and contents in safety. I gave her an account of my voyage to Malta and my opinions of that Island. If she got the letter it is all right, if not, I will give her the accounts over again at some other time. I had anticipated a beautiful sail among the 'sunny shores of the Grecian Isles' but soon after leaving Malta a gale sprang up and I may say has continued ever since. Towards evening I of course got sick and after taking as good a view of the storm as I could, I went quietly off to bed where I lay till next afternoon (Tuesday). I was not sick but felt that if I got up I was sure to turn so. After getting some dinner I got on deck, the moon as bright as usual, and a beautiful sight it was. The waves were going as high as the paddle boxes and rolling along with a white crest in the moonlight. I had enough to do to keep my feet but managed it very well for some hours. The gale was rather worse next day. I got into my old state and kept my bed for the first time the whole day. One would think that a hardship but I can assure you it was a pleasure. I only felt sick when I attempted to rise and I lay quite comfortably in bed and heard all that was going on. No one could go on deck as the waves were washing it every minute; everybody seemed tired of the voyage, and next day even more so than this. Towards night it became worse, it was difficult to lay in bed, and the ship creaked so much that everyone had an idea it was going to pieces. About 12pm when all was dark a sea struck her and smashed a lot of crockery in the steward's pantry; you never saw such a row, everybody was slightly excited and highly amused. Another followed and I had a good laugh at Dr Struthers being pitched out of bed, under the table. Towards morning the steward's cabin which was on deck was carried overboard and fortunately for him he had left it a few minutes before, else he would have gone the same way. All these disasters amused me so much that I got quite well and was troubled with seasickness no more. The decks were still wet and as we had to stay below it was not at all comfortable. We saw Cape Matapan and a few of the Greek Isles but they all looked so bleak that we wished them far enough. Yesterday we came in sight of Mytilene but it was getting dark and we saw very little of it. It was still very rough but what was a great thing I was able to eat and felt very well. 'Oh the delightful sea, the blue, the fresh, the ever-free' etc. I don't believe a word of it except 'blue' and that is sometimes changed to black. A view from the shore during a storm is all very well and if any wishes more let them try the Grecian Archipelago in a gale and I am sure they will come to my way of thinking. This morning I got up early and going on deck found we had passed the island of Tenidos and were now in sight of ancient Troy. There was very little to be seen about it, a low range of hills ran along the shore, and over them you saw the celebrated plain of Troy, I had heard so much about when at Mr Low's. We wished very much for a copy of Virgil but of course no one had such a thing. The graves of Hercules, Achilles and Petrocules, were pointed out to us and some on board declared they could see 'To the memory of etc'. Soon after passing Troy we entered the Dardanelles between the Castle of Europe and Asia, which are two forts belonging to the Turks and command the entrance. It was here we first saw the Turkish flag (crescent and star) floating over the ramparts. After passing to the inner fort we had to stop for an hour, during which time the doctor of the ship went ashore and reported all well, after that we were allowed to proceed. When he returned, everyone crowded round him to hear the news but unfortunately no news had been got from Constantinople for a fortnight before; it had been so strong in the Sea of Marmara. Sebastopol had not been taken but they were busy at it. The Dardanelles are about three miles broad and, with the exception of the names of the villages as you pass up, very uninteresting. You have rocky hills and here and there a few cypress trees on each side. We passed Bessia Bay, Serios, Obydos and Gallipoli. There were a good many ships taking refuge from the gale here. Some Turkish boats came off to us, but no one came on board. Some of the boats are very pretty and others much the same as ours but not so good. In the better ones there was generally an old Turk in the stern and beside him his large pipe. They all wear Turbans of various colours, loose jackets, wide trousers, and something very like a shawl twisted round their waist. As yet I have seen very few and for further particulars you must have patience. The towns we have seen look very well from the water but I believe in reality are very dirty holes. They are generally built on the face of a hill, and the minarettes which to our eyes seem strange looking things – they are round, quite small, shoot up for about fifteen or twenty feet, and then a bartizan above which it tapers off. They are white washed and when seen at a distance they look so clean and contrast well with the blue slates or something like slates. We are now in the Sea of Marmara, as it is getting rough I assure you it is very difficult to write. I will not close this until we are at or near Constantinople and I will tell you anything new I hear in a short note. I have not as yet the slightest idea where we will be sent. There is a new hospital built on the Asiatic side of the Dardanelles and some say we will be sent there, but no one knows.

I hope you are all well. I would like very much to hear from you. I think a letter addressed to Dr G, Staff Asst. Surgeon, British Army in Turkey will find me out. I told Anne this but missed the Staff and any little error may send the letter wrong. I will write none of my friends until I am settled, you may tell them so, it is so difficult. Give my love to my mother, my aunt and Anne, hoping they are as well as I am, Dr Hill, cousins, etc., I do not know what it will be when we land but it is very cold here. If we are stationed at the Dardanelles I will be very near Charlie Boyd. Oh, how I should like to meet an old friend here, wouldn't I have such a shake of his hand. I am not like myself here, I doubt much if even my father would know me. We all at present look like a flock of savages, with bristly beards and mustachios. What a cargo we have, it consists of 18 doctors, from Inspectors downwards to Assist. Surgeons, 48 nurses, black and white nuns included, Protestants, Episcopalians, and Catholics, Sisters of Mercy, Nurses from the London hospital, etc. I do pity them during the voyage, they are all so sick. When they do get to Scutari or wherever they go, some ladies who are amongst them – even ladies of fortune and title – will, I am sure, very soon tire of their good works.

Since writing the above I find I must finish this tonight as the mail bag will be sent off tomorrow morning before we land, so the accounts of my first impressions of Stamboul must be told in another letter. I am very unwilling to finish and at present feel as if I could write the whole night. When one is between 2,000 or 3,000 miles from home it is a curious feeling, in fact I scarcely believe I am here. I suppose it is a fact however and when I mount the red jacket I think it will be proof positive. We are now sailing over the Sea of Marmara, it is calm and I have been well all day. It has been a day of excitement, everyone busy looking over our traps, putting our names on our belts, seeing our swords are not rusty from the sea air, and a host of nick-nacks too numerous to mention. It is expected we will be at Constantinople by 8 o'clock tomorrow morning. We will get breakfast on board and then be sent ashore. I am tired of the ship and my eight days voyage, yet I am unwilling to land, as long as I am on board I am amongst English and feel a kind of attachment to the ship which I cannot describe. However I must face the barbarian Turks and hope providence will watch over me in this strange land. Dr Struthers has great hopes, and so have I, of us being sent together wherever we may go, in fact we have agreed to petition if separated to be allowed to go together. If so we will be as happy as possible. Four bells have just rung and all lights are to be put out so I must conclude. I had intended to do so before and am as far from the end as ever. Excuse this rambling letter, my thoughts are so confused, and I wish to say so much. Good bye and compliments to all and sundry kind friends at home who may ask for me. Farewell.

You must not expect a letter like this every time. Anne must write me a long, long letter immediately as close as this, and I will return the favour. Good bye.

CHAPTER 2

Scutari

My dear Father,

As I have learned that a mail starts for England today I seize the opportunity of writing you again. I wrote you from on board the 'Vectis' on the 3rd and I suppose you will receive both letters together. As ill luck would have it my first sight of Constantinople was spoiled by an old dear friend being present, viz – a scotch mist, or to speak plain it was a beastly day. We anchored in the Golden Horn about 10am yesterday, about 12 the rain ceased and we had a view of the Queen of the East. Well named I can assure you. You would think it was fairyland but I believe the best view is from the sea, for in reality the mud in the streets is knee deep. I did not land and cannot tell you much about it yet. We were all anxiety to know where we were to be sent and about 2pm we received our orders for Scutari. Each of us got into a *caique* – small beautiful Turkish boat – with our luggage and sailed over the Bosphorus and in doing so, as it was now a fine day, we had such a splendid view of the city and bay. In crossing the old Turk was as delighted with the view as us. He talked to us but all we could make out was, with regard to the sight, 'Buono Stamboul' repeating it often and pointing it out to us, and with regards to us 'Buono Johnny' to which of course we replied 'Buono Turko'. Everybody here is called 'Johnny', the Turks call us all 'Johnny' and we call them the same. They are very fond of the English even more so than the French, and they are always talking of the 'Buono Anglis'. What a sight we met when we landed here, a steamer had just arrived from the Crimea with 150 wounded and they were transporting them from the ship to the hospital on stretchers, carried by four men each. You cannot conceive the feeling I had, the sight of man after man being carried on shore and the same continuing for hours as if it would never cease. This is the work day after day and is performed by convalescents. Talk of large hospitals, I wish our friends in Dundee only saw this one here. It is a large square, as large as the High

Street, three flats, and as far as I saw quite full. The rest of the wounded are in the Barracks, which are about a quarter of a mile from the hospital. Oh, what a sight it is, upwards of 2,000 men sick and wounded, I cannot give you the least idea of it and will not try. I do not know how many doctors are here but there are plenty, and plenty of everything, that is comparatively speaking. What a blessing it is to meet friends here, we had no sooner entered the hospital than we met Calder, an Edinburgh fellow, and then another Stewart, then a third Titterton, then a fourth Drysdale, and they were so happy to see us as we them. We retired to Calder's quarters to have some dinner. I must describe to you an officer's room. A shutter placed on two empty casks in the centre of the room, four bare walls, forms what is considered here a good table, trunks, empty boxes and beds so all very well for seats, pipes, swords, uniform, etc., are hung on pegs driven into the wall, and this is the furnishing and accommodation required and all that can be got. James Rogers will with difficulty form an estimate for you of what it costs. Dinner was ordered and a soldier (officer's servant) in livery – shirt and trousers both abominably dirty – sets a black tin pan in the middle of the table, three tin plates and as many spoons, and this was for 1st, 2nd and 3rd courses. I do not mean to say we ate the tin plates, oh, no, the pot contained something, what it was I do not know, nobody gave it a name and no one asked. I think it was beef boiled in water. This was followed by steak. Talk of tough steaks, I wish you had a chew of one here, leather is nothing to it. Will you believe it we enjoyed our first dinner here as well as ever we enjoyed one at home. I am in first rate health and believe at present I could digest pig-iron. Dr Struthers and I have put up together but it is doubtful if we [will] remain so as we have not got our wards pointed out to us yet. We have just reported ourselves and have been told we are to remain here for some time at least. A great many have been sent to the Crimea and they say it is well supplied now. Since reporting myself I have not had time to take off my uniform and here am I in 'full fig', writing, standing at a window overlooking the Bosphorus. The day is beautiful but how unlike a Sabbath at home, it is Sunday here and not Sabbath. No church and everyone is as busy as any other day. I am doubtful if half here know what day it is. I am going to Constantinople in the afternoon to buy some cups, plates, pots, etc., a work of necessity if not mercy. Oh, I wish I had father's canteen which is in the back shop press, it would be quite a treasure here. Post closes at 12 and as there is not another for a fortnight I must bid you good bye. Address Scutari Hospital and if I am sent any other place I will get it the same. I will write some of my Edinburgh friends next post. Good bye in haste.

My dear Father,

I intended writing you last mail but just as I had got through my work
500 wounded men were landed here from the Crimea, a small specimen
of the result of the glorious (?) battle at Sebastopol on the 5th inst. I had
to lend a helping hand and of course could not get writing. I have now
been ten days here, but as yet have had very little opportunity or time to
look about me. Of what I have seen I will attempt to give you some idea.
Just opposite Constantinople there is a small village – Scutari – and
about a mile or two to the East of this there is another village, Katcahn.
Between these two but nearer the former the large general hospital is
built, again between this and Scutari you have the Barracks. Both are
very large buildings, more especially the latter. They are built in the form
of a square with a large parade ground in the centre. At first the hospital
alone was used as an hospital but was soon found too small and the
barracks were turned to the same purpose, they are not nearly full also. I
think I told you in my last that Dr Struthers, Dr Mason and I had got
quarters in the barracks in the shape of an empty room and two iron
bedsteads. While we were making ourselves what we call comfortable,
that is, we had got three chairs and were making a table, we had got also
some pots and pans, we were quietly told to flit, as some wounded
officers were coming to take possession of our room. To flit was easy
enough so in the morning we removed to our new quarters, an old
summer palace belonging to the Sultan, or as the Turks call it a 'Kiosque'.
It is an old square building overlooking the Bosphorus, not large, has
evidently been once a very fine palace but now looks very seedy indeed.
We descend to it by marble steps, there is a marble font almost in every
room, the rooms are beautifully painted, and ornamented in Oriental
fashion. The floors are covered with fine matting, etc., but the place is
falling to pieces, and you would be amused to see us pulling off a shutter
when we want firewood. As a recommendation we were told it was very
airy, that's a fact, the place is all windows and the wind blows thro' it like
fury, not to mention the way the rain comes pouring in when it happens
to rain which by the by is very often. We are not to be long here however
for the officers are to be sent home and we expect to get our water-tight
quarters again. If you would only see our room you would be amused,

everything here is turned to advantage, we are constantly on the prowl and if anything we meet with which can be of use as a seat or anything else it is immediately captured. We are not in barracks but have to pass across a parade ground in front of the barracks to our quarters, which as I said are within 6 yards of the shore. I have only been once or twice at the General Hospital, all my work is confined to the Barracks and enough I have to do. We go at 9am to visit our patients, dress the sores, wounds, etc., and work away till about 1pm then we have lunch, at work again till 3, we have dinner at 5, tea at 7, evening visit at 8 and generally go to bed about 11, this is our plan, but we seldom get it carried out, something or other always comes in the way. The work is most pleasant and interesting. The wounds we see here are things we can never see at home, today for instance we had three operations, amputations at the thigh, excision of the shoulder, and amputation of an arm. This we have almost every day besides various other little things we do ourselves. What a scene the hospital here is – Dragoons, Hussars, Lancers, Riflemen, Guards, and common soldiers, all mixed up together, very few of them have clothes on as you see them at home, when they land they are generally in rags, and glad of anything to cover them whether regimental or not. When they are put to bed and comfortable it is not so much noticed. What a sight it is to see them landed, those who are not able to walk are carried up to the hospital on stretchers by 4 soldiers, those who are able look the worst, clothes hanging in rags and all muck, hats and helmets smashed that once had looked so beautiful, bloody bandages round their heads and arms, faces and hands not washed since before the battle, the men looking most miserable dragging their wearied limbs after them to die in peace. They all show a good deal of spirit and some are proud of their wounds rather than otherwise. They have suffered very much in the Crimea and besides the wounded we have now and then a ship-load of sick – chiefly diarrhoea and dysentery. The wards of the hospital are not large – generally hold about 30. We have them also placed in the passages which are broad, extending half the length of a side of the building and as many as 180 may be placed in a passage. How many patients we have altogether I cannot tell but I think about 2,000. I have charge of 2 surgical wards and half a passage. I have plenty to do and like it very well. We have about 70 doctors but I do not know about one half of them, we have no mess and therefore never meet together. The want of a mess is not much felt altho' many would like to get one set a-going if they could, it is very expensive and would soon run away with money which is no use to throw away here. We get what we call rations, that is, a loaf of bread, a pound of tough meat, and some other things, coffee, candles charcoal, etc., and all the rest we have to buy. We get tea at 1/- per pound, sugar at 2d., out of the army store, butter, cheese, fish, etc. are bought at the village and are very dear, the two former 1/6 per pound. All we buy from the Turks is dear and they know how to take advantage of us. When we go to the shops for anything we ask the price, offer half what is asked and after squabbling for a while generally get it. The Turks are a dirty abominable looking set, constantly smoking thin long pipes and looking as lazy as you possibly could imagine. Their dress looks well in a picture but the reality is far from pretty. All wear the fez or turban, a loose jacket showing a bare breast, and dirty shirt, trousers as if the fellow had jumped into a deep sack, pushed his feet through the corners and had drawn the mouth tight round the waist, sometimes he has stockings, sometimes leggings, and last of all his feet are covered with old shoes or backless, generally the latter. As for the ladies all you see of them is a dark coloured gown with a hood covering the head, and instead of a face two stripes of white linen and a pair of eyes between. Sometimes the veil falls down and we then see a face, generally an ugly one. The Greek ladies look very well and smart, more especially the little girls who are neatly dressed and very like our English Miss out for a holiday. I have been once or twice at Constantinople, it is a most beautiful city when you see it from the sea, but when you enter it you never saw a more abominable place all your life. To describe it would be impossible but just imagine to yourself a large town with a street like the Overgate [in Dundee] the best street in it, every house seemingly built in the very spot you would have chosen to have had the street straight for 50yds, streets running into each other at all sorts of angles, and no arrangement whatever, regular or irregular, everywhere looking as old and miserable as possible as if a breath of wind would blow it down. The roads not repaired since the time of Constantine, and you will have some slight idea of Constantinople. When you land you tuck up your trousers nearly to your knees and stumble along the streets. If you venture to look into a shop or forget your feet you are immediately into a pool of mud or you trample on some dogs which are constantly in your way, and while you are – to say the least of it – in a stew, more especially if you have on uniform, you are very much provoked to see three or four Turks all squatted on mats in front of their homes smoking their Turkish Chibouks and looking as contented as princes among the mud. All the filth is pitched out of the houses into the streets, the dogs eat what they can, and what they can't is made into mud of which everybody must take a share. No one here thinks of keeping a dog, all the dogs belong to the State if I might say so, and act as scavengers. There are hundreds of them in all directions prowling about, sleeping or munching at bones during the day, and kicking up awful rows at night. We have a large common adjoining the Hospital and a very common amusement at night is to have a 'Chevvy' amongst the dogs, sticks and stones fly in all directions as many a poor canine skin catches it. They are ugly mongrels somewhat like our collies, smaller and always a thievish look about them. The Turkish horses are small and shabby. Dr Pirie's 'Donald' would have been a perfect beauty amongst them. Bullocks are always used in the carts, they jog along as slow as possible, and that pleases the lazy Turk who generally sits in front with his pipe shank stuck down his back and the pipe head high up in the air. Oh, they are an inactive set and it would have been telling us if we had had the Russians as friends and the Turks as enemies. Some of the soldiers exercise under our windows every morning, they wear tight dress but do not look at all well or smart. They are drilled into exercise but it is hard work. I do not know if I told you I had taken out a dress and some other things to a Miss Scott who is at boarding school at Constantinople. I had met her friends at the Young's last winter and when I called at Miss Young's before leaving and saw them I was asked to take out a parcel which I was most happy to do. I found out the place the other day when I was across the water and saw the young lady and also Miss Walsh who has the school. I had on my red jacket and Miss W evidently thought I was a dangerous character to have in a school, we came to a good understanding however and I am going back very soon again. Miss W is a sister of Mrs Dr Kaydysides of Edinburgh. Dr Struthers has met her in Edinburgh and what is very strange Dr Mason has a letter to her from some of her friends in England, so we are all to visit her together. I commenced this letter yesterday and changes for the better have since taken place. Last night was a very stormy night and an old Kiosque was nearly blown bodily into the Bosphorus, at any rate the roof was torn off – it was dreadfully cold – we applied to Dr McGregor our Director General here, and have now got a very snug barrack room and as a change from the beautiful (?) white the walls are painted yellow and a few big nails driven into them which is rather luxury here, and also a large press. We have a Dragoon servant who cooks our food in many a curious manner, which would make the good folks at home open their eyes a bit. Tom [their servant] however is not good at foraging for us and we have to do that by turns, sometimes a disagreeable business when one is busy, we are to dismiss him therefore and try for a better. It feels very curious for a green-hand to be under military law, when you are doing your rounds at night to be challenged at every corner you turn by 'who goes there?' and the salute you are constantly receiving from sentries and all the soldiers you meet. The climate here is very good but very changeable, you may have an almost beautiful afternoon when a sail on the Bosphorus in a *caique* is most acceptable and you are complaining loudly of the heat, next day may be as cold as the former was warm, and when it does rain, it does and no mistake. The Bosphorus is very like our Tay but narrow. When we go to Constantinople we get into a *caique*, a neat Turkish boat, sharp at both ends like a whale boat but more turned up, they are beautifully carved and manned by either one or two Turks who pull two oars each. They would be easily upset but there are no seats except for the boatmen. We squat down on a cushion on the bottom of the boat and talk and laugh at the boatmen all the way. You no doubt wonder how we manage to talk, it is very easy, for instance – you step into a boat and tell him where you want to go with a 'Hallo Johnny, Galata Johnny', Turks answer 'Buono Johnny', you answer 'Buono Johnny'. We 'Buono' one another the whole way and are as happy and jolly as if we understood one another perfectly and were old friends. I have learned some Turkish but it won't go far yet. Oh, I am anxious to hear from home. I suppose you have written already but I have never received any yet. Tell Anne and mother to write me long letters, all the sense and nonsense going. Newspapers also will be very acceptable. A great want here I feel is the want of postage stamps. We cannot pay our letters and I have to send them all unpaid, please send me some. I will try and write you every fortnight but you need not be disappointed if I often miss, the mail may be too late or I may be too busy, but I will try and do what I can. We are all in first rate health and like the style of things very well. We have of course a great many hardships but I can tell you we enjoy them gloriously. As for news I can give you very little as to the war, all our news we get from the wounded, and if any engagement takes place the folks at home will hear as soon as truly as we will do. I hope you are all well, mother, aunt, Anne, cousins, Mrs Hill etc. etc. Tell Dr Pirie I will write him sometime but it may be a while yet. It is very difficult writing here, your time is so much broken up and it is a treat to get a table to write on. Some good folks may be wishing to make extracts from this but I would rather not, more especially anything about the hospital as I might get into trouble about it, so use your discretion.

Do write soon. I do not think we will be sent to the Crimea this season at least. When I came out first I was anxious to go but could not get, now I have no wish, but may be sent up in the spring if required, I should like to see the fun. When the wounded were coming in I kept a look out for George Fenwick but I am happy to say I could not see him. Should he come I will take care of him.

My dear Anne,

You have no idea the pleasure your kind letter gave me. When in
Edinburgh a letter from home was a matter of course, here I can assure
you it is something more. I was not content with simply reading it
but have scrutinised it over and over again and yet feel pleasure in
reading it. I was very glad to hear you were all well and sincerely hope
I may receive no worse news. In my last I think I told you we had got
comfortably settled at last and so we have. If you could only drop in here
and see our room, wouldn't you be amused? It is a very snug apartment
indeed and the ornaments on the walls, from military cloaks and red
jackets to swords and revolver pistols, give it such a comfortable military
appearance as you can have no idea of. Dr Struthers, Mason and I are
as comfortable as we could wish considering the circumstances. Our
servant Tom has now got better into our way of working and we have
got a Sergeant Major's wife who cooks for us and barring the tough
goat's flesh, which here passes for the name of mutton, I may say we
have very good living. Tea, bread and butter is our staple commodity
and I am sure you would be frightened if you saw how that, and eggs,
go down at breakfast. Along with your kind letter I was glad to get
one equally so from mother and I hope she will repeat the dose often.
She tells me father would like to know what encouragement I get here,
that is a difficult question but I will try to answer it. My great object
in joining the army was, in these active times, in the first place to get
surgical practice, to see the world, to get the éclat of being at the war,
and to get a year or two's recreation before settling in practice. When
I entered the army I never thought what pay I would get, but since I
have learnt that we staff men get 7/6 a day as pay, 3/6 a day to keep a
servant, and 2/6 as war allowance, in all we calculate it at 18/- per diem.
Our expenses amount to about 20/- per week and various little odds and
ends besides. As for money it is far better than we – at least Dr Struthers
and I – expected. If we have the bad luck to be gazetted to a regiment
as our friend Dr Mason has been we immediately lose 4/- per day and
in view of that we get a soldier servant, if we are sent to the Crimea
we save money for the simple reason we cannot get it spent. Dr Mason
joined a fortnight before us and has been gazetted to the 18th Regiment.
For all I know I may be gazetted to one even now. When we came out

Dr Struthers and I volunteered for service in the Crimea, which I am now happy to say was refused. The work and hardships in the Crimea just now are awful but in the Spring, if I am not sent up before then, I will volunteer again and kick up a row if I do not get, when I am here at any rate I should like to see the actual fun. The wounded who come here tell me that Sebastopol is nearly as far from being taken as ever and will not be so before spring, so I am very glad to escape the bad weather in comfortable quarters here. John Erskine is not here yet, I have heard nothing of him, but he may have been sent straight up to the Crimea without landing here, as many have been. I saw a newspaper addressed to him here and took the liberty of opening and closing it again, newspapers being very acceptable articles here ... From mother's account of Dr Johnson's brother I think he must be very like the Doctor. Dr Struthers and I very soon tired of him, he is a sly, selfish kind of fellow, and that sort of thing won't do with us, more especially in this part of the world. We never gave him any encouragement to come with us and were very glad when he got quarters out of the barracks away from us. We are of course on good terms with each other but go no further as intimate friends. Since writing last we have had several peregrinations thro' the country and enjoy ourselves, we get ponies of an afternoon and have very pleasant rides. The ponies are small ragamuffin little animals but possess great spirit and go at a very good pace. The Turks are quite amazed at us riding so fast, their great delight is to ride as slow as possible. To see an old Turk driving a bullock cart is quite a treat, the oxen go at the same rate as a cow at home, and here is Johnny sitting cross-legged on the front of his long rickety cart either smoking his long chibouk or when not doing so having the long shank stuck down his back and the pipe head high in the air. Oh, they are a lazy set, one feels often inclined to kick them. They seem to pass their whole existence in a brown study. When two or three are walking together in the country instead of talking – why the fellows have nothing to talk about – they jog along the road singing together, not a stirring song but a kind of low drawling chant. The ladies are I think as bad as the men, since I came here I have never seen a woman working. No crochet work to make people think they are busy. Some of them wear very thick veils, these we know are the plain looking ones, any who are good looking wear thin veils, and very often as if by accident the veil drops down as we pass. The Greeks are not veiled and we always get a good look from them; in passing thro' the streets of Scutari on horseback the other day I came upon two little girls playing themselves in a cart, and Dr Struthers stopped to admire the little things when one of them looked up in my face and lisped, 'Buono Johnny' to which I returned a 'Buono Johnny' and passed on while they kept on calling the same after us. I cannot tell you how I am looking but I believe very well, I have never shaved since I was in Paris and I am sure you would be frightened to kiss me now. I would like very well to write to Dr Pirie but I hope he will excuse me now and I will promise him a long screed some fine day when I have less work to do, when that may be I have no idea, my wards no sooner get thin than down comes another batch of wounded from the Crimea and I am as busy as ever. I have been searching among my patients to see if I could find a Dundee man but I have never met one yet. I wonder if Andrew McNab is out here, do you know to what regiment he belongs? George Fenwick, I hear from some men of the 1st, is very well and not likely to come under my tender care. I am searching as much as I can for curiosities but pick up very few as yet. I have got a first rate revolver pistol which was taken from a Russian General at Sebastopol and which may yet be of use to me. Also a lot of bullets which I and others have taken out of the wounded, some smashed bones and such like. It is no use getting large things for you cannot keep them and cannot carry them with you on a campaign. I am very glad you are pleased with your watch, the one which mother was so kind as [to] lend me goes 'like a brick'. Everyone has their time here but I may say mine is the standard. I know this is a short letter but I will write a longer one next time. I will if possible write twice a month and you may do so every week and I will be much obliged to you. I hope you, father, mother and aunt are all well, Mrs Hill, Dr and Mrs Sandeman, Miss and Agnes Pirie, ask the latter if she remembers giving me a bosom friend. I find it very comfortable here. Remember me to all kind enquiring friends and hoping to hear from you very often. I will number my letters in future and you do the same. It will let me know if I get them all.

My dear Father,

As I expect it to be past the New Year, or at least very near it, when you receive this allow me to wish you all a very happy New Year and as the saying is many very happy returns of the same. There is very little word of any rejoicing here, the only thing that at all puts me in mind of the scenes at home at this time is our servant having invested in two ducks which he is to fatten and kill for a Xmas dinner. I tried to explain to the fellow that as Scotchmen we intended to hold the New Year and not Xmas, he is not very sharp in the understanding at any time and certainly the idea of keeping the New Year puzzled him. He compromised however by resolving to kill one on Xmas day and another on New Year's Day. In this country time passes in a curious manner, indeed, every day is alike and there is no break seemingly from one year's end to another. The New Year will however be a mark, and by the time I come to the next I in all likelihood will have the pleasure of being amongst you again, that however will depend on how the war goes. From all I can learn here you may expect to hear very important news from Sebastopol soon, shiploads of troops are passing this every day, both French and English. They cannot remain long in the Crimea as they are so soon reduced by sickness as to be of little use, it is supposed the town will be stormed very soon. Since the battle of Inkerman filled our hospital with wounded it has been gradually emptying itself of them, by curing some and sending others to Malta and England. People at home think we have nothing but sabre cuts and gunshot wounds, but that is a great mistake. Sickness which prevails in the Crimea is far worse than Russian bullets. As soon as our wounded are sent off, their place is immediately taken by the sick. We are all far fonder of the wounded than the sick, in other words of the surgical cases than the medical, but of course the sick soldiers must be attended to and we must take the unpleasant with the pleasant and interesting work, if these terms are at all applicable. When Sebastopol is taken however there will be awful slaughter and lots of wounded going. Struthers and I are very anxious that we should be sent up to the Crimea but we can't get at present, it is to be hoped however we will get sent up. From what I see here I think I could save both lives and limbs to some poor fellows. If you were here I am sure you would be very much amused with some of our wounds, and the effects of the rifle balls would astonish you. The Russian bullet is a good deal larger than the English one, the latter weighs in general one ounce, while the Russian one is one ounce and a half, and some which I have seen and extracted here have weighed an ounce and three quarters. You may imagine how uncomfortable one of these feel when lodged in a fellow. Our small balls do as much damage every bit as the large Russian's. The round musket ball gives a severe whack but woe betide the poor fellow who receives the contents of a menie or needle rifle. They are all conical in form, sometimes they lodge but in general they pass right through what they hit. You can have no idea of their effects. If one strikes the femur that bone is done for, and the sooner the thigh is amputated the better. When a conical ball strikes the femur it is shattered sometimes from top to bottom, a civil accident cannot be compared to it, when you look at the limb there is nothing but a small round hole seen, all the mischief is internal. So much for the bullets, and now for something softer and more agreeable. I received Anne's second kind letter in safety and also a very kind one from cousin Anne for which I have directed George to return her my sincere thanks. Since writing last I have as usual enjoyed first rate health and been amusing myself during my leisure hours at pistol practice, shooting dogs, and often air exercise, when I can get it. The weather here is in general wet but we have some very fine days somewhat like June days at home. About a week ago I had a Turkish bath which I must tell you about as we have nothing like it at home. I and other two Staff Asst. Surgeons made a small party and went to have a scrubbing in a 'hummam' or bath in the village of Scutari. The exterior of the bath is certainly not very imposing and looks somewhat like a dirty bakehouse. We entered and were met by an old Turk who directed us to undress on three soft couches at the side of a large room, a towel was then put round our bodies and wooden pattens on our feet and we were marched into a dismal small room which felt very hot and moist, in fact it was with great difficulty we could breathe at first. Three naked young Turks seated us on cushions, and presented us with long pipes and coffee. This put off about half an hour when you may imagine we were in a precious stew, the sweat was pouring from us. I did not feel at all uncomfortable but very languid. The young Turks then began shampoo- ing us, pressing all the muscles of our legs and arms, making our joints crack etc. After this had been done for about a quarter of an hour we were marched into room No. 2 which was far hotter than No. 1, not a dry heat but a moist heat. There was an elevated platform in the centre

[made] of marble and around the room were fountains of hot and cold water. We were directed to lay down on the marble platform on our backs, we did so but immediately sprang up again declaring it was by far too hot, and burned our backs. The Turks seemed determined to give us the full benefit of it and pulled us down again, we very soon got accustomed to the hot marble. Here we were kneaded and shampooed in a severer manner than in room No. 1. We were turned over and over, squeezed, punched, knelt on, and even our ribs cracked. We were roaring and laughing all the time but felt very sore and weak after it. We were seated each before a fountain and the Turk after putting on a glove of a rough kind began to rub us all over and you can have no idea of the amount of matter he took from our skin, it came off in rolls, at first I thought it was the skin itself but then there was no pain so I kept my mind easy and let him rub away. When he had fleeced me to his heart's content I was then plastered over with soap, in fact I never got such a lathering, I was then soused with hot and cold water, alternately from the fountain, and this finished the scrubbing process, and you may believe I felt considerably mollified. We were then conducted into room No. 1 again where we were carefully dried. Out of this we marched into the room where we undressed at first, we found the couches transformed into light beds, each of us had a shawl rolled round him, and a turban placed on his head. We jumped into these beds and in a sitting posture smoked long pipes, and drank coffee until we had completely recovered from the operation. The Turks talked and laughed to us the whole time and seemed as much amused with us as we were with them. The coffee was splendid and drunk out of small cups like eggcups. A bath I believe is one of the most pleasant things you can get here and I am sure I found it so. The only objection is that when your skin is so clean and fine the fleas bite easier thro' it. I suppose you have heard of Turkish fleas, my eyes, if you could only feel them, wouldn't they astonish you. We are very lucky at present as it is cold weather and we have few of them, i.e. ten may perhaps be caught in a shirt before tumbling into bed. We generally have a flea hunt before going to bed and then make out a return of the killed, wounded, etc. They are larger, slightly thinner than the common flea at home, but they bite and leap amazingly. The poor fellows who come down from the Crimea are covered with fleas and vermin of all sorts and in working about them we must get our share of what is going. The Crimean fleas seem to be starving like the men they come on, and when one has the good luck to be billeted on any of us he seems to make

up for lost time and lay in a store in case he should be sent up again.

Dr Mason and I had a long stroll in a Turkish cemetery last Sunday and then stumbled into a Mosque. A place of prayer – you can scarcely call it a church but it is something like it. We have a good many here and some very handsome, but in Constantinople the Mosque of St Sophia is almost one of the world's wonders. A mosque is generally in the shape of a dome, or miniature of St Paul's, and one or two minarettes attached to it. I have made a sketch here which will let you understand what I mean. The Mosque is where the service is conducted and the minarettes are where the cryer or as he is called the Muedyin, ascends four or five times a day and calls the faithful to prayer, when all who are disposed come in from the streets and join in the service, looking towards Mecca. Muedyin calls in a very pleasing style – rather romantic. I cannot tell you what like it is just now but if you can make your imagination intertwine the Edinburgh cry of 'Caller Ou' and the first line of the Old Hundred you will have something like it. We were not at all sure if we would get in, we peeped in and then made a bolt when we saw an old priest, he seemed quiet enough and we returned again, he signed to us to enter and after making us take off our boots we were conducted thro' the Mosque. The floor was covered by a most beautiful carpet, and about two hundred lamps of various colours were hanging about 9 ft above the floor. The walls were beautiful marble and so were two small pulpit-like places and a gallery used, I suppose, on high occasions. We of course admired everything, which pleased the old priest. A young fellow then took us up one of the minarettes from which we had a splendid view. The minarette is very slim and the stair goes up almost perpendicular and there is a small door looking towards Mecca which leads out to the bartizan. The Muezzin, for he it was that was with us, pointed to his watch and made us understand if we would wait five minutes he would call out, we did so and had an opportunity of assisting in calling the faithful to prayer. When we came down we found prayers begun. We stood at the door but were not allowed to enter as we had on boots, every time our feet touched the carpet the priest warned us off. The priest read the prayers which sounded very pretty, there were about 20 hearers who stood in a row behind him and followed all his motions such as prostrating them-selves, kissing the ground, etc. Every person immediately he came in cast off his shoes and running forward joined in the movements. As soon as service was over we bolted and astonished Dr Struthers by telling him as it was Sabbath we had been to Church.

I cannot tell you how much annoyed I am by my letters being published. I have seen one in the Mercury and heard of one in the Courier. I do not wish to say much, but this I must say, that if I hear of such a thing again you alone may expect to hear once a month, I am well and nothing more. It is against all army regulations and might get me into no end of rows so do not allow it to occur again. Since commencing this I have received a letter from Dr Pirie. I am much obliged to him but he is at his old tricks again, crossing letters. I sent one off a fortnight ago to him. I think a great deal of his letter but it is far too short. Mother and Anne of course will write me soon, and I would also like you to do the same. Many thanks for the plan of Sebastopol and the Courier which you sent. I suppose it is winter here but it is more like a mild autumn than anything else. We have some beautiful days and a great many beastly wet ones. The Royal Albert (131 guns) passed up here today with 1,700 troops on board, chiefly guards and the 71st Regiment. I was through her all, she is a splendid ship. I hope you are all well and that Mrs Hill is better. Give all and sundry my kindest wishes and many Happy New Years to them all. I will write to Anne on or about the 30th and with a farewell to her, mother, and aunt, believe me to be,

Ever your affectionate son,
David Greig

NB – the top passage about publishing.

I cannot send mistletoe or holly but I enclose a sprig of cypress and myrtle. I send you something for your New Year in the shape of a ten piastre note, value 20[s].

My dear Anne,

I am sure one of your letters must have gone astray, as I have had none since the one of 22nd November and what makes it worse I have seen by a newspaper that Mrs Hill is dead. I need not say how sorry I was to see it. I have looked for a letter post after post in order to get some intelligence about it but as yet have looked in vain. I can easy fancy however that it was in one of her ill turns. Mother told me she was ill when she last wrote but hoped she would get over it. Poor kind hearted creature, she suffered a good deal and altho' it is with pain we part we must be consoled at the same time with the assurance that she is now permanently relieved and happier than we. During the last fortnight I have felt more uncomfortable and low spirited that I have done since I came out and that from three causes – Mrs Hill's death, my letters being published, and on my being on the sick list. With regard to my letters, oh, I could eat my fingers could I recall them. I know Mr Lindsay and you all thought it was a kindness but I can assure you it was a mistaken kindness, the greatest kindness you can do me is never to think of such a thing again, if it is done I give you my word of honour I will never write a single soul again. I won't mention this painful – to me at least – subject again but I trust you will attend to it. About a fortnight ago when out shooting dogs I got cold in my left eye, it was slightly sore for two or three days but I did not much mind it, and from conjunctivitis it went on to teloritis and then iritis. I was in bed for four days but through the kind management of Dr Struthers I was able to enjoy a plum pudding on Christmas day. Oh it is disagreeable being sick so far from home, more especially if you are in bed, then comes the full appreciation of the comforts of home. I was as comfortable as anyone in barracks could have been, I had Mason and Struthers beside me, and a kind sergeant's wife to attend on me, a thing I never saw any other here have. The eye was very painful and as I lay in bed I reasoned thus – 'Well if I was at home what would my father do.' He would bleed me, accordingly I had myself bled from the arm, that gave it a check, well what next, 'He would leech my eye' so on went 6 leeches. I felt a great deal better after that and I then allowed Dr S. to treat me as he liked. The eye was dim for a day or two after but is now quite well and in truth – no blarney – I am as jolly as usual. Everyone here says I am getting fat and I am frightened my fine tight uniform will soon be useless. I was only four days when I am sorry to say Dr Struthers took with fever and I have now ample opportunity of repaying his kindness to me. It is not typhus, we have very little of that here but a peculiar kind of typhoid fever which is very common here, attended by great prostration and restlessness. Our men suffered greatly from it at Gallipoli and also at Bulgaria, and many take it immediately on coming down from Sebastopol. Very few die of it but they generally have a slow recovery. It is not considered at all infectious. As yet I cannot say how he will get over it but I hope easily. I have written by this post to his brother telling him about him. Johnston is also ill but it is only a slight feverish attack brought on it is said by plum pudding – don't mention this to any of his friends. I had a note from Major Fenwick the other day asking me to go to Constantinople and look after a box which he sent to George sometime ago, I have not yet got down but will go this week and see about it. I was happy to see that George had got promotion the other day and is now Lieut. I was very much surprised on Xmas day to get a visit from a Mr Laird who turned out to be a cousin of Miss McDowell's. She had been visiting him and told him to be sure and call for me here, which he did. He is a jolly young fellow, an engineer, I think on board the 'Italia' one of the Austrian Lloyd's steam vessels. He was just going off to Alexandria and is to call for me when comes back. When you write to Mr M. give her my kind compliments and thank her for her kindness. You may also tell her cousin is in first rate health and spirits. I have heard no word of going to the Crimea yet, there is plenty to do here, chiefly medical practice and suppose will continue so till we have a battle again. Struthers and I both wrote to Syme and Simpson asking them to get Lord Blantyre to send us up some time ago, and I hope he will do so. We volunteered for service in the Crimea twice and were told we were required where we were. Johnston says he won't go up, I suppose he would bolt home if there was any chance of it. I am very much obliged to Mrs George Baxter for her kind and constant enquiries about me. My life isn't insured but when I do get home, which must be some time, I hope to have a long-winded crack with her. Remember me to her, Mr B. Crichton, Mary etc. That puts me in mind of Charlie Boyd, I should like to have his address in case any chance should blow me near Syria. We have got a hospital there or at least there was a talk of one. What a difference it is here from a Christmas at home, our ideas of Christmas is cold, crisp weather, jolly fires and happy parties, here we have neither the one nor the other. The weather is beautiful and mild, and as for a fire when I was on board the Royal Albert nothing pleased me more than the sight of the large fire they were looking at. All we have here are small charcoal furnaces, and when it is cold at night we get one brought into our quarters and we all sit round it, and smoke like Turks. By the by if you look in the 'Illustrated London News' for 16th December you will see a view of a part of Scutari Hospital, it is one of the passages and the view is taken from the door of Miss Nightingale's quarters, just where I live. The picture is not good but will give you some idea of the place. The passage is not nearly so high nor so broad, in the centre between the two rows of beds we have only two or three feet, while in the picture you would think it was eight or ten. You see the first arch crossing over the passage, well, on the right hand side you see a fellow entering or about to enter a door, you may say that is me for he is going into my quarters. The beds are placed close to our doors and of course all the moaning of the patients at nights is heard to the best advantage while we are in bed, in general however, I sleep so sound that that never disturbs me in the least. Liff will be looking just now as when I saw it first twelve months ago, remember me to the inmates of the said cottage and tell the Costor I hope to hear from him again soon. Of course Aunt will be fretting herself and wondering how I am in regard to clothing, tell her to keep her mind easy I am very well off in that respect, only I wish all my white shirts were home again as they are of no use here, we all wear these coloured woollen ones and very comfortable things they are, saving their own in washing in less than no time. Socks I have in plenty. I hope father, mother, aunts and cousins etc., are all well. I should like to hear from father and mother often – ditto you – I have heard there is a mail just arrived at Constantinople. I hope there may be something for me. In future I intend writing uninteresting letters that will not be worth publishing but I think it would be difficult to do that. You asked me by the by about Miss Nightingale – when on board the 'Vectis' I did not know who or what she was, but since then we all know her very well. She is a very kind lady and what is more has £8,000 a year, which we all joke about here. The nurses are all under her charge, sometimes we get a visit from her in the wards and if a nurse is required for a patient she sends one. At some parts of the hospital they attend every day and dress the patients, but to do that at all the hospitals would require 50 times the number. She keeps strict watch over them and they work very well, but I think just the same could be done by the orderlies which we have always in our wards (soldiers who act as nurses). I had a farce with Miss Nightingale today, she was visiting some of my patients who were very bad and was asking one poor fellow who had got his leg shot off and who was complaining of thirst, if he would like rice water or barley water to drink, he thought for a little and then said he would prefer brandy and water if it was all the same to her.

CHAPTER 3

Kulalie; Death of a Colleague

KULALIE, (NEAR) SCUTARI
14TH JANUARY 1855

My dear Mother,

Since I have never yet had the pleasure of writing you since I left home I intend now to give you the first letter this year, and a long screed, I will try to make it. I was very happy to receive some days ago such a long letter from you and Anne, and many thanks for you all for it. I brought in the New Year very quietly indeed, owing to Dr Struthers being ill, in fact at that time I scarcely thought he would live. I had to sit up the whole of New Year's night with him and had to cut out all his hair myself. I am glad to say he is now past the worst and when I heard last he was progressing very well under the care of Dr Mason. You will see by this letter I have changed my quarters and I must tell you how that change took place. There were so many of us at Scutari and we had so much to do and were so knocked about that I must say I was beginning to get tired of it, and heart-ily wishing myself at the Crimea – I had been exactly two months there on the 4th – I had just asked leave to amputate an arm and on being refused must say I felt snubbed, however, I assisted at the operation as it was one of my own patients. After the operation I was going to my own quarters in a demure state and wishing Scutari and all its inmates – at least all its first class staff surgeons – to the mischief, when I was touched on the shoulder by our principal medical officer and the following conversation took place.

'You are Dr Greig?'

'Yes.'

'You are ordered to proceed to Kulalie immediately and take charge of Russian prisoners'.

'I can't go, Dr Struthers is very ill and I can't leave him.'

'You must go when the Service requires you.'

'Very well.'

'You give over your present charge and proceed tomorrow'.

If Struthers had not been ill I should have been most happy to have gone. Poor Struthers was far worse about it than I was. I packed up my traps next morning and also my blankets which I had got out of store at Scutari. I had no qualms of conscience about stealing the blankets, oh no, I was determined to make myself comfortable wherever I might be sent. As the grand rule here to keep health is to eat well, drink well and sleep well, and it was impossible to do the latter without good blankets. The weather had suddenly changed and it was very cold and snowing. On the 5th I was furnished with a boat by the Commissariat and taking some of my things on board I started for Kulalie which is situated five miles up the Bosphorus. I was fully equipped, sword and all, covered up by my military cloak and a waterproof over it. It was snowing and very cold but with a short cutty pipe in my cheek I must say I enjoyed it. As I passed up the banks of the Bosphorus it looked most beautiful. The Turk who took me was a jolly fellow and talked the whole way. As we started he put his large cloak over my legs, and in his own way made me feel very comfortable, intimating at the same time he expected a 'Bucksheish' for it, I said 'Buono' so off we went. In passing up a Muezzin was calling the faithful to prayer from a minarette on the banks of the Bosphorus. I asked him about it but he told me it was a 'Yok Bano' and that he did not believe in it as he was an Armenian Protestant. He was coughing and I explained to him I was a doctor, he coughed and pointing to his chest always cried 'No Buono' and then followed it up by 'Buono by and bye' to which I of course assented. After about an hour and half's pulling we reached Kulalie and I landed at my new quarters which I must now describe. Kulalie is a small village situated five miles up the Bosphorus on the Asiatic side, it is peopled by Greeks chiefly but also by Turks. It is most beautifully situated in a kind of Bay with hills behind, from the top of one it is said you can get the finest view in Europe. In a clear day you see far down the Sea of Marmara, the whole of the Bosphorus and as far up as the Black Sea. At the northern extremity of the village there are large cavalry barracks close to the water's edge, and as there is no ebb or flow in the Bosphorus the water is always within a foot of the path in front of the barracks. A part of this barrack is set aside for the wounded Russian prisoners and more of it is to be appropriated as an hospital for the English, both barracks and hospital at Scutari being full. It is a most romantic place and I am very glad I was sent to it. There are only two other English army surgeons and a French one here at present. We have got what we call a scratch mess – that is everyone brings his own tin plate, cup and saucer, etc. I and the other Asst. stay together in a very nice room overlooking the Bosphorus, and our mess is held in our room. It is smaller and more comfortable than we had a Scutari, our mess table it is true, is as usual two shutters placed on a box and a cask, but when it is covered over with a BA [British Army] bedcover I can assure you it is a swell table. My companions are the other two medical men, a commissariat officer, and the Commandant (Capt. Brendon, 1st Royals, G. Fenwick's regt.), all jolly fellows. They all meet and smoke in our room at night and every second night we are honoured by a visit from the Bey who commands the Turkish Cavalry here, he brings his long pipe and we are as happy as princes. Besides we have the Turkish band performing during dinner and also in the evening, they play very well, waltz, polka, etc., and by way of honouring us 'God save the Queen' is attempted every evening with 'Partant pour la Syrie' in compliment to our allies the French. Oh, it is jolly. We are quite isolated here and as happy as I could wish. The other Assistant Surgeon comes from Corfu and talks Greek which is of great use here. Already I have seen more of Greek and Turkish customs than I did all the time I was at Scutari. No sooner was I landed than Dr Temple (Assistant Surgeon) and I went out to see an old Turk who was sick. His name was Ali-bey – of course I was very willing to go in order to see the house. All the Turks here as soon as they enter a house cast off their shoes and then go upstairs, we don't do it, but wipe our feet as clean as we can. Well we did this in Ali-bey's house and entered his parlour as I suppose where we found the old chap comfortable enough I assure you, beautiful ottomans all round the room, and a large brass charcoal burner in the centre. A servant brought long pipes and a small cup of coffee and we sat and examined our patient, rather a comical medical visit I must say. There was very little the matter with him so we cleared off soon. I did nothing the first night but next morning I went to Scutari for the rest of my luggage. The morning was cold but very fine. I took a soldier with me and after getting my things all square about 3pm I wished to go back. However it had come on to snow and although there were about 30 boatmen all smoking round a fire none would move, so here was a fix. I did not care for myself but the soldier I had for a servant would have been put 'in quod' if he stayed away all night from Kulalie. After a great deal of trouble I succeeded in getting two at about six times the usual price to row me up. I have been in a great many of the Greek houses, they are as it were the Town houses, rickety affairs, generally built of wood and brick. The rooms are small and in those houses which we would call the better class, you find ottomans round the rooms the same as in the Turkish houses. The Greeks are a lazy dangerous set, very much given to use the knife, and therefore not at all comfortable to deal with, however they are very kind to us, I suppose we do them good. As we passed along the street the other day, I and a friend, some Greeks pulled us into a tavern and insisted on treating us to wine, etc., they also presented us with flowers. I discovered afterwards I had prescribed for his wife the day before. The Greek girls are most beautiful and quite some up to Byron's description, there is a laughing merry-hearted English look about them which I can't describe. I am sorry I cannot talk to them but my companion does for me and we get very good friends by laughing to one another. They are very neatly dressed, the dress is plain and generally ornamented down the front with a neat small apron. When they are going anything such as cleaning about the house the dress is tucked up on each side and by this management is shown short petticoats, beautiful wide white trousers, fringed with lace, white stockings and slippers. I think I hear you say these are things you have no business with, but since I have been blessed with eyes I can't help using them. The head dress is very simple and very neat also, a coloured muslin handkerchief with flowers painted round the margin, is put on the head in such a manner that it can be tied tight round the head and allow a corner to hand down over the back, covering the back hair which is put up in two long plaits, sometimes the hair is ornamented by artificial flowers, wrought into it, oh, I wish I could only bring home some of the beauties of the Bosphorus to show them to you, I am sure you would like them. As for their customs the best thing I can do is to give you an account of my first visit to one of their houses. Dr Temple and I went to see an old fellow with liver complaint. We knocked at the door and it was answered by a very pretty girl – daughter of the patient – she wished us good morning in her native tongue. We brushed our boots as clean as we could at the bottom of the stair – they always remove their shoes until they go out again – we are however excused from doing this – we went upstairs and saw our patient curled up in the corner of a room squatted on an ottoman. The old lady was there nursing him, also another daughter and a son. We sat down, looked at his tongue, felt his pulse, and then we admired the girls. I looked at them and they blushed, I laughed and they laughed. I told one she was like a pretty English girl and she seemed to understand me and looked flattered, the old folks looked fierce and I thought I had better stop my flattery. The prettiest then went out and returned with a small tray on which was placed a glass jar of jelly or rather jam, somewhat like conserve of roses, two tumblers of water and 4 or 5 teaspoons. She presented it to me and I could not make out for the life of me what to do. I could do nothing but laugh so she showed me what to do much to the amusement of all. I took a clean teaspoon, took a large sup of jelly, replaced the spoon on the tray, took a drink of water, and so ended the ceremony, everyone present did the same and the tray was carried off. Each of us then had a small cup of coffee, we talked for a short time and then took our leave. In all the Greek houses we always get a 'cup of jelly' and in most coffee, and also sometimes a smoke but very seldom that is a Turkish custom. I enjoy this place very much and a more beautiful place you could not well see. I was over all the hills the other day with the Commandant shooting. There was about two feet of snow on the ground in some places, it was so jolly however, we hurt nothing, as for fishing none of us try it, but I suppose it would be good, the fish aint 'gackly niggers' but lots of beautiful mackerel we get. I was down at Scutari yesterday and saw Struthers, he is better, but I cannot say he was looking well. There was a large abscess formed on the side of his face. He is very weak and quite unable to get out of bed yet, he will I hope get over it but I don't think he will be much use here. Johnston is also knocked up. He has been confined to his quarters since Xmas and when I saw him last he was in bed. He had been out one day but took ill immediately again. He has been ill but more frightened than hurt I think. I think he will be home very soon, the only thing that keeps him is the question 'What will Simpson say?' I heard two days ago from a fellow who had come from the Crimea that Erskine was lying very ill of typhus fever in a tent at the camp. I am in most splendid health, in fact, I never was better. I must say I look coarse but nothing comes wrong to me. I can eat and drink at all times and any quantity. The work here is very pleasant. We have 221 Russian prisoners and I have charge of 77 of them. They are very comfortable and what is more very happy. They are smart good-looking fellows, some are very badly wounded, more especially the Cossacks who were engaged in the Cavalry charge at Balaclava and who have got some very ugly cuts especially about the back of the head. At home they talk of Russian serfs etc., all the men we have here are smart fellows, almost all can read, and many can write. They are little or no trouble, give them plenty to eat and drink – and all's well. They are in two large wards, the most of them are able to walk about and they spend their time as they like. Some mend shoes, some clothes, some play cards, some smoke, and all are happy. The only disagreeable thing is the sentry walking at the door with a drawn bayonet. One of them, a young fellow can talk a few words of English, he acts as my servant in the wards, and I am picking up some Russian words from him for the benefit of my patients. I suppose you have heard of the celebrated Major Alexander Ungelisopilo who was found stabbing the English lying wounded after Inkerman. He had received a wound through the shoulder joint and died under my charge three days ago. I took his shoulder as a souvenir – a memento of the brute. This place will very soon be turned into a general hospital and the Russians removed to the arsenal at Constantinople. Two days ago we got 268 English sick from the Crimea, a great many having lost their toes etc., from frost bite in the trenches. Since writing the first part of this two other Assistant Surgeons have also come here to help us and joined our mess. Oh, what a strange thing the army is? Change, change, we got notice yesterday to flit again. We are now in the Sultan's quarters (the Sultan has quarters in every barrack) and swell quarters they are, exactly in the centre of the barracks over-looking the Bosphorus. It is no use singing 'I dreamt I dwelt in Marble Halls' for it is I actually dwell in marble halls. The roof and walls are most beautifully ornamented (I only wish cousin David could see them) and the star and crescent look you in the face wherever you turn. As I lay in bed this morning I actually counted about three dozen stars and crescents on the roof. The Commandant occupies the best room, and it is most beautiful, paintings (fresco) and gilded flowers, urns, etc., in great profusion. I cannot describe it but I enclose a plan which will give you some idea of it. In your last letter – (the Turkish band is at present playing an opera air below my window, Sunday night though it is) – excuse the interruption – you were all very kind in asking me to allow you to send a box, all I can say is I will only be too happy and I enclose a list of things I would like sent out and you can pack the box with anything you think proper if there is room. I do not require any more uniform but if I should at any time I will direct it to be sent to you from London. I am only very sorry I can't return the compliment and send you a box also. I will write to father next. I hope aunt, and Anne, are very well. Kind love to Mr and Mrs Sandeman, David George etc. Remember me to Mr McIntosh, Dan, Mrs Boyd, uncle, aunt, cousins and all kind friends in Dundee. Also when you write to Miss Sclater remember me to both the Mr and Mrs Sclater and thank them all for their kindness to me. I suppose you have not heard what a row one of Dr

Struthers' letters caused, it was to Simpson and the War Office folks heard that he had said something about Miss Nightingale in it, a correspondence ensued and the letter had to be sent them before they could be satisfied. Luckily there was not much in it and the accounts they had received had been exaggerated. Government are on their P's and Q's at present, and so they well may, such blundering and bad management I never saw the like of – so no more publishing – I was sorry to hear that Stuart Lithgow had volunteered as a dresser here – he is a great fool – anything after passing but not before. They are looked upon as camp followers, are bullied by everybody and as for £1 a day, that he will find to be all humbug and no mistake. Anne tells me of a lady who was visiting Miss Pirie – I can't think who – and who has fallen in love with me, do tell me who she is. I suppose she has an eye to the 'Patriotic Fund'. I am very sorry I have never yet had time to look after G. Fenwick's box at Constantinople. I have not been in that place for weeks now, and I do not know when I may get, but I will do so as soon as I can. Address my letters as usual Asst. Staff Surgeon, Kulalie by Scutari. I am a step nearer Sebastopol and at present am thankful I am no nearer, however if I was ordered I would go with great pleasure knowing I would be of use to our poor men who are suffering unknown hardships and being extirpated by degrees by sickness and not by wounds. I had intended to have finished this long ago and felt as if I could write all night, but I must stop. I will be writing to John Lindsay soon. Please give Dr Pirie a fillip and tell him I am at Kulalie.

> 'Singing Ala, Ala, Ala, Be,
> Ain't I jolly at Kulalie.' (Nigger song)

I am being drilled in sword exercise at present by a Sergt Major of the Guards in case I should require to use my toasting fork, as swords are called here, when I am sent to the Crimea which will be some time I have no doubt. Good bye.

List of Articles required.
1. A thick coarse pea jacket with lots of pockets.
2. A pair of jack boots to come 4 inches above my knees.
3. A pair of leggings like what Dr Pirie had.
4. The canteen (special).
5. A knife having corkscrew etc. you know what I mean and I must have a hole bored through it so that I can tie it on and not lose.

6. A dozen short cutty pipes, get Dr Pirie and Joe Rodgers to pick them
    for me.
7. Etc. etc. etc.

Dr Mathieson has my measure for my clothes, and Mr Scott for the
boots. When you send them off write and tell me what ship they go by
and who they are consigned to.

KULALIE
21ST JANUARY 1855

My dear Father,
   My dear friend Dr Alex Struthers died in my arms at Scutari yesterday morning at 2.45am and was buried this afternoon on a height close
by the shore of the sea of Marmara. I have written to his brother by this
post and will write you soon again.
   This leaves me in first rate health.

KULALIE (NEAR) SCUTARI
30TH JANUARY 1856

My dear Father,
   I suppose by this time you will have received my short note informing you of the death of my poor friend Struthers. He died of typhoid
fever, he took ill the day after Christmas and the fever ran its course as
we thought very well, unfortunately he had a relapse which was again
followed by a large abscess on the left cheek. This was opened and large
quantities of matter was discharged, next day he became comatose and
continued so for two days when he died. Dr Mason sent for me about
midday on the 19th I rode in as fast as I could but he was unable to
speak. I asked him if he knew me and he said 'No'. When he was becoming comatose he was anxious to see me and the last words he said were
'Is Greig come yet?' I stayed all day beside him he gradually became
worse towards night, about half past 2 in the morning I was lying on the
top of a bed beside him when his breathing altered. I jumped up and
raising him up I thought to give him a little relief, he had a short strug-
gle and fell back in my arms dead. Mason and I arranged his things that
night and wrote to his brother for instructions about them. Next day he
was buried on a height close by the sea of Marmara. It was a melancholy

sight to me, the 'Union Jack' covered his coffin and he received a soldier's funeral. I cannot tell you how his death affected me at the time, but I am now jogging on in much my usual way. Johnston has been confined to his quarters this last month, ill of remittent fever, as soon as he is able he is going home, and I must say it is the best thing he could do for he is little or no use here. He gets frightened about every little thing that affects him, and to joke him about going to the Crimea lays him for a fortnight. Johnston is a strange fellow and one who I must say I can't admire. Poor Struthers and I pulled well together, but neither of us could with Johnston, so we let him go where he liked and choose his own companions. Hearing about Struther's death you will I have no doubt be very anxious about me, well I am in as good health as ever I was all my life, I eat, drink, smoke, and sleep to any extent and am as happy as I could well expect to be. Of all the stations which a fellow can be sent to here I believe Kulalie is amongst the best. We are out of the way of the big-wigs and wear what clothes we like. When I am going about my usual work I am dressed in a rough warm shooting coat and trousers, a red sash round my waist which we term a cholera belt, and my forage cap, (which is the only article of my uniform) with a gold crown and a thundering V.R. on the front of it showing that I belong to the medical service. Add to all this a moustache, beard and whiskers, and I am sure you will say the good folks in Dundee would be astonished if they saw me. Do not be frightened for me killing myself with work, oh, no, you may keep your mind easy on that point ... I have, I must say, plenty to do for we have now about 500 sick English here. I am generally amongst my patients until between 12 and 1 o'clock. I have lunch and off I go to amuse myself on the hills shooting or doing anything I like. I borrow a gun or if I can't get one I take my pistol, ramble about till between 4 and 5 then don't I pitch into dinner. In the evening I visit my patients about 8 o'clock and after having a talk about things in general, a glass of grog, smoke and off to bed at 10 o'clock. You will say that is early but going early to bed and having a good sleep is one of the best things for preserving health here I know of. Poor Struthers erred here, he would sit up till all the hours, the same as he had done at home. It was no use talking to him, I told him he would hurt himself but he only laughed at me and I am sure this tended very much to weaken him.

Many thanks to you for your kind letter and postage stamps. Your letter has the same fault as all the rest, viz. too short. It is dated 5th December and you may imagine where it had been, at no less a place than Sebastopol. I do not think it was actually in the town but it was picked up in Balaclava post office by a friend of mine there and reached me today. All the letters which have been sent me as well as the newspapers have come very irregularly but still I am very thankful they do come. Dr Pirie's letter also reached me today. It is very pleasant to hear of parties etc going on as usual. I am not sure if I could speak to an English lady now, I am sure I would feel very awkward. The only English ladies I ever see are the nuns, ten came here about a week ago under the charge of a Miss Stanley, a daughter I believe of the Bishop of Norwich. She is a very nice person and all under her are anxious to do good. The first night they came we told the Bey to give us more music at night. He said that instead of the band playing three tunes they would play five, two for the gentlemen, and three for the ladies, and weren't they astonished by hearing 'Buffalo Galls' and 'Lucy Neal' under their windows. The nuns are dressed in black and these tunes were very appropriate. Lady Stratford de Redcliffe has taken a fancy to this hospital and has taken it under her special protection and we are honoured by a visit from her every three or four days. She comes in a splendid *caique* – 10 oars – very often accompanied by her two daughters, kicks up a row about this and that, gives us all a most gracious bow and we wish her ladyship 'good luck' till she comes back again. A great many of our cases now are cases of frostbite and we have a few operations. I seem to be a 'don' here and am consulted by my superior on every case, one of which I must tell you about. A man of the 30th Regiment was brought down from the Crimea with his feet frostbit and was put under the charge of one of the doctors here. I had nothing to do with him but one day the surgeon who has charge here took me to him and asked me what should be done. I told him he ought to amputate one of the feet at the ankle joint after Syme's method. He said he would rather amputate below the knee as he was not acquainted with the operation, having been all his days at the Cape of Good Hope. I took him to the dead house and showed him how to do, he said, 'My fine fellow, it is a beautiful operation but I can't do it, if you like to take the risk and say it should be done, you must do it.' Just what I wanted. We had a consultation of all the staff and everyone spoke against it, but as I insisted on it the patient was taken from a fellow senior to me in the service, put into one of my wards, the operation performed and I am glad to say I have saved a nice young fellow's leg, besides getting a great deal of credit from all my companions, and the result is all the bad cases are sent to me, which is very good. The amount of practice I see here of all kinds is immense and I hope may be of use to me in after life. I am as comfortable as possible but I should like to go to the Crimea soon, all the talk just now is medals, and if I am not there before the war is over I will not get a Crimean medal. Some say we are to get one for service at Scutari from the Sultan and the joke goes we are to get one for attending to his Russian wounded from no less a person than the Czar himself.

We have had some very cold weather here but it has now passed off and we have as it were alternate wet and fine warm days. Very little has occurred here worth mentioning except a ceremony which I witnessed about a fortnight ago, viz: – The Christening of the Bosphorus. Two days before the ceremony we had a young Greek in our quarters, talking about things in general, he told us that the ceremony was to take place and if we like he would come and take us to it. We all agreed to go although he told us it took place at 6 in the morning, and there was snow on the ground. There is an old saying that it takes two good fellows at night to wake one in the morning, and so it proved, in fact we forgot all about it and were quite astonished and could not understand what the fellow wanted when we found him in our bedroom when it was yet quite dark, we reasoned the thing and at last I and two others did get up and off we set. The ceremony took place close to a wooden jetty close to the shore of the Bosphorus, luckily a steamer was lying at the jetty taking in cattle and we went on board of her. The morning was very cold and hard frost had made the roads like glass. Some young Greek ladies had managed to get out of bed and appeared on the beach in 'full fig' as we say. To describe the dress of the young ladies I suppose I must – shortly however – one had a very pretty small bonnet on the back of her head made of blue and white silk, blue satin dress and white scarf, another had a tartan silk etc., etc., I can't be bothered talking about these, well to show them our gallantry we got them all on board and gave them seats. Of course this gave great éclat to the affair. The morning was cold and we were very glad when the mate of the vessel gave us what he called a 'nippen' to keep cold out. We waited about half an hour and then saw a good many *caiques* arrange themselves off the shore, and some of the men began to take off their clothes, soon after the Bey – who is our friend – and is governor of the village, and a party of Turkish soldiers arrived followed by their priests and a procession bearing crosses, lanthorns, etc., followed by a mob. The priests came close to the water's edge, one said a short prayer, another said a kind of proclamation, and the third taking up a small silver cross threw it with a cry into the water. Immediately the fellows we had seen undressing plunged and dived into it, there was of course a scramble and an aqueous fight, one young fellow got it and swam to his boat, the cross was seized and eagerly kissed by all on board and then handed round. The procession then moved off to the Church to finish the ceremony. We wished to go but the Bey persuaded us rather to go with him. He took us to a grand house where he introduced us to a General (Turkish). We had of course long pipes and coffee sat for about half an hour and then got so hungry that we were very glad to get the termination of the ceremony alone and bolt home to breakfast, and you may believe we were quite ready for it. I had the pleasure of seeing my old friend Dr Miller, surgeon on H M S Simoan, who used to attend the infirmary in Dundee when I was there. I cannot tell you who he is but you will know who I mean. I heard he was in Constantinople, he invited me to dine on board with him. I had a first rate dinner and then we went to the Opera. The Opera in Constantinople is on the whole very good. It is small and the company are chiefly Greeks with a sprinkling of Italians and also an English prima donna who calls herself Madam Alba – Alias in plain English Mrs White. The scenery is very fine, in fact much better than we had in Edinburgh, the singing is good, and on the whole I enjoyed myself very much. I slept on board the Simoan that night and returned to Kulalie next morning. Dr Miller is looking as stout as ever and we had such a long talk about Dundee. I was very lucky also in knowing the Asst. Surgeon who I found to be an old Edinburgh friend and we were all so jolly. A good dinner wets a fellow on his feet for a week here and as a general rule whenever a ship is landing sick here I go on board and am very often asked to breakfast or dinner and all know that dinner on board ship is no humbug. I am much better off in regards to living than I ever was before, we have a regular mess established and I can assure it is much better and more pleasant than taking food by yourself. When a person is alone he makes anything do for dinner, but when in a mess you must always take a good one. We have only breakfast and dinner, no tea or supper, in fact everyone is so hungry that he eats so much dinner it would be impossible to take anything but punch after it.

In one of Anne's letters she tells me about a Captain Daws whom Anne Pirie knows. What about him? I have never seen him yet. Many thanks to mother for her long letter. I hope she received mine which I had sent off before I received hers. Mrs George Baxter wishes me to bring back a turban for her, a real Turkish one, give her my kindest compliments and tell her the ladies do not wear turbans here, and as for those of the gentlemen they simply put on a fez and then twist a shawl round their heads but nevertheless I shall keep a look out and if I should see anything like what she wants I shall remember her. Just as I am finishing this I have received Anne's letter of no date, and your short note enclosed of 15th January. I am very glad to hear you are all as well and hope you may long continue so. Tell Anne her letter is a capital one and since I have discovered she can write such a long one, just let me try and catch her writing any other kind after this. We have very few flowers here just now but I will remember her request and always send her a leaf. The first opportunity I get I intend to send home all my white shirts and my black dress suit, also a Russian sword picked up on the field of Alma, and some charms and trinkets taken from Russian prisoners, curiosities perhaps in their way. I fear it is time to draw to a close. Please remember me to all the many kind friends who may ask for me. Continue to send the newspapers and you will oblige the whole mess. I see by then the town has come out very patriotic and recognise the names of my two cousins and lots of my friends as subscribers, it seems to be quite the fashion now-a-days. I think I deserve some of it. What is Dr Crockatt about? I suppose he is trudging about as usual, every old wife's servant. Tell him to get a cocked hat, and a red jacket and to come out here to serve her Majesty. Oh, how some of the doctor's patients would stare if he came to see them in a red jacket. How is uncle and aunt Pirie? How are all my cousins? How is everybody? Mr and Mrs Sandeman and family. Mr Justice, John Thoms, and a host of others too numerous to mention. Mr McIntosh, Mr Baxter, John Stewart, etc. etc. Write me often and give me all the news and nonsense going. I will always write on the 15th or 30th of each month and give you all my chit-chat. Good bye, may you all be as well as this leaves me.

ps. I shall keep a look out for my box which I have begun to take a great interest in, send the key in a letter if it is at all a small one.

pps. Lord Kinnaird's offer has just come in and I wish you to forward the enclosed to him. To stay in a large hospital in the heat of summer would be clear murder. I am very anxious to get to the Crimea and tho' I wrote to Syme and Simpson to get me sent up I have never yet heard anything of it. Dr O'Connor our chief medical officer advises me to get attached to a regiment by all means if I go to the Crimea because when you go to a regiment you are the same as going to a ship, you belong to the regiment and the regiment belongs to you, and you have brother officers who take an interest in you. Whereas as I am at present I belong to nothing and I may be shipped here, there or anywhere, at an hour's notice. I do not much mind to what regiment I am appointed but if I had my choice I should prefer the Rifle Brigade which is a very fine regiment. As for mess there is none to pay so that would not be expensive and as no uniform can be got here what I have at present would do. A regiment during peace is a very expensive thing but just now it is very different. I do not ask your opinion on this matter because you are not in a position to give an opinion, but you may believe me it will be better for me afterwards, so please send the letter, do not keep it back, or I will be very much disappointed indeed. At the same time do not mention to anyone what you have done. I may be gazetted to a regiment before this reaches you, if so, do not send it, but if not send it. If I am appointed I will go up just at the beginning of summer to the Crimea which will be very nice, thereby escaping the cholera, plagues, and other nice diseases which go about Turkey in summer. Dr Watson, an old fellow clerk in the Edinburgh Infirmary has arrived here and curious to say added to the staff at Eulalie. Enclosed is the smallest Turkish gold coin value 1/- it will do for mother's watch as an ornament.

My dear Father,

Dr Mason died at Scutari on the 8th inst. of fever. Oh, father I leave you to judge the effects which the death of my two (only) friends here has had upon me. I am in first rate health and what is more I am in comparatively good spirits. If you have not sent my note off to Lord Kinnaird please do so immediately. If we are to have crowded hospitals during summer I can assure you it will be far worse than in camp. I have seen very few here who would not infinitely prefer the camp to an hospital. Dr Erskine called on me the other day, he has been ill, but is now better. I will write to Anne on the 15th. Good bye at present. Love to all.

My dear Anne,

I suppose you received the notice I sent you of Dr Mason's death, poor fellow he was only four days ill. I saw him the day before he died and he commissioned me should he die to bury him beside Dr Struthers and to write home to his mother. Both were difficult tasks more especially the latter as he was an only child and his mother a widow. I wrote her two days ago and gave her an account of his illness in as tender a manner as I could. Only think a month ago three young fellows in the very best of health living as happy as possible together, and now two are dead, and I am alone. When I look back on the last month and a half I am struck with the wonderful manner Providence has preserved me. Dr Struthers took ill of fever and I was just beginning to get fagged nursing him and thereby more liable to take fever, when without any cause I was forced to leave him and come to as healthy a place as you could well choose. Dr Struthers was so restless that I must have sat up night after night with him and had I done so I in all probability would have shared Dr Mason's fate as it was he who was left. He removed to another quarter and got a companion with him, he took ill – died – and now I believe the companion who nursed him is ill too. When I left Scutari fever was just commencing to attack the medical men then, and since then 10 have got my share of it. However as it is I am still in the land of the living and in first rate health. Since coming out here and witnessing so many melancholy and sad sights, and seeing every day so many dead and dying men, I must say my feelings are now very much blunted, in fact I do not know what would make me cry, you would have thought the death of my two friends would have been an awful blow to me, it was so for a day or two, I found new companions and I and the world around me as if my two companions had never been known. Were I to get into low spirits here I do not know how I would stand it at all but I never am, there is so much change – away on the hills – sailing on the Bosphorus – shooting – reading novels, etc., so I keep in the very best of health and am happy. When I wrote last I think I told you the weather here was very cold, now it is quite changed and you could imagine yourself in the middle of summer in Scotland. Some of our fellows bathe every day and consider it warm. All the hills are beautiful and green and the trees begun to bud. I am sure this must be a beautiful country in summer for even now we have so many evergreens that it looks well. Our hospital here is now full, we have about 1,000 English and upwards of 100 Russians, and what is more I am allowed to perform my own operations. I had the pleasure of performing an amputation at the thigh on a poor unfortunate Russian this forenoon and tomorrow I am to perform my second amputation at the ankle joint. This is something like work and recompenses for our many weary medical cases. I had the pleasure of meeting Dr Erskine about a week ago. I found him in my quarters seeking me. He has been in the Crimea but has been sent down sick. He is now much better and like all who come from the Crimea would much rather prefer the hardships of the camp than the dangers of an hospital. He was expecting to be sent to Smyrna for a while to do duty there and recover his health but I do not know more about him. I wished him to stay for a day or two with me but he could not. He promised to come back soon again but I have never seen him. When I was across at the other side of the Bosphorus yesterday I met some English sailors and by way of saying something I asked them when they were going home. They said they were to sail tomorrow morning, so as the ship belonged to Hull I asked the mate if he could take a parcel for me and he said he would do so. If I had had time I might have sent a lot of things. I had to bundle what I could into a canvas bag and send it off, however with what I had. I scarcely know what I put in. My black suit and some white shirts which are quite useless here and which are a burden, I stuffed in a Russian sword from Alma, a string of Russian charms and amulets taken from the prisoners, some half dozen bullets and anatomical preparations, there is also a whip rather the worse for wear from thrashing dogs but which may be of some use to Dr Pirie and an old curiosity in its way, having come from Kulalie, in fact I wished to send him something and there was nothing else I could lay my hand on at the time. My black coat and shirts you may put past until I turn out a civil swell again, and how I shall feel then I have not the slightest idea. I wonder how a hat would feel on my head, what an idea, a cocked hat is comfortable enough, but oh, crikey, think of a round tile. The sword was taken from an artillery man (Russian) at Alma and is by no means a bad blade. The crosses etc. may be hung up in the cabinet and the anatomical preparations and bullets put in a safe place. Take care of them for everyone has a history and must not be lost. I do not think they will be home for at least eight weeks but you can keep a lookout for the bark 'Expert of Hull'. The mate said he would put it aboard one of the Dundee and Hull traders. I know it was a great risk sending them home so but I could not always carry them about with me and I thought it a good opportunity to give them a change, if they reach Dundee, well if not it can't be helped. Nothing of any very great importance has occurred in my sight-seeing since I wrote except a visit which I made along with two friends to the Palace of the Sultan. He is not yet living in it himself, it is newly built, situated close to the water's edge – an ornamental garden and fantastic grass plots, and fish ponds give you the first idea of grandeur. A look at the ornamental and pillared front of the building makes you open your eyes a little and made me exclaim 'Well I am blowed if the Turks are such heathens after all.' Yes they are. If they only made gutters and streets instead of palaces it would be much better. However we got a guide and entered first a large hall which we understood to be the Throne room. It is in the form of a dome, beautiful marble pillars, fluted and corniced with white and gold. Room lighted from above by coloured glass windows, the whole of the roof appearing as if (from painting) it was covered with rich satin crimson drapery, an immense glass chandelier hanging from the centre – this was covered with a cloth but which was removed to let us see it – and the Turk with a grave look informed us that it was 'English Candle'. I expected to see Price's Patent but to my surprise discovered he meant gas – the first I had seen in Turkey – a small gasometer supplying the palace. We then passed up a staircase – stocking soles of course – and it was beautiful and the immense pillars which supported the railing were of cut crystal. The different rooms we were in were in general small, and looked like so many beautiful ornamented ivory cabinets. We visited the bathroom which was made entirely of porphyry and of course cut into baths and basins of all sorts and sizes. I jumped into a bath and of course others followed saying, they could say we had been in the Sultan's bath. The Turk looked in amazement at us but we hinted bucksheish and he was content. Altogether the place was worth seeing even the floors could not be plain and were highly polished and composed of numerous small pieces of wood, all colours, something like the tops of our small tables and as fine every bit.

We have now a good many nuns or rather Sisters of Mercy and nurses here and each of us have two who attend to our patients and do what we bid them, cook extras etc. The nuns are meek quiet creatures and although very willing can't do much. The nurses are like our better class of nurses at home. All are sadly disappointed at what they have come to and wish themselves home again. One told me it was a great mistake, they were little or no use. They were carried off by the excitement at home and instead of coming out to attend noble fine fellows they have to attend poor miserable wretches, covered with fleas, lice, etc. etc. They do their best however and in doing so set the barracks on fire the other day and a pretty mess we had to go through before it was put out, so much for females when they find their way where they have no business. I hope father, mother and aunt are well, remember me kindly to my cousins etc. I should like to get a glimpse of old Dundee again. I often dream of you all and have long talks with you, sometimes start up in bed and instead of the Tay find the Bosphorus rolling under my bedroom windows. However by and bye I hope to see you all, so here's to a happy meeting, when it does happen, be that when it may. Excuse shortness this time as this is a short month and I will write again on the 28th. So good bye.

CHAPTER 4

Sickness, Near Death

Dear Sir,

As your son David has been by no means well and as I am sure it will cause you far less anxiety to know this and to know at the same time how he is getting on, than a post should be allowed to pass without you hearing of him. I have proposed to him to allow me to write to you and to this he has consented. Last Thursday (20th) he was in Scutari making some arrangements about poor Mason's things and when he returned he complained of not feeling at all well and of feeling cold and chilly. Next day his stomach was very much out of order and since then he has been suffering severely from gastro biliary derangement. Yesterday morning he was much better, but having been a good deal annoyed by a proposal on the part of our RMO Dr Tice that he should be removed from his quarters along with the rest of us to give better accommodation for the ladies under Miss Stanley's care, and when he got this order countermanded upon your son's account, by the noise of removal of things in the adjoining rooms, he felt uneasy and restless all afternoon but slept soundly last night. He seems a good deal better today and I hope that in a few days he will be quite himself again. He only now suffers from lassitude and a feeling of weakness. We have had a very severe earthquake today, the house rocked backwards and forwards in a very alarming way. There are several cracks in the walls the result of the shock. It lasted about a minute. I am glad to say there has been no accident here.

I hope you will excuse the liberty I have taken in thus addressing you, and believe me, yours
Very sincerely,
Patrick Heron Watson

[Appended note by DG]

You know when I have a gastro biliary touch it is generally pretty severe, but complicated with an earthquake I can assure you it is no joke. Yesterday as I was lying in bed just imagine the roof of my room dancing and all the walls setting to each other. Last night I had a dreadful nightmare which turned out to be an earthquake again. I have scarcely got over the shake, but this morning I felt very well. I will give you a short note every Monday and Thursday if I think necessary until the 15th. Good bye. I am, my dear Father, your son,

David Greig

Dear Sir,

I regret that I have again to write to you instead of your son, who I am very sorry to say has been very seriously ill indeed. His illness which at the time I wrote, I along with all his other friends regarded as simply a severe case of gastro biliary derangement very speedily showed itself to be neither more nor less than Typhus fever. Last night and the night before he was really alarmingly ill but I rejoice to be able to tell you that there is a marked improvement in all his symptoms from this morning at daybreak. This is now the eleventh day and from the comfortable state in which he now is, that of a quiet natural sleep, I expect that tomorrow and next day will find him better and better. He is in good hands as Mrs Tice, the wife of our principal medical officer is most unremitting in her attentions, and the servant and the nurse and I should add the Chaplain are no less so. He bids me tell you that as soon as he is able he intends to start for Smyrna to spend his sick leave with I think he said Charles Boyd. I daresay you will know to whom it is he refers, and that should he not speedily get strong and well there he will quit the service and return home without delay. I do not think there is any room for anxiety for him now though of course at this stage of his illness it is impossible to speak with that certainty which I well know you long to possess. He is comparatively little brought down by the attack, his tongue, appetite, and pulse, are much improved, and his intellect is becoming quite clear and acute while the drowsiness is gradually passing off. I will leave this letter open until the despatch of our letters in the morning to give you the latest intelligence of how he is. Pray accept my most sincere sympathy with you in the anxiety which I regret such a letter must necessarily cause, and remember that in all probability he will be on his way to Smyrna by the time this reaches you.

Believe me with sincere respect,

Yours most truly,

Patrick Heron Watson

Dear Sir,

As I had anticipated he awakened this morning both in feeling and in reality a great deal better. He awoke only once or twice during the night asking for a drink. He had some appetite for breakfast and looks forward to the forenoon when he is to have a good plateful of porridge and milk which I think he enjoys more from home association than from anything else.
Yours sincerely,
Patrick Heron Watson

KULALIE
7TH MARCH 1855

Dear Sir,

I regret exceedingly that I can give you no favourable account of my dear friend, in fact we all consider him to be in a most dangerous state. Since I last wrote his serious symptoms have continued unabated. We have had to shave his head and apply one blister to the crown of his head and today another to the nape and back of the neck. He lies in a dreamy state but when roused answers questions slowly but collectedly, but often in the middle of some train of thought of his own starting, forgets what he was saying and cannot finish the sentence. The worst symptom of all however is the constant though slight twitching of his fingers and arms, while his pulse keeps up at 120 and is very weak. I do not think that his case is by any means hopeless but I think it is only right to let you know the worst, that should our dear friend be taken away from us you may not be unprepared for the severe blow. One Presbyterian chaplain who sees him frequently speaks of his state of mind as most satisfactory which I am sure must be a very great consolation to you in your affliction.

Pray accept of my sincere sympathy with yourself and Mrs Greig in this severe trial. May you receive strength to endure it from Him who alone can give it and with whom are the issues of life, and believe me,
Dear Sir,
Very sincerely yours,
Patrick Heron Watson.

I am glad to be able to tell you that we all think David decidedly better this morning and Dr O'Connor has such a favourable opinion of the improvement that he thinks him out of danger. David says he feels much better.

Dear Sir,

I am very glad to be able to communicate good news to you by this letter.
Since I wrote last David has made slow but most satisfactory progress. All
his unpleasant symptoms are now gone and there seems now every prospect of
a speedy convalescence. His memory is not yet very strong. He sleeps soundly
and well, as he himself says 'fully eighteen out of the twenty-four' which I do
not think is by any means an exaggeration. His appetite is still capricious, his
great desire is for oatmeal porridge, which he generally gets once or twice in a
day from Mrs Tice who continues to tend him most devotedly. As soon as he
is strong enough to bear removal a board will be held on him to invalid him
for several weeks, and grant him sick leave. I think that in all probability he
will go to Malta, which of all places is I think the most pleasant and the most
convenient when one's time is limited. I am sure he deserves every indulgence
in the way of relaxation, as none could have been more thoroughly devoted
to his most onerous duties than he was just before he took ill. I will leave this
letter open as I have done in previous ones to the last moment to give you the
latest accounts, and
With best regards,
Believe me, Yours most sincerely,
P H Watson

12TH MARCH
David is quite out of danger. He bids me tell you he won't bother himself
writing to anybody till he feels quite well. He says he has such an appetite that
he could eat a horse. He has taken tea, bread and butter, and eggs and enjoyed
it exceedingly.

My dear Madam,

I know you have accounts by every post of your son's state but knowing how valuable every detail is I venture to write.

I sincerely trust that your son will be spared. That his state is very precarious cannot be concealed but I see that Dr Tice, the chief medical man, hopes that the worst is over. I am here as superintendent of the nurses and ladies who came out to attend upon the sick and wounded soldiers. Your son is in the room next to ours. It is a large high room with a range of windows on one side commanding a magnificent view of the Bosphorus and Constantinople – there is always a fresh breeze coming from the water. Your son's bed is moved into the centre of the room with his head towards the windows – it is a small camp bed with a grey rug.

For the last ten days he has required night as well as day attendance and as Mrs Tice and her maid undertook the day my staff undertook the night. We have but few hands but each has gladly taken her turn, both nurses and ladies. I am not strong enough to take my turn I am sorry to say. He is so patient, no expression of murmuring ever crosses his lips I believe even when he has wandered. I truly believe had he been at home he could not have been nursed and attended more carefully or had more comfort. The medical men have been most attentive. Dr Tice is in the same passage and can be called any moment. Mrs Tice has had the chief charge of his sick room and when he spoke on Saturday about his things saying that such directions would not impede his recovery but that he should feel glad to have given them. He has always thought so much of you. Miss Taylor, one of the ladies who was sitting up with him one night was much affected by hearing him, as he was half asleep murmuring 'kiss me, mother.' The Presbyterian minister, Mr Johnson, who has lately come out here has been constantly to visit him and therefore I feel he has had every spiritual consolation. We all feel deeply interested in his case. He was so much respected by all. This morning's account is that he is decidedly better and has eaten an egg and some toast for breakfast.

Dear Madam may God be with you in this great anxiety and may He give you strength to say 'Thy will be done.'

I will write again by the next or following post. Any letter sent to me (Miss Stanley) to Grosvenor Crescent, London, will be forwarded.

Believe me to remain yours with deep Christian sympathy.

M Stanley

Dear Sir,

I am truly glad to be able to tell you that David is making most satisfactory progress towards a complete recovery. He sleeps soundly, has a capital appetite, and is now perfectly composed and tranquil. I think there can be little doubt but that he shall be able to get a board to send him home on sick leave, unless they rigidly adhere to the rule that no officer shall go further than Malta on sick leave. I regret exceedingly to think that when we are now rejoicing in his recovery you will just be receiving my letter in which I felt it my duty to prepare you for the worst. He is very much brought down by his illness, but has improved most wonderfully in appearance, as in every other respect, within the last few days. We have had a great deal of sickness among us of late, out of eleven asst. surgeons three are sick confined to bed just now from fever and other affections more or less serious and I think I may say with truth that not one of us has escaped from some digestive derangement more or less severe during the last two weeks. I believe this to be owing to the quarters into which we were put after being ejected from the Sultan's quarters by Lady Stratford's orders for the better accommodation of Miss Stanley and her nurses. Your son however still continues in our old quarters and he will do so until his convalescence is complete.

I will as usual keep this letter open until morning, not as before to give you the latest intelligence but to tell you anything he has himself to say to you,
And believe me,
Yours most sincerely,
Patrick Heron Watson.

This morning up to the last moment I can wait he is sleeping so soundly that I think it is a pity to wake him.
P.H. Watson

Dear Sir,

I am glad to be able to continue a most favourable report of David's health. He was sitting up in bed for three or four hours yesterday for the first time. Today he will sit up in another room, so as to have his own room well ventilated and put in order.

He sleeps very soundly and his appetite still continues to improve. I assure you we all rejoice most sincerely in the restoration again to health of our friend who has been so seriously ill. Now that he feels well I don't think he is so anxious to run off to Scotland but as far as my influence goes I shall urge it very strongly, for though I believe that long before he gets home, he will be as strong as ever and fit for duty, still I think it a mistake in anyone to begin hard work again too soon after having been so long laid up, (just a month tomorrow.) It is so near the post hour that I will not have time to see him this morning before this must go.

And believe me,
Yours most sincerely,
Patrick Heron Watson.

My dear Father,

I suppose you will be very glad when you see my handwriting again and I can assure you I am just as happy I am able to write to you once more. It is now a month since I was seized with Typhus fever and I believe I have been very ill, indeed. I do not remember much about it now but I am, as the saying is, as weak as water at present and as hungry as only one recovering from fever can be. Dr Watson I believe has been kind enough to tell you how I have been progressing and I fear he at one time gave you very bad accounts indeed. That is all past however and with the exception of extreme weakness I would be as well as ever. Dr Watson advised me not to write this post as my hand was so shaky but I am sure you will excuse this my first attempt at letter writing after my illness. I have been most tenderly and carefully nursed by Mrs Tice, the lady of our chief medical officer here. To describe her kindness I cannot, she was constantly beside me and I am sure I may say I wanted for nothing. Dr Tice was very kind also and but for him, his lady, and Dr Watson I am sure I would now be sleeping quietly on the hill above Kulalie. As it is however I am getting on jolly well. If I recover fast I will not come home yet as the best of the weather is coming now. I intend going to Therapia for a week or two and then I expect I will be as strong as ever, if not, I will get leave home, but I think it would be a pity to leave just now when everyone is expecting something to be done. I am tired of hospital work now and wish I was out to the Crimea, all say it is a healthier climate during summer than the shores of the Bosphorus. All this is to be seen however and will depend on how I fatten up. During the time I was ill all my letters were kept back and when I got them some days ago I had such a feast of kind news, the newspapers I also receive regularly, and all enjoy them. So you are to leave Union Street at last, I for my part think you are making a good move, I will write mother and Anne by and by. Many thanks in the meantime for their long letters. Some of mother's last letters have been a good exercise to me in a theological point of view. I was very sorry indeed to hear of the split of the Churches and I sincerely hope and trust it may yet be put to rights. As for my part I think it is going rather far, and since the Church is so small already everything ought to be done in order to keep it together and preserve its strength. However it is none of my business.

A great many doctors have been ill at Scutari, chiefly of fever, here we have suffered also and one of our number a Dr Graham died this morning. He had not been out two months and was like my friend Mason the only child of a widow. It is all very sad that sort of thing but we get quite used to it. Mother, aunt and Anne will no doubt be wishing they were here to nurse me but it is perhaps just as well they are not, the nursing part is past now, it is cooking and eating I need. I have never heard anything of 'the box' as yet, but I have no doubt it will cast up in due time, and the things will keep, but I wish I had the gingerbread and marmalade – wouldn't I pitch into them. I have been up for the last three days and spend the most of my time in Mrs Tice's room at present, I have just finished dinner with them and am writing before the fire, while Mrs Tice is bustling about the room giving it such an appearance of home, when tells me not to write too much or fatigue myself after dinner. What a kind creature she is. I believe Miss Stanley wrote mother about a fortnight ago but whether she had the right address or not I do not know. She is a very peculiar kind of lady. I had a long letter from Dr Struthers, I forget the date, as it was amongst the bundle I got the other day, his brother James was complaining at that time but I hope he is now well again.

So, Dr Crockatt has become one of the Parochial Surgeons. I suppose it is the first step to being physician or surgeon in the hospital. How is he keeping? Give him my best respects. Liff Cottage will be looking very pretty now. I suppose you often pay the Dr a visit. Oh, if only I was there for a fortnight I think I would soon fatten up. The Dr knows well what weakness after fever is and when I tell him this is the third day I have been up he will easily imagine my picture. A soldier gets a hold of my arm and so keeps me up and so I stump about in a funny manner I can assure you. I will write soon again. Remember me to mother, aunt, Anne, cousins, etc. etc. and hoping you are all well.

My dear Anne,

I am very happy I am able to write to you once more. How are you, how is father, mother, aunt, how is everybody? Oh, how I long for another letter from home. I wrote Father about a week ago giving him as well as I could an account of my illness. At one time at home I thought after being so much about the hospital and never taking fever that I was proof against it, it seems however that I was mistaken and I have come through as sharp an attack and been as near dead as anybody could well wish to be, it is all over now and I am as jolly as ever. On Sunday last the Inspector General had an inspection of the Kulalie hospitals and of me at the same time. He was very kind, he asked if I wanted home (this was my idea when I was ill but it passed off as I got better) he said he had heard very good accounts of me and would be sorry if I ran away so soon. He gave me a fortnight's leave to come here. I am then going back to Kulalie and as soon as I am strong enough he has promised to send me to the Crimea and I am sure camp life during the summer will be far better than staying in an hospital. I am getting stronger and stronger every day and can now take pretty long walks, but if you could only see me I am sure you would laugh, my head was shaved when I was ill and the hair has not yet grown, while my whiskers, beard and moustache are very long. I often take a good laugh at myself when I look in the glass. With regard to questions etc in your letters I can tell you nothing about them, while I was ill all my letters were kept back, and when I was able I got a bunch to read which nearly took me a whole day to read through. The only thing of any consequence is the box – there is no word of it yet. Many thanks to you for the many nice things it contains. I wish I had the marmalade.

I think I hear you say tell me something about Therapia, well, look in the map and you will see that Therapia is a small village, but beautifully situated at a corner of a small bay. The hotel is close to the water's edge, and we see all the war steamers etc., constantly passing up and down to the Crimea. The country around is very pretty. The weather is very warm and if there is any place where an invalid should come to I think it is Therapia. The hotel is very good, clean, comfortable beds, real English cookery, and don't I walk into the eatables, I think that is my only disease now, what Father would call a galloping consumption, taking both my hands to supply my mouth. I am very glad you are leaving

Union Street. Oh, that abominable passage, just a facsimile of the streets of Constantinople. I won't know the road home now, when I do come you will need to be in waiting at the train. So there has been publishing again, confound Master Croal. I am not very strong just now but I think I could manage to pitch him into the Bosphorus if I had him here. People always say 'do let us publish some extracts and we will be careful what we publish' now what could have been worse than publishing that the Russian Major had been cut up and his shoulder kept as a memento, it might have offended some of our Government men as being a thing to irritate Russia. I see nicely how it will end – I will only require writing a few more letters and then I will give up correspondence with everybody. The best joke about the Russian Major is that I have not got his shoulder after all, for when I put it into a jar to macerate the rats took it out and devoured it. I do not know if you heard of the earthquakes we had here about three weeks ago. At Bruca – which is further south in Asia Minor – it was very severe and destroyed about 60 villages. With us it was not so severe no damage being done, probably on account of the houses being chiefly composed of wood. I was in bed sick when it took place, the whole hospital shook, the walls of my room I saw moving whilst the roof seemed quite undecided what to do, this was in the afternoon, we had another shock during the night. I was asleep but it awoke me in a dreadful fright as if I had severe nightmare. A regular earthquake is not what a person meets in with every day. I am sure you will wonder how I spend my time here by myself, well I will tell you. I get up about eight and having got dressed and a good breakfast swallowed by half past 9, I then go out and walk till between 11 and 12. The coffee shops are close to the water's edge, I drop into one of them and have a pipe and a glass of lemonade, which is very pleasant by the water side. I then come home and read or write for a while, have lunch, take another walk, a rest before dinner at 6pm – coffee after it – there is always a good many at dinner so there is no lack of conversation, lounge on settees till about 10 and then off to bed. Rather a nice kind of life you will say. Yes, but remember it is only to last a fortnight. You will be frightened of me talking about the Crimea so soon after being ill. Keep your mind easy I will not go up till I am quite strong. Everyone is wishing to get to the Crimea since the warm weather has come in. Do write me soon a long letter, give me all the news. Love to Father, Mother, Aunt, cousins, etc. I will write again before I leave this place. Of course address to Kulalie as usual. I will tell you as soon as the box casts up.

Dear Sir,

I have heard from Lord Raglan relative to your son – when he says he has received my letter about David Greig 'and I have in consequence made arrangements with the principal medical officer that he should be brought up to the Crimea very shortly'. I only hope he may keep his health and enjoy his agreeable service.

Your obdt.

Kinnaird

KULALIE
15TH APRIL 1855

My dear Father,

Here I am again at the old place Kulalie and have resumed my writing of letters on the 15th and 30th of the month which indicates I am off the sick list and all right again.

I returned here three days ago and when I reported myself our RMO wished to place me on duty and kindly offered me a fever-ward. Of course I rebelled and insisted on the Crimea, an order, the RMO at Scutari settled the dispute by telling me to apply for a passage immediately. I have done and expect to be at Sebastopol in 3 or 4 days. In the meantime I am a gent at large, and have nothing to do until a ship casts up for me. I am sure you must think me a (what shall I call myself) mad fellow? for going to the Crimea but I have been so petted of late that I have grown so self-willed and I suppose like a petted child instead of coming home when I am told I go further away. However I will be a good boy in future and any future commands will (perhaps) be attended to. I spent sixteen happy days at Therapia and must say I had a very rapid convalescence. I am quite strong now, can climb hills, walk 10 to 12 miles with ease, ride on horseback etc. We have very fine weather now and I have no doubt by the time I am a few weeks in the Crimea I will be stronger than ever I was. Just as I have written this I have got my orders and start tonight, so next letter from camp.

My dear Father,

I suppose you were more surprised than amused by my last abrupt epistle, but such is the fact just as I was writing to you as I received my final orders for the Crimea. They do things very quickly (sometimes) in this part of the world and I was ordered off at four hour's notice. However I postponed by embarkation until Monday morning when I took leave of all my friends at Kulalie, glad that I was going and sorry to part with them. I got my traps on board a *caique* and along with a R.C. clergyman bound for the same place as myself, got on board the 'Canadian' a large screw steamer, 2,000 tons, and having on board about 24 officers, and 420 men. To say the least of it, it was a beastly morning and rained 'pigs and whistles' as the saying is, until we started which took place at 11pm when it cleared up and we had a most beautiful sail up the Bosphorus. In passing Kulalie as you may well imagine I had a good look at it, and had the satisfaction of seeing Mrs Tice and the Dr waving a farewell to them with my handkerchief, which they returned. The 'Canadian' is a very fast steamer but she had a large barque to tow with Government Stores and Turks on board, this protracted the voyage for three days, instead of 36 hours. We reached the Black Sea about half past two and the vessel of course began to pitch and I got squeamish. I managed my dinner very well and also my tea and immediately thereafter tumbled into bed. When I awoke next morning I was not at all surprised to find I was sick and no mistake, I got up and attempted breakfast, 'No go' lunch was the same, dinner however I managed. I have the great satisfaction in informing you, I continued in first rate health ever since, eating like an elephant. The second day of our voyage we were closed up by a Black Sea fog and saw very little indeed. Next morning the fog cleared off and I got my first sight of the Crimea. At first it looks like any other coast but when you get nearer to it the coast is seen to be very bold and rocky. The entrance to Balaclava harbour is quite invisible even at a short distance from the shore, you get nearer and nearer and at least you see an opening between the rocks in you go and find yourself in a very good natural harbour where men of war are lying close to the rocks in deep water. The forest of masts in this harbour is quite amazing and at first sight it seems as if 200 or 300 vessels had been tied into a knot and placed there, if one was to take on fire I am sure almost all would be destroyed. We were kept dodging outside the harbour until afternoon when we got in and made fast to a man of war. There is no Inn in Balaclava and of course we had all to remain on board that night. Next morning I set about getting ashore to report myself to Dr Anderson the BMO [Brigade Medical Officer] here and see to where I would be sent. I walked here and there for a while and then found the gentleman, a polite enough fellow, who told me to return on board and wait for orders, so here I am still on board the 'Canadian'. The village of Balaclava is situated up the bay or harbour, as it is called, and is a curious place indeed, it seems as if the village had been ruined except a few houses and wooden huts and tents erected instead. The houses are occupied by the chief nobs, the huts as stores and houses, and I do not know who occupy the tents. It is a very confused place and at present very dusty as it is very hot weather, in wet weather it must be ten times worse. Looking up the valley from Balaclava you catch the first view of the camp and a curious and pretty sight it is, tents covering the hill sides, and here and there wooden huts. The railway passed through the town but I saw no trains running. One feels very curious being so near the far famed Sebastapol and that feeling is increased still more when you hear the constant boom of the guns and think the Russians may attempt Balaclava again. Oh, what an idea. A trip to St Petersburg. I do not know if you will understand my description of Balaclava but I have given you a plan which will assist you. I have no doubt you as well as all Britain will be very much interested in the place which I may call the key to our position. The Russians are very anxious to get Balaclava but as that is the only part through which we can get our supplies we cannot afford to gratify their wishes. There is no pier at Balaclava only two or three wooden jetties and there you land. As you wander through the streets, if streets they can be called, one is highly amused by the curious sights he sees, soldiers in all uniforms driving carts, carrying guns, driving canons, piles of shot and shell, are seen in all directions on each side of the street. Here – a heavy ammunition wagon drawn by six horses and as many artillerymen make you move out of the way. There as cart load of bread comes thundering down for the camp direct. A dragoon nearly frightens you out of your wits as he flies past with despatches, you jump aside and come in contact with a Turk or Greek driving some oxen in a cart etc. in fact Balaclava is 'Multum in parvo' much in little space. All the supplies required in the English camp passing through a small village twice the size of the American Muir. Where I may be sent I have no idea but in all likelihood I will go direct to the camp, there are a number of medical officers here, in the hospital, but I neither wish nor expect to be kept here. However I do not know and therefore cannot say. I do not regret at all my coming to the Crimea, I am I can say as strong as ever I was and the voyage has done me a great deal of good. I do not know all the kind friends who have written me, my correspondence has got into such a confused state, during the since my illness, but if I am right I have had three extraordinary correspondents – if I may so term them – very – Mr Sandeman, David R, and Mr Crockatt, as a reply to the two first I must return my sincere thanks for their kindness, and as I know they see all my letters it would be just the same story over again if I were to write to them, therefore I hope they will excuse me. As for Dr C., I can give him some medical news, so you may tell him I shall give him a screed soon.

Dr Watson is at present at Therapia recovering from an attack of fever. I do not know if I told you he had been ill but he has had a pretty smart attack of fever, not very bad or dangerous but still bad enough. I hope you are all well. No news of my unfortunate box yet although I have no doubt it will cast up in safety before winter, when I suppose the ginger-bread will be like a 12 lb shot if so, I will put it in a gun and present it to Prince Gorkshochoff or whoever has charge of Sebastopol.

Address: Dr Greig, Act. Staff Asst. Surgeon, Balaclava, Crimea.

Give me a long letter soon.

CHAPTER 5

Siege of Sebastopol

—

My dear Anne,

You see where I am now and I do you the honour of giving you my first letter from camp. About a week ago I wrote to Father from Balaclava and if the letter went safe you would learn that I had set foot in the Crimea and that I was still on board ship when I wrote. Acting up to my instructions I remained on board the 'Canadian' until Sunday morning when getting tired of my lazy life I and the Dr of the vessel started to visit the camp, it was a beautiful day and very hot. We could get no horses so we had to drive 'our own pair'. The road from Balaclava to the camp is, to say the least of it, a weary wander, it winds amongst the hills, and in a hot day such as we had the dust is very annoying. What it was in winter and during the wet weather I leave others to tell. Nothing of any consequence occurred to us on the way except that we went into a French Vivandier's tent and had a glass of wine, there I came in contact with one of the navvies for the first time, he was sitting in the tent in what we call a rascally state of beer, while another companion of his was fast asleep beside him. He (the former) was very polite however. He offered me a seat beside him which I declined. Nothing daunted however he would have a talk – 'They's agoing to send us home, sir,' 'Indeed is the railway finished'? 'Yes' (not true). I told him they had better stay as soldiers and serve the Queen, 'no' said he 'we are damned glad to get home and we'll see the Queen and the sodgers' to some place or other, I am not sure where, for I got tired of my acquanceship and walked off. We went to the 3rd Division and had a long stroll through it. We visited various friends and always got something to eat or drink and amongst the rest I called on Lieutenant Fenwick. I found his tent first and then himself coming towards it, of course we had a happy meeting and a long talk together, a glass of cherry brandy and then we started under his guidance to have a good sight of the far famed Sebastopol. We went to a height among some ruins called the Pecquet houses and had a first rate view looking down into the town. You of course know the situation and shape of Sebastopol, well from what I saw by my naked eye and also by the aid of a glass, I must say it has been a very pretty town. Good houses in rows with terraces in front, large fine public buildings, streets and all what not. When I looked at it I was quite astonished to see the town in such a good state of preservation. There are of course ruins here and there and a good many at the north and south extremity, but on the whole the town looks not amiss considering the battering it has got. I could see no people in the streets however and no ships in the harbour. 'But where were the canons?' I think I hear you say. Oh, keep your mind easy they were busy enough, shot and shell going fast, the Russian flagstaff battery and the Redan (another battery) were blazing at us, whilst our Greenhill battery and another one belonging to the French were blazing at them. We were within Russian range although not under fire, still at the time I thought it was quite near enough. The bullets were heard whistling and the shells making their peculiar noise in all directions. The whistle of a large shot has a very peculiar and, I may add, disagreeable sound, to one unaccustomed to it. The sound seems as if the bullet was passing over his head and often I start and think myself too near when I hear a loud 'Whish'. When a person is frightened very little will make him useless. A good joke is told of one of the Asst. Surgeons just now – which illustrates this. He was serving one night in the trenches and was sent for to a battery to see a man who was wounded and bleeding to death, the man had been serving at a large gun and was lying close beside it, the doctor was just about to tie the artery when 'Bang' off went the gun close to his ear. He thought earth and sky had come together or something far worse, and of course he bolted. He soon recovered his presence of mind however and came back to his patient just at the same time the gun went off again. Bolt did he again a second time. He returned again but just as he reached his patient a shot struck the wall which they were behind and sent a deluge of brick and mortar flying over them, it is almost useless to say the former bolted for good and all, while the latter of course died. After having a good sight of Sebastopol I parted with Fenwick and trudged back to Balaclava tired enough but glad to be in time for dinner. What pleased me most however was my order which had just arrived, worded as follows:–

'On Her Majesty's Service. Immediate.'
'Medical Department Order.'
Staff A. Surgeon Greig will be attached to and do duty with the 17th Regiment
and will report himself to Staff Surgeon Roberts BMO 4th Division.'
By order, A. Anderson, MD, S. Surgeon and BMO
Balaclava 22nd April 1855

I knew what 'immediate' meant so I took my time and yesterday
forenoon (Monday) I got my luggage upon one pony and myself upon
another and set off for camp. After some labour I found the subjects
of my future labours the 17th Regiment. Before receiving my orders it
never occurred to me there was a 17th Regiment and of course I have
not been long enough with it yet to tell you much about it. I was told
before I came up it was a very nice one and as far as it goes yet I think
so too. I went to report myself to Dr Roberts but he was out so I left
my name. I then called on the surgeon of the Regiment and he was at
Balaclava. I then went to the Asst. Surgeon but he was busy construct-
ing a hen-house. We soon got acquainted and he introduced me to the
Colonel, Adjutant, and some other officers, and also to my predecessor
whose place I am to fill and who is going home for a short time. He was
an Edinburgh student whom I knew by sight and name before. Dr Pirie
will know him if you tell him it is 'Big Bone', 'Little Bone's' brother, and
in other words Dr Theodore Gordon Bone. Dr Crockatt knew him at
college. My fellow Asst. is a Dr Gibaut, pronounced Jeb-O, or as he is
always called Jib. He comes from Jersey and is a very nice fellow and he
and I are to Mess together, and what is very kind has made me free to
his preserved provisions of which he has a good stock. To be attached
to a regiment in the way I am is far better than being gazetted to one. I
belong to and go with the Regiment wherever it goes for the time being,
while I retain my staff pay. If I had only regimental pay I could scarcely
afford to live in camp. All our little comforts and necessaries are so dear.
Of course if one likes to live on hard biscuits and pork one need spend
little but I intend to live as well as I can and want for nothing which
I can get to buy. Well to continue my story I got a tent pitched for me
close to Gibaut's and got my traps put into it and after having dinner,
grog, and a pipe, I got into it myself, got my bed put up and was glad
to spring into it as I must say I felt the ground much cooler for my feet
than a carpet would have been. As I lay in bed I was quite amused with
a novel situation, the tent shivering as if it felt the night wind, the canon

blazing away just the same as during the day, the balls whistling, the rifles cracking in the trenches etc. I fell asleep however, dreaming I was a gipsy encamped some way or other near the Law of Dundee instead of on the battlefield of Sebastopol. To describe the camp to you so as to let you understand it would be a very difficult matter indeed and you will require to look at the map before you understand what I am going to say in trying to describe it. The Army is encamped along the east side of Sebastopol exactly in front of it, for about four or six miles the encampment also passes from this as far as Balaclava and guards this place. We have then a good extent of land and sea coast and two good harbours: Balaclava which is used by the English, and Kamish which the French have. In coming from Balaclava to camp the first part of the road is uphill for about two miles, you then come to a kind of undulated plain of great extent and this is where the camp is. The first look of the camp certainly astonishes you. What a multitude of tents and wooden huts everyone exclaims. Scattered in all directions as far as the eye can see, soldiers marching, bands playing etc., in fact it puts one in mind of a large fair more than anything else. The 17th Regiment is encamped on the face of a small hill looking to the Northwest, very near to the field of Inkerman, and it seems to be a very healthy position. The regiment have no huts as yet so of course we are all in tents. The tents of the officers and men form a cluster, then a little removed from that you have the Regimental Hospital consisting of three huts and a marquee or large tent, beyond that again at a short distance from the Hospital you have the tents of Drs Gibaut and Greig, and the celebrated hen-house made out of a couple of old provision boxes. In going through the camp you are often struck by its rustic appearance, cocks and hens in all directions, in fact one would think the poultry mania had reached the Crimea. Not Cochin-chinas but regular useful, laying barnyard chuckies. The camp is I must say a first rate jolly place and I hope to continue to like it as well as now. What we are going to do with Sebastapol now no one knows but I suppose something will be done soon. There is some rumour that part of the Army is to march and keep the Russians in check behind or something of that kind, but no one knows. If such is the case the 17th Regiment will in all probability form part of this as it is nearly as strong as any regiment on the field. But this may be all humbug. All the fighting goes on at present at the batteries and the trenches, no shot comes into the centre of the camp or at least very seldom. Last night hearing very heavy firing in the direction of the French trenches I went to the top of a hill and saw a beautiful rifle skirmish, the moon was shining so we saw a party of Russians and French pitch into one another, whilst the constant flashing of the rifles and the shells flying through the air and then bursting with a bluish light gave the affair the appearance of a display of fireworks. The French do not make much way but the English keep whatever they take. There has been some great fighting about some rifle pits lately, the French have taken and some of them two or three times. The English took two or three the other night and kept them. This seems to have annoyed the French Commander in Chief as he published a general order in the French Camp which was very cutting. I do not remember if I can state it correctly but it was something like this – 'The English have taken their rifle pits. When the English take rifle pits, they keep them. (signed) Camrobert.' – Now I think I have given you a long enough yarn about the camp, so now for a little chit-chat about things in general. How are you all, father, mother, aunt, uncles, cousins, friends of all sorts and sizes. Mr and Mrs McIntosh, Dan Menzies, Mr and Mrs Sandeman, and family etc., give everyone my kind compliments who ask for me. Have you ever received the parcel I sent home? No word of the celebrated box yet. Before leaving the 'Canadian' I got a pair of large yellow boots – don't require brushing, an entire waterproof suit, a pair of worsted drawers, worsted shirt, socks and mitts, all for nothing, so much for serving the Queen you see. I have got a lot of flowers for you and will send some every letter if I can remember at the time. On looking over this letter I think I have told you too much camp gossip but you must remember to keep it to yourself. To tell you the truth I never write a letter with the same pleasure as I did at first and often keep back amusing things I might tell you just in case they should find their way into those newspapers, so 'keep dark'.

Address, Dr Greig, Staff Asst. Surgeon, 17th Regt, 4th Division, British Force, Crimea

My dear Anne,

I can assure you I was very well pleased yesterday morning when I
received two of your letters from Kulalie, dated 9th and 14th April, also
a bunch of newspapers, all very welcome things in this part of the world,
not to mention a long PS from Father. Since writing to you last I have
been enjoying the best of health notwithstanding we have had some
very disagreeable weather. The Crimea in fine weather is a delightful
place but in bad weather it is quite the reverse. I suppose you have heard
of Crimean mud, but I can assure you you can have no idea what it is.
When a shower of rain falls the whole camp becomes a plain of mud,
not plain English mud which takes the polish off your boots and little
more, but Crimean mud as of a peculiar adhesive nature, wherever it
touches it sticks, and you have to walk about with four or five pounds of
mud on each foot. During wet weather we all go about in our big boots,
they are very heavy themselves but it would be quite impossible to walk
with anything else. The other night I tried to go to the hospital with
shoes with India rubber overalls on, but I was quite astonished when
I stuck fast, my shoes would rather leave my feet than the mud, and I
had to call my servant to carry me back to my tent – that is one item of
wet weather – another is having a wet tent over you, everything in your
tent gets as damp as possible and all the consolation you get is that you
must keep up your spirits the best way you can until fine weather comes
again. Perhaps your tent is not waterproof and then you have a mess.
Two nights ago I was awoke by the rain coming right in my face as I lay
in bed, at first I was very unwilling to believe it, but that trick was no
use so I had to get up and after getting a light I discovered that the rain
was dropping on the upper part of my bed, and that I was all wet about
the head and shoulders. I pulled the bed to the other side of the tent,
gave the clothes a shake, turned them upside down and went to sleep as
comfortable as possible.

Turn-outs are another set of disagreeable things. I suppose you do not
know what a 'turn-out' is, well if during the night the Russians attack
us we have all to 'turn-out' and give support to the men who are in the
trenches or batteries, no one at the time knows what it may be, it may be
simply a row, it may be an Inkerman. I had my first turn-out about four
nights ago. I had gone to bed about my usual time and about 1 in the

morning I was awakened by the noise of cannon and musketry. I started
up in bed wondering what the row was but it was pitch dark I could see
nothing. I was just on the point of quietly lying down again when our
bugle sounded the 'turn-out'. I jumped out of bed, you may imagine I
was in a fright, after hitting my head against my tent pole, and tumbling
over a box I got my tent door open. It was a beautiful dark night and the
sight I saw was certainly one I never saw before. The shells were flying so
thickly through the air, it looked as if the stars had got drunk and were
having a dance, they were bursting in all directions and the noise was
something grand. The whole camp was alive and lights were seen moving
and bugles blowing in all directions. I got on my clothes and then went
to see what Gibaut's opinion of this was, we agreed to sit still until we
were sent for, we lighted our cutties and took the affair in a philosophi-
cal spirit. The firing became less and less and in about an hour all was
as quiet as it usually is. I went to bed again and next morning I heard
there had been an attack on our Light Division and some 20 or 30 men
besides, 3 officers killed.

Since writing you last – I have bought a horse – a beautiful bay – I
bought him from a Captain of the Zouaves. He is a nice beast but being
a Frenchman he understands neither 'Gee' nor 'Wo'. The first night I had
him he bolted and not appearing for two days I came to the conclusion
that I had been sold a 'pup' instead of the horse and that my powers
as a horse dealer were not great. The horse however cast up – he had
gone over to the French Camp and was returned to me by the Zouave.
It is impossible to do without a horse of some kind here, if we march
he will carry my luggage, and as we are at present he is very useful and
is a pleasant amusement for the afternoons. Yesterday I had a ride to
Balaclava and a canter over the battlefields. I intended to have got a
flower for you but I was rather in a hurry to get home at the time, but
next time I will remember your request. Your last letter contained the
melancholy and dreadful intelligence that Miss McD was about to be
married. I leave you to imagine the quantity of brandy and water and
number of pipes I had to smoke before I could get my mind back to its
equilibrium again, in fact I am scarcely myself yet N'Importe – I think
of 'Villikims and his Dina' and 'the cup of cold pison' and so the Yankee
beauty is gone! and may Good Luck attend her. I believe the war has
produced a great scarcity of males in the United Kingdom and that
the civilians are making hay while the sun shines but wait a wee while
until the red jackets get home again. I have been told that gentlemen

are so seldom seen and are as scarce at home now, as ladies are out here, and I can tell you that is precious scarce, with the exception of French Vivandiers I think I have only seen two ladies during the last month. The other day Miss Nightingale rode through the camp, I was standing with some officers when she passed at a distance from us, immediately a cry got up 'Oh, there's a lady, oh, there's a lady' and everyone turned out of his tent to look the same as children would do if an elephant was passing through the street. I did not get spoken to [by] Miss Nightingale as she was a good way from me, but I am very sure it was her. I believe she has taken a trip up here by way of a change. But to return to Miss McD tell her from me that I wish her all joy, that I expect cards from her and that if she and her husband should think of taking a marriage jaunt in my direction I will be most happy to see them, at my tent, and give them whatever is going. Just as I am writing all this blarney a soldier comes to me and giving me a bunch of letters tells me I must go to parade immediately, so I jump into my uniform well knowing what is to take place when I am wanted, and off I go reserving the letters till I come back. When I reach the parade ground the regiment is just formed into companies – a cart is standing by – I have a talk about things in general with the Major who tells me no one in the regiment likes to see the doctor on parade as it is very ominous. The whole regiment then forms square, the cart is taken into the middle of the square and I follow the cart. The order is then given thus 'Attention', 'Right about face', 'attend to the proceedings of a court martial', etc. and then follows the sentence, so many lashes. I have just now seen three fellows flogged. A doctor, one of the Asst. Surgeons, must be present in case the prisoner turns ill or faint, when he orders him to be removed. As soon as the sentence is read to the regiment the fellow takes off his clothes, is tied to the cart wheel and gets what he deserves. One of the fellows got 25, another 15, and another 10, all being for drunk and disorderly as the police reports say. I had an idea that flogging was abolished in the army but we can't do wanting it, we have flogging matches every third or fourth day. I now take up my letters and find they are all four months old, one from Lord Kinnaird, one from Dr Alexander and another from James Rodgers – better late than never – I wonder where they can have been all this time. The one from Lord Kinnaird is I am sure very kind and I think it was by him that I was sent up here – I will write and thank him. As for Dr Alexander's it is just like one of father's. He has so much to say to me that he can get very little said, while kindness to me shows itself in every line to me. I write regularly to John his eldest son but I will write to the Dr personally also. James Rodger's letter contained a very welcome present namely a copy of the 'Group' which I have got suspended like everything else on the tent pole. In a former part of this letter I spoke of the French Vivandiers I suppose you would like to hear something about them. I know mother likes me to describe the ladies I meet, for what reason I do not know. There is one or two Vivandiers attached to each regiment. They are young happy girls, they may or they may not be soldier's wives. They have tents and each has a kind of stall before the tent with all sorts of drinks, wine etc. on it. We always call on all the French Vivandiers when we are in the French camp and have a talk and laugh with them. They are generally very good looking and their dresses set them off to great advantage. Each is dressed somewhat like the men in the Regiment, if the men have red trousers and black leather at the foot of their trousers (horsemen etc) so has the Vivandiers, but beside the trousers she has a skirt of the same cloth coming down to the knees. A small white apron, an embroidered jacket, and straw hat, in fact they all look very neat and some of them, the Zouaves, for instance, are regular swells. They are all great flirts and laugh and talk at no end of a rate. I think they might even beat English Ladies in the use of their tongues. Sebastopol is in the same state as when I wrote last, the men are working away in the trenches as usual, but we have no word of an assault yet. I wish Raglan would try it. I suppose there will be another bombardment and I hope with better success than the first. Dr Struthers made me a very kind offer to come back to Edinburgh and demonstrate for him, much as I should like another winter in Edinburgh I cannot think of leaving camp yet. How are all my kind friends in Dundee? Remember me to all. I will write father again at the end of the month. I hope mother and aunt are very well. You may all keep your minds easy I am as strong as ever I was now and since I have Donald (I call my horse Donald in honour of the Liff charger) I take plenty of exercise.

PS. Lieutenant Fenwick and I are often together now. He is quite well and his camp is only about half a mile from mine, he was calling on me last night. Dr Watson is I believe quite well again and has returned to Kulalie. I merely heard of him by chance but am very happy he is well again. I will write him some of these days.

Tell mother to write me a long story soon and I will expect the same from you. You can have no idea of the pleasure of reading letters from home in a tent. Newspapers are always very welcome, I do not get them very regularly, but I always know who they are from even without the stamp. Tell father not to mark them as I believe it is against Post Office rules and everyone here opens newspapers especially late ones as they pass through the post and I think many of mine have been thrown aside. All my postage stamps are done.

My dear Father,

Since writing to you last everything has been going on here much as usual. I am in first rate health and spirits and hope I may continue so. I received a letter from Mother two days ago dated 12th May. I was very glad to hear you were all well and that you had got changed into your new house. From mother's description I can form a good idea where it is, but I am not sure if I could find my way to it however I have no doubt that if I were once in Dundee again I would not be long in finding you out. Since getting a horse I have been riding over the Camps in all directions and two days ago I had a splendid ride all round the outposts. I and a Captain of the 17th started about 11 in the forenoon, passed through the French right attack and across the field on Inkerman. I have never visited this celebrated place yet thoroughly and this day we passed rapidly over it. Beyond Inkerman you come to a deep valley, then to a hill covered with brushwood and occupied by the French, and then to another valley through which flows the river Tchernaya. In these two valleys the vegetation is something extraordinary. Rich coloured wild flowers so high and luxuriant that it is difficult to make your way through them even on horseback, while the smell is almost overpowering. My companion had been a long time in India and Arabia and he said he had never seen anything like this in all his life, and we both agreed that it would be well worth John Bull's trouble to keep the Crimea although the trouble should cost him somewhat. The river Tchernaya is a beautiful small stream of which the French had only two days before taken possession. When I saw the stream I immediately remembered some scenes we used to have six or eight years ago on the banks of the Dean or Isla. The French are grand campaigners and already they had got all their tents pitched, cocks and hens running about them, and bowers made of the branches of the dwarf oak which grows in great quantities here, in fact they look as happy as if they had live for years there. Some of them were fishing in the streams with crooked pins and what is more catching fish, not trout, but a kind of perch. Our horses seemed to be as glad as ourselves at the sight of the stream, that it was with difficulty we could keep them back and when we did go into the water they thrust their faces up to the eyes among the water, drank till they were tired, snorted, kicked and drank again. The French were very busy throwing up earth batteries at the bridge in order to protect it, while the Cossacks were seen in great numbers on the hills close by. We then passed eastwards round the hills and entered Balaclava by the plain passing over the battlefield and a more delightful spot I never saw. The battlefield had been a farm and all the vineyards although much trodden down and cut up by shot, were now springing. We passed through miles of vineyards, I tumbling over large shot. As we passed along we came to the farm house, now a mass of ruins, such a sight is I can assure you a very sad one, everything looks desolate and mournful, even the very fruit trees in the orchard near the house seemed to understand their position, and although they appeared green and fresh they still seemed as if mourning over the fate of their native land. I rambled about while my horse made a feed on the vines, picking up flowers and looking for some trophy to carry off but the hand of the spoiler had been there before me and nothing was left except bleached horse bones relics of the celebrated cavalry charge. I picked up a piece of shell and carried it home to my tent, whether I carry it further remains to be seen. While I was hunting for some curiosity my companion was always pointing to some large shot and telling me to send that to Scotland. I told him I had no doubt it would be considered a great curiosity if it only could be got home, but that was the difficulty. In Balaclava after having tied up our horses at the store we went on board some ships in search of grub, and were lucky enough to find a Dundee ship the 'Sutley' belonging to Mr Clark. The Captain had some first rate beer on board, and I can assure you it was a treat. I bought three dozen from him and of course paid a Balaclava price for it. We got home about 7 o'clock hungry enough as you may suppose. These are the kind of jaunts we take and very interesting they are. Oh, what a thing war is. A country which had once been beautiful now looking so desolate. The inhabitants now fled no one knows where. Shot strewed in all directions and the eternal roar of cannon sounding in the ear. Well may you all in Scotland be thankful you have never seen war near your shores for it is certainly something awful. In a letter I had from James Rodgers a few days ago I was very much amused by the way in which he spoke, he says 'you must tell me all that is going on' 'I have a right to know, I pay double Income Tax.' I intend asking the young man if he would rather see the Russians in England than pay double income tax or if he would rather come out here and fight. I mean also to ask him quietly how he would like to come out here and fight and pay double income tax as we do. Every shilling of pay that an officer gets, double income tax is deducted from it, this I think is very hard, and I wonder who has most cause to grumble. There are a great many grumblers at home who would be much improved if they were only one night in the trenches here. I am sure they would never grumble about income tax again. Talking about trenches I must tell you how I got on my first night in the trenches which was the first time I was ever under fire. About a fortnight ago when I had just returned from a journey to Balaclava I was informed I had to go on trench duty for the next 24 hours. I took my dinner and a stiff 'tot' after it, then filled my haversack with bandages, lint, tourniquets, biscuits, chocolate, etc not forgetting a short pipe or in the words of Beatties Minstrel:–

'Dainties he heeded not, nor gold, nor toy, Save one short pipe.'

I mustered with the men (1,500 guarded our left attack that night) at 8 o'clock and marched down the ravine or as the soldiers call it 'Down the valley of the shadow of Death' from the number of Russians shot in it. The ground is regularly paved with large shot for about a mile, just behind our Greenhill trenches. I went to the surgeon's hut and deposited my burden, then had a look about me at the large guns, mortars etc. When coming down the valley the Russians threw two large shells amongst us, the first fell short, the second burst close to us, we all immediately fell flat on the ground until we heard the piece 'whirr' over us, and none were hurt. After being satisfied with my examination of the guns etc., as it was getting dark and above all other reasons as the shot and shell were coming over us I retired to the hut. The Surgeon's hut I must describe to you. Just at the centre of Greenhill trenches is a hole dug in the ground for about six feet, there is then a wall made of sandbags and a roof of sandbags. In the burrow the doctor for the day retires and the wounded are brought to him, except in severe cases when he has got to go to them. In my burrow I found two gambions (wicker basket kind of things used in making breast-work) and by partly squashing these I made a springy bed and in spite of the noise of guns going off in all directions around me and comfortable Russian bullets coming over me I fell asleep. I was roused up about six times by men with choleric symptoms etc., and just as day was breaking I was finally roused by a shell bursting close to the hut. I felt very uncomfortable so I thought I would wash myself. A broken beer bottle served me as a basin and a sandbag pulled from a battery did for a towel. Some of our officers dropped in to see me and we had breakfast, rum, biscuits, and preserved salmon which one of the officers had in his pocket. Very little occurred during the day I wandered about the batteries etc., munching biscuits and smoking myself into dyspepsia and such like little luxuries. At midday it was very hot and not a gun was fired for two hours and all wore the aspect of peace. In the afternoon the roaring began again and as there was a mortar close to me pitching shell into the Russians they began to pitch round shot into us and the first shot they fired came slap through an embrasure close to me caught one poor fellow in the face, took his head off, wounded another, and dashed into a powder magazine close by sending the stones flying in all directions. I attended to the wounded man as well as I could considering the state I was in. I then went to look at the one that had been killed. The whole of his head had been knocked off except his right whisker. While I was looking at him another shot came 'whizz' over my head, I thought I had quite enough so I retired to the furthest corner of my hut and remained there till I was relieved and jolly glad I was to get into my tent again. Shot and shell look very well at a distance but they are anything but pleasant when they are flying about your head. From appearances here I believe something is to be done very soon and bloody work it will be, quite different from the taking of Katch. I wish they had a regular engagement. Everyone feels confident that we could smash them if they would only come out to the open fields instead of keeping behind their batteries. I forgot to mention when talking of the trenches that about 4 in the morning twenty of the Russians came over to us, they were stupid and all came in a body. Our sentries, seeing so large a number come, fired on them and only two succeeded in deserting. They were quite young fellows and seemed glad they had escaped from Sebastopol. I am sorry to say we lost our Surgeon from fever a few days ago. I attended him to the last, poor fellow, he is a great loss and what is worse he is an only child like poor Mason. We have at present got a Dr Inglis, 60th Rifles (pro.tem.) he is soon going to India to join his Regiment. He made me a very good offer today, viz:– he would get me appointed to the Regiment he is in if I wished. He is going overland and the Regiment is only to be four or five years in India and then come home. Oh, wouldn't it be jolly. I would have jumped at the offer 'like a cock at a grosset' but – but – but – I knew you would not like it so I refused, if he is very pressing however I may – may – I'll not say what. We have no green coffee now as we used to, we get salt pork, salt meat, mutton sometimes, biscuit, white and brown bread, all by way of variation you know. Also a ration of rum, besides all these we get beer, brandy, sherry etc., to buy at Balaclava and altogether we manage to live pretty well. I had the honour of dining with our Brigadier Major the other day and a jolly good dinner he gave us. Soup, salmon, roast mutton, fowls, etc. Champagne, port, sherry, claret, beer and porter. Oh, ye powers didn't I pitch into them all. I was none the worse but I must say I had an awful hiccup that night. He is a jolly old fellow Brigadier McPherson. He was ill a few days before and (I do not know why) he sent for me. He soon got well and his servant taking ill a few days after he sent for the Senior Asst. Surgeon. I thought he looked rather disgusted but I said nothing so we got both a dinner for our trouble.

I hope you are all well. I wrote to Lord Kinnaird about a week ago thanking him for his trouble and kindness. I hope you will excuse this rambling letter. I have been disturbed so often while I was writing it and one of the disturbances was to go and visit the regiment. This is done twice a week by one of the surgeons. He goes into every tent to see if it is clean. All the men have to show their feet, legs, arms and hands and if I think it necessary they must strip naked to see if they are all clean. If a man has dirty feet he gets extra drill, is sent to the river to wash them, or if he is very bad he may even be flogged. What a splendid thing military law is, eh?

Remember me to mother. She tells me to write every week but I can't do that. I will rather write every fortnight and give you long letters. I hope aunt is well. Tell her my stockings sadly need to be overhauled and I am sorry she is not here.

Compliments and flowers to Anne, tell her to write twice a week, what does she get to do? Cousins, Dr Crockatt, etc. have all my very best wishes.

My dear Father,

Since writing last I have received two letters, one from Anne and another which I received this forenoon from mother. I am very glad that phantom ship the 'Expert' has at length turned up and that you have received the parcel. It is not much worth but you have it as it is and if I had not got the clothes sent home I do not know what I would have done with them here and they may do for me should ever I be privileged to come into civilised society again. Yesterday as a friend of mine was going home I took the opportunity of sending by him poor Dr Struther's snuff box, a lock of his hair, and also Dr Mason's ring. As I was making up a parcel I thought I might send you something also but did not know what to send, so got hold of a Russian knife which was captured at the taking of the 'Mamelon' on the night of the 6th. I made them all up in one parcel and directed it to you. When you receive it you will send the box and hair to Dr Struthers, 19 Abercromby Place, Edinburgh and the ring to Mrs Mason, Surbiton, Kingston on Thames, Surrey. I was writing to Dr Pirie last week and I gave him an account of the taking of the 'Mamelon' and Quarries in front of the Redan the other night, and I suppose I need not repeat the story suffice it to say it was a glorious sight. To give you an idea of the firing and noise would be impossible not to mention the roar of the batteries on all sides. I thought we were to be engaged that night but we were kept in safe but inglorious reserve under arms and ready to turn out. It is very dangerous to go near the Mamelon and I have not seen it yet but from the description which some of my friends give who have seen it, it seems to be a regular model of engineering and would do credit to any nation. There was a truce for two days after the fight and our surgeon visited the Mamelon and had a talk with some of the Russian officers. They were very civil, examined his sword and everything about him, and in bidding them goodbye he expressed the hope that they would soon meet as friends 'Oh, no' said one of them, 'That can never be' 'Our Emperor has ordered us to keep the town, Providence has been kind to you in giving you the Mamelon, and you may get more advantages, but whenever you come into the town we will all go to the clouds together.' So we may expect a good blowing up. However I am very sure we will have the town before another month is over. Our guns have nearly ceased at present. There is only a shot fired now and then but it is expected we will open fire again next week and walk into the town. No one believes we will winter in our present position again and many say we won't even winter in the Crimea. The general opinion is that as soon as we take Sebastopol Russia will come to terms and that we will all be home by winter. Won't that be jolly? Be what may we are evidently preparing for a move. We have been ordered to get all the horses we are allowed and also to stable what quantity of luggage we must leave behind in store, so you see these are symptoms. We Asst. Surgeons are allowed a charger and a pack horse. I have got the first which is a useful kind of animal and can carry baggage very well at a push, although he does not like it much and I suppose I must get the second. In the meantime my name has been sent in for a medal in the way of recompense and I suppose they will give a clasp for Sebastopol, if so I will get it also. In one of Anne's letters she began tell me a very melancholy story and told me to hold myself in readiness to faint or something far more stupid. I must say I began to think that my favourite Gibbie was dead, but as I read on I was glad to find that was not the case, but that it was a misfortune of a far lighter kind – Anne will understand what I mean.

I intended to send this off by today's post but as I have received an order to convey a cart load of wounded to Balaclava I fear it will not be in time, however I will try. When our Field hospitals become full of wounded they are sent off to Balaclava in what we call ambulance carts. And an assistant surgeon is sent with them. We rather like the job as it saves us trench duty. The carts hold ten, six sitting in front and four on beds on the inside. It is drawn by four mules and the surgeon rides alongside clears the road of Turkish donkey carts and uses his authority in monopolising the whole road. Just as I supposed, I have missed the post and it is now Sunday evening when I finish this. Oh, what a change from a quiet Sunday evening at home. This morning I was awoke not by the sound of church bells but the roaring of cannon. We have opened fire again and are to take Sebastopol tomorrow. Before another 24 hours thousands will have fallen. Where I may be I do not know but I will write by next post again, so good bye with love to all.

My dear Father,

I sent off a letter to you three days ago and in it told you we were
going into Sebastopol on Waterloo day, the 18th June. There is an old
saying about the plans of mice and men etc., and I suppose by this time
you will know all about its failure. When I was finishing my last letter
everyone was in high spirits and all believed we were going in next day.
What a curious sight it is the evening before a battle. Everyone knowing that many will not see another evening yet all as jolly as possible
and hoping for the best. Some writing letters telling their friends their
last wishes should they fall, others joking with the surgeons and telling
them to be kind to them if they should require a limb amputated and
so on. As for myself I was as cool as possible because I was to remain
at our field hospital, our surgeon going down with the regiment. Our
troops paraded at midnight and marched down. I went to bed in order
to be fresh for next day's work. At 8am I was roused up by the rattle of
musketry, I dressed and went out to see what was going on but could see
nothing but smoke. On the left attack the 57th were the attacking party
and the 17th the support, the French were to take the Malakoff and we
the Redan. In this however the French failed and no sooner had we left
our trenches than a perfect shower of grape shot took the shine out of us
considerable. The 57th got very much cut up and so did the 17th, besides
different other regiments. Sir John Campbell in leading the attack got
shot amongst the very first and as no one knew very well what was to be
done and as the men were being mowed off the face of the earth by the
shot, they retired. I am not soldier enough to know where this fault lay
but everyone here says it was a bungle and I fear it will tell sorely against
Raglan. The 17th Regiment had one captain shot dead, 10 men killed
on the field, and 38 wounded. I believe there was no want of courage on
the part of the men, it was all the fault of the Generals. About 9am our
wounded began to arrive at the hospital and then we were busy enough.
We three assistants had to manage everything and of course I had the
lion's share of the operations. I had one amputation at the shoulder
joint and another at the forearm. The wounds were chiefly inflicted by
grape and beastly wounds they were. Others by menie balls and a few
by round shot. The men came to the hospital in a most melancholy
condition, covered by blood and dust. They were dressed, put to bed and

any operations which were required were immediately performed. The severe cases were brought on mules or in the ambulances and the others walked up themselves. I was very much amused by a Jack Tar, he was the first wounded man I saw that morning, he was trudging home to his camp with his head all covered with a bandage, his moustache and beard clotted with blood but still looking the very picture of contentment. Smoking a short cutty pipe he asked me for some water and was highly pleased when I gave him some grog. What we are to do next seems a puzzler to all. Still all are of the opinion that if the attack were properly conducted we could easily gain, and I hope they will soon attempt it again. The camp on the whole is very healthy at present. We have about 70 in hospital and every now and then we have a case of cholera which generally finishes the patient in a few hours, this I must say is rather unpleasant. As for me I am very well and could never wish to be better. I enjoy myself here and am always learning something professionally, at least I hope so. I expect Dr Watson here in a few days at least he told me so in a letter I had from him, I am very glad of this for he is a very nice fellow. You must excuse this short scrawl at present as I am very busy and it is fatiguing work, besides this is an extra letter. Remember me in kind love to mother, aunt and Anne, cousins, etc. Do write me a long screed soon, all letters are so very welcome here, not to mention newspapers which I receive very regularly now.

PS. I will write mother (next week) a long letter giving her an account of my domestic arrangements here and how I manage when clear of 'petticoat government'. I have just received a letter from Dr P and another from Anne with a lot of stamps for which I thank her.

My dear Mother,

According to promise I now sit down to thank you for the many interesting letters you send me and in return give you as well as I can a sketch of my domestic arrangements. You can form no idea of the pleasure it is here to get a letter from home, when you tell me about the little chit-chat that is going on in Dundee I often am like to split my sides with laughing at, I do not know what, and I am always in very good humour for the rest of the day. What you can find in my letters to make them so welcome I cannot make out, writing from an outlandish place and always talking of horrible things, seem to please you so much that I have begun to take an interest in writing home again. How do you like the accounts of our doings on Waterloo morning? Rather a large butcher's bill I hear you say, however that's nothing now-a-days. John Bull likes that sort of thing and why not indulge the poor old fellow occasionally. Oh what a splendid thing war is for the advancement of the science of surgery. Is it not?

In a letter I had from Anne a day or two ago she expresses her surprise at me having a servant, does she imagine I cook my own food, or does she think we are as cannibalised as to eat it raw? I have always had a servant ever since I left home and like you at home sometimes I have had a good one and at other times a bad one. First of all at Scutari I had an Englishman, a downright humbug who could do nothing but get himself into scrapes of all sorts, I left him at Scutari. At Kulalie I first got a Greek Flunkey who was very willing but as he could only speak modern Greek and Turkish, neither of which I could understand, he was very little use to me, however by means of kicks and signs I did make him understand what I wanted. He was with me about a month and I was very glad when he burnt his foot once and left me. So much for Yanko. I then had another Greek for a short time, a first rate cook etc. He stayed with me until I took fever. I then got a soldier belonging to the 79th Highlanders, a very attentive fellow he was and how I did bother him, at nights, I could not sleep and of course I never allowed him to sleep either but he always took it in good part and often put me to sleep by talking of Scotland. He was rather religiously inclined although very fond of whisky when he could get it. He would often read me a chapter from the Testament and that time I felt myself as safe in old Fraser's hands as in any of the four Divines who were visiting me every day. I had one Roman Catholic, two Church of England, and one Church of Scotland. Rather well supplied. When I joined the 17th I got a servant from it and I have him still, he is a bit of a jockey, a first rate cook, a good forager, and does very well as groom and waiting man. Gibaut has of course a servant too, so that we two living together we are very well served. Neither of our servants are teetotallers, we give them warning that they must never get drunk at once or we will immediately have both flogged. One must always be able to wait on us. This arrangement seems to answer well and on the whole we are very little bothered with them in that respect. When I joined the 17th, Gibaut and I had each a separate tent as bedroom tent and our servants stayed in a tent at the hospital about 150 yards from us. This was inconvenient and as their tent was one day turned into a store tent I gave up my tent to them and had my tent removed beside Gibaut's. It is a much better arrangement, our servants are always at hand and all we have to do is to bawl out for them when we want them and besides we are more comfortable together. Our territory is a neat little spot close to the hospital and overlooking the 2nd Light Division with a fine view of Inkerman, the ruins of the Picquet House, the celebrated windmill etc. The small tent in which we dine and in which I am writing at present is not a regimental tent but one that Gibaut brought out with him. It is an octagon and we have ornamented it with a weather cock and a N.E.S.W. affair. We have a small table in it and it is such a jolly little place that it puts me in mind of the back shop on a winter's night. When the weather is very hot, which is every day at present, we get the sides of it tied up and the cool draught passing thro' it is very pleasant, at least comparatively speaking, whilst the top acts like an umbrella. In this we take our meals, read, write, drink brandy and water and pass the time the best way we can. Our bedroom tent is just opposite the door of this one or rather vice versa. There is a large hole dug and this is our wine cellar which we always try to keep as respectable as possible. It is the coolest place in the tent and cold drinks are everything. I know you are very anxious to know what we have got in our cellar, are you not? Now confess and I will tell you. Oh, how miserably we poor fellows in the Crimea do live, fighting for an ungrateful country, just think what a miserable cellar we keep, it only contains sherry, Marsella Brandy, whisky, rum and home brewed lemonade. No wonder we look so thin etc.! With regard to the food we get a ration of salt pork every second day, and sometimes mutton, and as we live beside the Hospital we always get tit-bits and good measure. We get white bread, brown bread, and hard ship biscuit at different times by way of change. So much ground roasted coffee and a gill and a half of rum. On the Queen's birthday we all got a pint of sour cask porter to drink her health with which gave half of the men colic. Everything else we want we must buy and things here are rather dear, but as we are told to use the world and not abuse it we never sacrifice comfort to expense. From the beautiful mezzatint engraving (proofs £1. 1/-, prints 10/-) I hope you will be able to understand what I mean. The best kind of tents are those that are dug out to the depth of 3 feet like our bedroom tent, it gives a great deal more room and the only drawbacks are that instead of going upstairs to your bedroom you have to go down two or three steps and in fact sleep in a big hole which you are very apt to find turned into a big pond any morning after a shower. We had a stable dug at 4 feet at first but one morning finding our horses nearly drowned in a small pond we had it partly filled up again and after condemning a lot of hospital blankets and taking them for roofing and sides we have got a first rate stable now. Our beds you must understand are not four posted ones nor even cribbed. They consist of two poles for sides, three legs and a piece of canvas, they are very jolly little things, and when we get the route they are soon packed up and off we go. Everything we have must be portable. You see a small table between the tops of our beds that was put up to hold the candle when we read in bed. The small square table in the centre of the tent is placed on an old wine cask and supports our tent pole. It is a very useful table and is always covered with innumerable pipes etc. The square table near the door is a portable one and doubles up into less than nothing. You see our trunks and you see these things marked 'boxes'. These are old hospital boxes fitted into the ground and act as presses etc. We also have a small stove, a hospital comfort of course, very small and useless at present. This will give you a very good idea of our tent. You would be astonished how comfortable we are and I am sure I would rather stay in a tent than a hut. It is true we often find centipedes 4 inches long who think they have as good a right to your bed as yourself but we soon convince them they are mistaken. As for ants and flies why the whole place is alive with them. Sometimes a field-mouse takes up his abode with you. These are always treated kindly and looked upon as pets. We have one great pet, however, a Russian dog. He is somewhat like a Scotch Collie and was a deserter from Sebastapol. I wanted to call him 'Vipy' but as that name did not end with 'off' or 'dorf' or 'ski' he could not understand it so we always call him 'Ruski'.

With regard to money matters I must say I possess a great deal of father's spirit, the less said about that the better or I am afraid you would call me an extravagant fellow … I'll say no more.

We have very hot weather at present, everything is burned up, we expect rain however in the beginning of July and then commences the second summer here. During the last month I have been regularly stewed. I have now discovered I cannot stand heat that well and would never do for India. Of all the wants I feel here none is so bad as the want of milk. I have been wishing to get a goat but can't and that preserved milk we get in tins to buy is beastly. I often think of father's copious draughts and wish I was beside him. I have never tasted good milk since my last night at home. Another want of mine is oatmeal but I am happy to say I succeeded in capturing an oatcake at Balaclava the other day, which was a very great treat indeed.

I have never heard from Dr Struthers since I refused to come home in October. I have no doubt he will be angry with me but I can't help it. Dr Watson has not made his appearance here yet but I expect him soon.

How are all my kind friends at home? How is Mr and Mrs Sandeman and family? Give all my best respects. I would like to write to David but he must excuse me …

Are any of them much taller yet? If they continue so small they will never be taken for 'sodgers'. I hope you remember me now and then to the Misses Sclater and also all my lady friends. Bless me, to think I have not spoken to a lady for months now. Well it is curious to think how well we get on without the darling creatures. Smoke when and where we like, when tired, throw ourselves on the top of our beds with dirty boots on, no washing days, no scoldings. Man, I have come to the conclusion is only seen as Lord of the Creation in his savage state. There is no aunt here to bother me about brushing clothes, shirt fronts, neck ties, etc. and of course I have no one to blow me up if a shirt button is wanting. I can only give a growl, sew it back on myself and there is the end of the matter.

I calculate we show an amount of independence here which would astonish some of our fair tyrants at home. The officers of the 17th have voted Dr Pirie an awful animal, only think what he said to me in his last letter – 'There are lots of ladies still here who would take even a red coat when they can't get anything better.' Oh, the unpatriotic monster. He ought to be sent to the advanced trench for a week and I am pretty sure he would alter his tune. I do not think I have any more commands or grumbles to get rid of and now I have one favour to ask, do not ask me to write every week. I am often tired, busy etc. and I am sure weekly letters would too much resemble weekly police reports that no one would take the trouble to read. Oh, me, I thought I was free from female government but I find I am wrong.

Do continue to write to me every week. Remember me to all my cousins and all who may take the trouble to enquire after ...

IN THE TRENCHES BEFORE SEBASTOPOL
3RD JULY 1855

My dear Anne,

I suppose you will be surprised at the place from which my letter is dated, but such is the fact. I am at present in trenches for 24 hours and in order to pass the time I have brought writing materials with me and am now scribbling to you. I hope from the letter I sent mother a week ago you will fully understand all my little domestic arrangements, and you must tell me what you think of them and if you think they could be improved. I received a long letter from mother last week besides three newspapers all of which were very acceptable. I was very sorry to hear of Mr Mathewson's accident. I hope he will soon be well again.

She tells me that a Mr Smith had called who was coming out here. All I can say he is a great fool. He has only been two years at college and must be coming out as a dresser and the dressers at Scutari were none of the best conducted youths. He may have got a diploma, still I think all who hurry through their college time like Lithgow and Sharp will regret it all their lives. They can't know their profession their patients won't trust them, and in fact they can't trust themselves. Smith is a soft kind of boy and I think his parents are little better.

So I see by the papers that Mr Langland has lost one of his Russian relics. 'Serve him right too' for making such a fuss about the confounded things.

Mother tells me that Dr Erskine has asked to be appointed to a regiment and asks what good it can do him? I cannot explain in a letter what good it can do him but I may mention with regard to comfort, being with a regiment and on staff duty there is almost as much difference as East from West. So Mr Croal is married by this time. 'Serve him right too' like Mr Langlands for publishing my letters. I do not know when I may meet him but when I do I calculate I won't be what mother would term 'a very amiable state of mind' however time may improve my feelings … but I do not think so. I am sorry Mary Baxter has been so ill. I hope she is better now. Please give her my best wishes for her recovery.

4th July

The foregoing part of this letter was written in the trenches but I am now in camp attempting to finish it as I found it was no easy matter attempting to write whilst under fire. The day passed over very quietly. The Russians did not fire much at us and we were only giving them a shot every now and then. What amused me most the whole day was the firing of one of our largest mortars which they have placed on the top of the doctors' huts. It was throwing a shell into the town every half hour and of course it was impossible for me to sleep although I had managed to convert a powder case into a kind of pillow. I would drop off to sleep at times and would be roused up by some soldiers either sick or slightly wounded. Of course I growled but could not help it. I would be going off again when 'bang' would go this mortar making me fancy all sorts of mischief had befallen me. You can have no idea of the sound a very large mortar makes. You never heard anything like it, and I am sure from descriptions I can give you no idea of it. A railway train rushing past is something like a shell going thro' the air and should the boiler of the said train burst that would complete the illustration as it would represent the bursting of the shell.

As I could not sleep I went beside the mortar and studied mortar practice for an hour or two, strutted about the batteries, etc. smoked, and so filled the 24 hours. Not at all displeased with them, yet very glad as everyone is when they have done their turn over. As for news in this letter upon my word that puzzles me. Every day is very much alike, at present there is no talk of taking the field, storming the town or in fact doing anything!

Lord Raglan is dead of course you have heard this, everyone here regrets his loss as a kind hearted man, but very few regret his loss as a general. I hope we may get someone with more spirit in him. Waterloo morning seems to have been too much for his Lordship before breakfast.

In one of your letters you are very anxious to hear of my coming home. Well that is rather a difficult question but still it may be satisfactory to you to know that I have come to some conclusion on that point, viz, should I like the winter in the Crimea very much and if there is anything going on I will all winter there and see what next spring will produce, but if I do not like the winter and if there is no chance of anything being done, if I am not in good health, then I will offer my services to take sick home and if they won't send me home that way, I will resign. Some of our fellows tell me that as I witnessed all the Crimean diseases last winter and therefore must know something about them then I ought to stay next winter and show a patriotic spirit whether or not I liked it. A patriotic spirit is all very well but as we do not get very much credit for any good we may do either here or in any other way in the army I have no idea of making a martyr of myself. Oh, no, I have some idea of a comfortable home yet.

I was very much pleased yesterday by receiving two newspapers, a letter from you dated 16th June, one from Mr Sandeman, one from Mr Struthers and one from Andrew Rodgers. I luxuriated in them all the evening and have now very nearly got them all by heart. I am very much obliged to you all for remembering my birthday. I gave a small party that day and enjoyed myself very much. So you have struck up an acquaint-anceship with Miss Alexander. I should think it would be rather a dif-ficult matter to write to a stranger. I cannot imagine what you get to talk about, her brother tells me that she is as unreasonable in London as the Emperor of all the Russians, as she has put a stop to his smoking in the parlour! I am sure you will find her a very nice person for all that, and as for a hearty welcome to Wooler, that you may be sure of, should you ever cross the borders. I am glad Dr Ramsay has turned up again although it is not at Hong Kong, he still seems to have a hankering after home. I do not know what has become of Dr Watson, I suppose he is still at Kulalie. I expected he would have been up here long ago. With regard to Mr Sandeman's letter I must say I am in a fix. He has made a request which I rather he had let alone, to burden myself with more correspond-ence more especially as that would be to write news for a newspaper from a place where no news are going. As he is very anxious however I have no objections to his publishing descriptions of country etc. but to publish such things as 'me having received a pistol for having dressed a patient's wounds', 'that I had the shoulder of a Russian major' (confound the impudence of Master Robert Croal) or such-like, any person in their sober senses must have seen how absurd it is, and how vexing to me. He of course sees my letters and mother can pick out parts that may suit and it is by her permission alone they are to be published, and my name and profession must be kept secret so that no one can form an idea who writes them. I am sure you will say 'oh, no his Lordship is relenting'. Not a bit I am as furious as ever at these Edinbro' papers.

My dear Father,

I received a letter from mother yesterday dated 23rd June and I must say I was very glad to hear you were all so well. I suppose you received my letter last week, after I sent it off I must say I repented it heartily wished to withdraw my stupid permission again but you all seem so very anxious and I cannot refuse and all I beg of you to remember is that it will please me far more if my letters were kept strictly private. When I was sent up to the Crimea I had not the slightest idea that Lord Kinnaird had done it but I am quite sure it was him now and I am much obliged to him for it. Dr Watson is here now he came up from Kulalie about three weeks ago but as he is stationed at the hospital at Balaclava and I in camp we never met until a week ago. He is quite well and seems to like the Crimea very well. He and another two friends dined with me yesterday and keeping in mind Anne's birthday a very merry evening we had, and as we sat over the coffee afterwards we discovered a curious thing, viz that four out of five who were in my tent had been made MDs in Edinburgh on the same day. There is very little new in camp going on at present, we are just at the same old work. When we will go at the Malakoff or Redan again no one knows. Every now and then we are getting two or three men knocked over, and yesterday we had one killed and three wounded. I believe the French are making two batteries on their right attack which will destroy the ships in the harbour and then we will go at the Malakoff again I suppose. Mother seems very much frightened for me getting shot. There is not the least fear of that for it will be a very smart Russian that will manage to hit me. I have seen men knocked over close to me and I must say I do not like it much, and will always try to keep out of the way more especially of round shot. Dr Innes has left us and we have at present got a Dr Crerar 2nd Class Staff, but he is going off very soon and then we get a new surgeon who is, I believe, gazetted to the 17th. There is also another Assistant Surgeon gazetted to the regiment, so that I may expect a move again – perhaps not – I do not know. I had no intention of writing a long letter just now. All I wished was to send you a curiosity. I know you are fond of these sort of things, and I am sure it is the greatest curiosity I have sent home yet. If you present it to the Eastern Bank they will explain to you what it is. Do anything with it you like and if you do not require it keep it for me till I come home. I have no use for it here, and keep quiet. Do not mention this to anyone. I will be writing to Anne very soon and then you will get all the news. This letter is intended for your own quiet perusal and I hope you will give me one in return. I will not send compliments to anyone this time as you need not mention you have got a letter at all. I am in first rate health and hope you are all the same.

My dear Anne,

I have no doubt you will be wondering why I have been so long in writing to you this time, and to tell you the truth ever since I have made that promise to Mr Sandeman I feel as if a load was on my mind and I have postponed and postponed writing until I can do it no longer and I wish you to bear in mind that however much I shall like to please you all, I must still tell you that if you wish me to write you often and give you all my little outgoings and incomings my letter must be kept within the family circle and whenever I see anything of mine in the newspaper it immediately goes into the fire, and I feel ashamed of myself for a week afterwards and I make of course my next letter a precious short one and take good care there shall be nothing in it worth publishing, so please yourselves, if you are content with letters half a page long I am very willing to publish them. How would you like if I wished to publish some of your letters to me? I have no doubt our fellows would be very highly amused by them. Since writing home last I have received a letter from you another from father and another from mother, last night besides various newspapers. In the Courier of 11th July which I have just received I am sorry to see a letter extracted from the 'Times' headed 'Neglect of the wounded in the Crimea' on the 18th June. I am sorry to see such a letter as I can tell you it is a lie from beginning to end and calculated not only to alarm the good folks at home but to hurt the Service itself. Of course Mr Stafford must bring it before Parliament and make a world's wonder of it. The Service is much obliged to Mr Stafford for his tales about the state of Scutari Hospital, I lived longer in Scutari Hospital than Mr Stafford and I must say I never saw what he describes. The gentleman who writes the present articles must either be mad or a most consummate fool, and ought to be drummed out of the Service to the 'rogue's march'. He says he could not get drinking cups, water, food, splints etc. Why? Because he was an ass, and did not know where to get them as he should have done. I have never yet applied in vain for anything which would be of use to my patients even to calf's foot jelly, lemon jelly, soups, turtle soup, or even champagne! Everything can be got if you go rightly about it. Now to tell you what I saw in our Division on the morning of the 18th June. We had a very large tent on the Worongow road within Russian range and while the Russian shells were bursting amongst our tent ropes, there were a lot of surgeons in that tent attending to the wounded brought to them, dressing them in such a manner as they might be brought in safety to the camp assisted by men, or carried by mules or in carts. And you will ask had they everything they wished in the tent? Everything. A continual supply of water, tea, coffee, wine, brandy, in fact there was a glut of everything. When the wounded came up to camp they were attended to, properly dressed, washed and put comfortably to bed, had food given them and if a man was severely wounded one of his comrades was placed as guard beside him, to feed him, give him a drink, and assist him to turn in bed etc. We never feel the want of attendants. All we have to do is ask for them, however, the fellow, whoever he is, has got himself into a nice scrape which is being investigated into here and I have no doubt the fellow will curse the day he even took to publishing letters.

I am very much amused by your description of Mr Croal's marriage. I wonder the young man isn't ashamed of himself, but as the saying is 'he's been and gone and done it' and I suppose he must stand the consequences whatever they may be, that's very certain. Did Mr James Croal remember me? I suppose not, he never was a great favourite of mine, and from all I have seen of him I do not think he ever will be. I was glad to hear Miss Mary Baxter was well again, give her my best thanks for the flowers and in return take these to her and tell her I gathered them on the battlefield on Inkerman. They are not very pretty but I hope the name of their native place will make up for their beauty. What they are I do not know. You ask me how often I go to the trenches. It is very irregular, but in general it is once in ten days and often enough too. Sometimes we escape the trenches by doing division duty such as taking the sick to Balaclava etc. but that is all chance. In the letter which I received from mother last night she mentions that my Cousin Anne would like very much to come out and attend to the poor wounded fellows. I have no doubt she would be like some of our nurses at Kulalie who came out as they thought to attend upon brave heroes, and instead they found the most miserable specimens of humanity one could well imagine. The romance of war is only seen at home when the Queen gives medals to those who return from the Crimea, while the poor in the Crimea have to live in hope. However, we will all get medals some fine day if we ain't knocked over before the time. I keep my mind very easy on that count for 'a man who is born to be hung will never be shot'. I do not know what death Dr Johnston will die but he may thank his lucky stars he is out of the reach of shot, tell me all about him, how he is etc. etc. should you see him. Dr Watson is now attached to the Artillery. It is the best branch of the Service and I have no doubt he will be very comfortable. He is stationed in Karari near Balaclava and has no trench duty. Dr Erskine called on me the other day, he is appointed to the Regiment and seems very much pleased with it. He was in first rate health but had skinned his nose in a fall from his horse in leaping a ditch. We (the 17th) have got a new surgeon, a Dr Ward from the Artillery, he is newly promoted and is just like one of ourselves. We are constantly in each other's tents, smoking, chatting, etc. in fact he is an in and out brick and has been at Alma, Inkerman and Balaclava. He is a very happy fellow and makes us all so hearty when he comes beside us. I am glad Charlie Boyd is getting on so well. I have never heard from him but should anything send me to that quarter I will seek him out and try if possible to spend a few days with him. I should like it very much.

Since writing mother an account of our tents etc. Gib and I have erected a hut, and are, comparatively speaking, settled for the winter. It is very much cooler than a tent and what is more we have got a large fireplace i.e. a hole in the wall but what a jolly thing it is. In my next letter I will describe the said hut. I am all safe and sound in body and limb as yet and intend to remain so. I had a narrow shave the other day however, or in other words I was regularly fired at. I and another sawbones were riding round the French outposts on the Tchernaya, we were the only two mounted officers near, it was a calm afternoon and we were looking at some Russian tents when 'bang' went a field piece and I heard a round shot coming slowly to us over the plain. I could not see the confounded thing but I knew from the sound that it would pass us, and so it did, diving into the ground about 25 yards behind us. I must give up as there are three officers sitting beside me in the hut, who suspecting I am writing to a lady insist upon me sending you their compliments and hope you are well, so I must give up, Good bye. I hope Broughty Ferry will restore you all to health.

My dear Father,

I returned last night from the 24 hour trench duty and was very glad
to find a letter from Anne dated 4th July. The two last times I have
returned from trenches I have found a letter from home waiting me
and you can have no idea how jolly it is to get into bed and read them.
I generally read them twice and then fall asleep and dream I see the
realities. I am very much obliged to you for your kind letter and I wish
you would write more oftener. One thing in the way of good news is
that I have hopes of getting the unfortunate box at last. Dr Gibaut, my
fellow assistant Surgeon, has started for Constantinople this morning
(he has got 15 days sick leave) and he is to hunt for it in the parcel store
there. I hope he may get it. Anne's letter is a good long one but there
is very little news in it except that mother and she have got lodgings at
the Ferry. I hope it will do them both a great deal of good. It is quite
provoking to hear her talk about strawberries and cream. Oh, how I
should relish a dish. Only think it is nearly two months since I have seen
cream. I have been trying all I can to get a milk goat but have never been
able to get one as yet. All our tea, coffee, rice etc. we have to take with
water and think it is very good too. My last trench was, I must say, the
worst one I have had yet. The weather had been broken for two or three
days and of course the camp was covered with mud. An hour before
parade time (7pm) it began to rain and oh such a rain, bricks and mortar
are nothing to it, in fact you would think no mortar would face it. I was
clad top to toe in waterproof and did not mind it much, but my horse
seemed to have a decided objection to it. However it was no go and off I
set with 500 men from our Division. When we got to Greenhill trenches
the rain ceased. I gave my horse to my servant and went to the Surgeon's
hut, alas, this little comfort of ours I found in ruins, the large 18" mortar
had shaken the roof in. It certainly was not a palace but I was sorry for it,
in fact I was in a regular stew where to put up, so I applied to the Field
Officer who told me I must go up to the third parallel No. 7 battery near
the caves and stay there all night. Says I 'what must be must be' and off
I went. I had never been so far forward before. I passed through the
covered way to the second and then through the zig-zags to the third.
You will know what I mean, I believe you have got plans of our works.
Well the zig-zags were in a precious mess something like knee deep with

mud, and I found the third parallel not much better. When I got to the No. 7 battery I enquired for the doctor's hut, not that I expected to find a hut, but expected some shelter. I was sorry to find there was none. To sit down on the ground was impossible as the mud was 4 inches deep. I therefore made the best of a bad bargain, sat down on the trams of a 32 pounder lit my pipe and made the best of it. It soon got quite dark, I stretched myself on the gun carriage, and fell asleep. I did not sleep long when I discovered it was raining very hard and I had better change my quarters. A powder magazine was close by and by making love to the magazine man I got in beside the powder boxes. The magazine was full and there was not much room for me, however I coiled myself on the top of a box and had a very good sleep taking everything into consideration. The powder magazines in the trenches are formed of sandbags the same as the parapets and are very snug places. They blow up every now and then but that is not much, the man who has charge of a magazine is never allowed to take lucifer matches or a candle in with him, not even his sword in case it might strike fire against a stone. I was very glad when daylight broke. I got out to look about me, it was a fine morning and continued all day. The Russian pickets were moving off and you could see them very well. I thought of taking a shot or two at them but as one always has a chance of getting a shot or two in return I did not do it. They had been amongst the bushes all night and were carrying bundles of the twigs home with them for firewood I suppose. During the whole day I was very much amused by the shot and shell going to and fro from the batteries behind us, passing over our heads and none coming into our battery. The Menie bullets were not so good however and at times would come over our parapet in half dozens whistling as they went along with their musical 'ping'. One passed by me, struck a bank and threw the mud in my face, rather rude I must say. One great benefit with No. 7 Battery was that no one knew where to find me and I had very little to do. I had only one wounded man brought to me and he was shot close by me and I could not well help seeing him. He was shot through both thighs and all I could do was to send him home

Well after all would you believe it I have first rate health, and I enjoy this kind of life very well. How I may like the winter is another question. However if I stay where I am as I have got a hut now, I think I will be very comfortable. You ask me if I could better myself by interest at home such as Lord K etc. No, I do not intend to stay in the army very long and it would be no use if I was promoted to a permanent appointment and gazetted to a regiment, it would cost me about £60 or £70 and my pay would be worse than it is at present. So 'let well enough alone'. As I am at present I am very independent and do not care a button for anyone. If any of my superiors bully me I tell them I came out here for fun and not for a livelihood and as soon as I am tired of them I will go home and if they are tired of me I am very willing to go. In fact it would rather please them otherwise, so of course everyone is shut up at once.

There is no news what we are to do yet but I suspect we are to open fire very soon again. Yesterday the Artillery man told me that the magazines in the trenches were quite full and that shot was being brought up in very large quantities every night. I think or rather I hope our next assault may be more successful than the last. There is another small parcel on the way for you which I think will turn up some fine morning. There was a friend of mine going home to London and taking the opportunity I made a parcel of pieces of shot and shell etc. from different parts and sent them with him, if they reach Dundee they may be looked upon as curiosities and if they do not it will be no great loss. Amongst them are one or two rifle balls from Inkerman. They are very much squashed having struck stones, firelocks or some hard substance. The specimens of shell splinters will give you an idea of the things which fly about a fellow's head when a shell bursts near you. Pleasant looking things I must say.

I am glad you enjoy your new house, I should like to see it. I will give you a description of my hut in my next letter. I must draw to a close. I know this is a careless rambling letter but as it is only intended for the dear folks back home I suppose it will do. I will write soon again and hoping Mother etc are all in a state of high authority. I am your affect. son DG.

PS. There is a band playing Scotch airs beside me at present, quite enough to drive a poor fellow mad. 'Maggie Lauder' is just finished. DG

My dear Mother,

I received a short letter from Anne dated 28th July enclosing a shorter one from you and one from Mrs Mason. I am very sorry I fear I can do very little with regard to her son's effects as I am not on the spot now, but I will do my best and write to some friend of mine at Scutari and then send her word whether the things are sold or not which I do not think is the case. I am very glad to hear the sea bathing has improved your health and I hope it will keep as well as mine is at present, and I can have no better wish I can assure you. For since I ceased to drink that beastly champagne I have never even had a headache. Anne says she is very sorry I have no one here to listen to my complaints. I am happy to say I have very few to bother anyone with, except that the Russians have begun to fire round shot into our camp which I must say is very unpleasant. I am in great fear my nice hut should be knocked down some night, shot has fallen in all directions round it but never hit it as yet. About a week ago as I was lying on the top of my bed I heard one coming directly over me (we get wonderfully knowing whether or not they are coming directly at us), I jumped up and looked out of the door and saw the shot plunge into the ground close beside one of our Hospital huts and bury itself below it. It was a large 32lb shot and had it been a shell all our wounded men would have gone sky high. Rather a nice mess for an hospital to be in and only think what a state of mind our patients were in. Anne tells me that Dr Johnston is compelled (?) to come out here again, a very fine story. I have no doubt the folks at home laughed as much at him that he was very glad to come out again to save being called all sorts of nice names. If I wished to get home I have not the slightest doubt I could get home any time I liked. Johnston repents going home? All that I can say if he comes to the Crimea he will never leave it, he will die of pure fright if nothing else – don't mention this to any of his friends. Last Sabbath evening about 7 o'clock I was starting on my way for the trenches in a considerable state of excitement as we had been informed that we were to have a general attack from the Russians that night which we had learned from some intercepted dispatches. I immediately began to think of the quiet Sabbath evenings at home, and that it would be just the time you would all be going out for a walk with no ideas of danger of any kind. I can tell you it was a strange feeling.

That night everyone in the Army was under arms and of course we were on the outlook in the trenches. All the guns were manned at midnight and everything in readiness, and in that darling No. 7 Battery where I was stationed the spikes were also in readiness to spike the guns in case the Russians should take it. Fortunately for me the night wore over very quietly and during the forenoon I went to sleep below a big gun with my jacket folded on a round of shot for a pillow. About 3pm there was a party of men repairing our advanced trench and the Russians began to fire on them. After wakening from a sleep I felt very weak and I swallowed all the brandy I had in my flask (about one and a half glasses). I had scarcely done so when I was startled by a few rounds shot bounding over the parapet and immediately one of the 17th came and told me that a batch of our own men had been knocked over. I do not know whether it was the brandy or what it was but I felt uncommonly brave. I immediately rushed down and as I was passing along I was remarking that the parapet of the 4th parallel was very low, when something loped over us, down all went like a shot and kissed the ground very keenly. 'It's a shell, sir, keep close,' cries one of the men, and so it was for it immediately exploded covering us with dust. 'It's all over sir' says one. 'Good luck to it' says I, and bolted on as fast I could. I found three men in a kind of hole and a large newly fired shot between them. Just before I got to them I met one of our Lieuts rushing up as pale as death – 'Oh, Greig. For ***** sake go down, there's the very devil in that advanced trench.' I found two of the men belonged to the 17th and were only bruised, the third belonged to the 21st and was knocked to smithereens. Before I had time to examine our men 'Bang' came another shot and struck a cask which formed part of the parapet close to me which was filled with earth etc. and we were all immediately buried amongst dust and stones. I shook the dust off me, felt their pulses, and giving directions to have them carried up I hooked it as fast as my legs could carry me. What an awful feeling it is when a round shot strikes an earth work beside you, and you screwing yourself up into a small a bulk as possible. When I was buried by that round shot my only feeling was 'well the day of judgement can't be much worse than this'. It is certainly something beyond description, it requires to be felt in order to be understood. Well with all these things I am as happy as cricket and the more dangers we run the more I hope to enjoy home when I get to it. I believe we will have an engagement soon – (I am always open to an engagement, you may inform my lady friends) – and this is the opinion of everyone. There was a very smart engagement at the Tchernaya this morning, about 50,000 Russians came out to the right of Inkerman, and forded the river, they were met by the Sardinians and French and driven back. The French threw some rockets among them, which astonished them a bit. We are at present all confined to camp and ready to turn out. The Cavalry are all in Balaclava plain, and the Field Batteries have all their guns ready, and the horses standing with harness on. All our men heartily wish they could get a fair slap at them and none has the slightest doubt but that we would beat them, on the open plain. How this night will pass over I do not know but as the post does not leave until tomorrow I will finish this tomorrow.

[On 17th August over 700 allied guns commenced the Fifth Bombardment on Sebastopol, which was to last four days.]

17th

The night passed over quietly and the firing I heard yesterday now proves to have been a great victory on the part of the French assisted by the Sardinians. About 4,500 Russians killed, wounded or prisoner (600 of the latter) and 500 French killed and wounded. The Russians seem to have got an out and out thrashing. I rode over the field of battle today and must say it was a very curious sight. I would say a horrible sight but nothing is horrible in this quarter of the globe. Russians were lying in all directions and in all kind of attitudes, they had all been killed and the most had lost their clothes. I could pick up little or nothing but just as I was coming away I saw a dead Russian embracing his water flask and with a 'hail old fellow, what have you got there?' I walked off with the flask and also his cap-pouch. Before I came out here I never could understand what people meant when they talked of the attitudes of the dead on the field of battle, but I can assure you it is something very curious, some were in sitting positions bending over their arms, as if they had been wounded and their life gradually ebbed away, the most however were lying on their backs as if they were basking in the sun, and their arms folded over their faces to protect them. The masses of dead Russians were something wonderful and every here and there a Soave amongst them. We came to a mass of dead bodies which were being buried in a pit and from one of the Frenchmen who was burying them I got a small medal which he had taken from the breast of a Russian soldier, it may be a small curiosity in its way, and a memento of the Battle of Tchernaya, if it be called so.

Dr Gibaut is going home on sick leave and I sent by him a Russian gun and bayonette which may cast up in Dundee some day and be another 'week's wonder', as it also was taken yesterday at the Tchernaya.

With regard to my box, you may keep your mind easy as I have learned it is somewhere in Turkey and I have no doubt it will turn up. I must defer the description of my hut until another time and I will write soon again and tell you what is doing etc Regards etc ... and hope you will excuse the abruptness with which I finish this as I fear it will be very heavy. I am very sleepy and the additional consideration that I may be roused out of bed to the tune of the 'assembly bugle'.

My dear Anne,

How to write a long letter to you this time beats my comprehension but if I did not I suppose I had better look out for a blowing up or at least some very severe remarks, now, as I do not like these things I must do my best and when a person does their best I am sure you can say nothing to them. Well, I am always fated to receive your kind letters when I come off trenches and your last I received on Tuesday night; although I was very tired I managed to keep my eyes open until I had read it twice over. On looking over it again I must say I could easily have digested double the quantity of news which it contained, however I was very thankful for what there was. And I sincerely hope you and mother will never let a week pass but that some of you will drop a note.

So Mrs Baxter wishes to see me in my uncivilised state. It is certainly a compliment but I cannot promise her her wish. As the saying is when a person is in Rome do as the Romans do, and I say when in Turkey I do as the Turks do, but when I come to the civilised country again I must appear somewhat like a civilised being again and therefore she will see much the same as I was before. As for Cousin Anne she seems a perfect Amazon. I do not know how she would like to live in a tent and be in a state of perpetual picnicking, and singing the 'days we went a gypsying' and such like. Since I have got a hut I am sure she would be very comfortable so far as shelter went but I could not guarantee anything else. I think she is far better at home, at least until the war is over, and then a jaunt to the Crimea and a visit to the battlefields would be a very interesting thing.

Talking of my hut I do not think I have ever described it to you and I suppose I must do it now. My friend Gibaut is a very mechanical genius and one day he took it into his head he would have a hut. I told him it was too early to think about it yet as no one knew what would happen before winter. However he would not listen and I agreed to help him – in other words, to become his partner in this building speculation. We got two or three men from the regiment to assist us and we dug a large hole in the ground close to our tent, 12ft long and 10ft broad. Around this we built a wall about a foot high and also two gable ends, as for a roof we got a piece of tarpaulin and some condemned blankets and now when it is finished it is quite a stunning mansion and is as neat an amateur constructed hut as there is in the Crimea. Gibaut did not enjoy the hut long and when he left it he gave it all to me until he came back, when that will be I do not know. Before he had left we had got another Assistant Surgeon (Dr Hooper) he slept in a tent close to my hut. And messed with me. After staying a month he got gazetted to the 10th Hussars, joined them, and I am now all alone. There is another Asst Surgeon gazetted to this regiment but he is still at Scutari, and never joined yet. His name is Mr Walker and poor fellow I am sorry to say he has got a wife. I do not know if he will bring her with him but as our own Surgeon said when he heard it 'Oh, won't we have stunning parties in you hut when she comes up.' As far as I can learn I believe she is still in England. When you see my hut from the outside there is little else to be seen but a roof but when you get into it it is quite a snuggery, and I can stand perfectly erect in all parts of it. It has all been whitewashed and smoothed down in the interior and I have covered the walls with pictures from 'The Illustrated London News' and 'Punch', mixed them all up together and they do look so comical making one laugh whither he will or not. Here is a sketch of the said hut and I am sure that you must say it is an elegant looking article in the hut line. In my next letter I will perhaps send you a drawing of the hut which may give you a better idea of it than this ground plan will do, as it is domestic arrangements and I hope you approve of it. I have erected a porch and two seats and it is such a jolly place to sit and smoke in the evenings. I have got great furniture in the way of tables you will see, but sorry to say I have not even a chair but perfectly content with three or four stools. At present I am seated on top of a box. The fireplace is something out of the common run of things and will be a great treat when the cold weather comes on. The weather is not so hot as it has been here and the last night I was in the trenches I got it very cold although during the day again it was what I might term 'stewing'. Since I got the hut it is much better than the tent. I received a letter today from Mr Struthers as kind as ever. He has received the box all safe and he tells me he has seen Johnston but that he does not intend coming out here again. Dr Struthers is still asking me to tell him more about his brother as Johnston could tell him little or nothing. The more I see and hear of Johnston the more I am astonished at him. You tell about his teetotal brother, the name is quite enough. He must be a fool who cannot take care of himself without pledging himself on oath to do so. If he converts the fishermen at Ferrymen I'll eat my cocked hat. I think you have certainly come down a peg in the world by the Auchterhouse picnic if I could not get to a picnic like our former ones I would not go at all. I think I told you about Dr Watson. I have not heard about him since he went off to Scutari. I hope he is better by this time. He was very ill before he left this. We have had very little news since the Battle of Tchernaya. We have been expecting an attack every day and had different 'turn outs' but the Russians seem to have given up the idea now and I believe that their large army has withdrawn towards the Belbie again. There was a tremendous explosion of gunpowder three nights ago which shook the whole camp. I believe it was about two tons which the French were taking up to the Namelon. A Russian shell struck it, it exploded and sent a great many Frenchmen to their last home. I hope you received the Russian medal which I sent home. When you receive this you may be expecting the gun which Gibaut has taken home for me. Enclosed in the same parcel is a small stick which was cut from a vine on the field of Inkerman by our own Surgeon soon after the battle and while he was exposed to a very heavy fire from the Russian batteries. It may be a bit of a curiosity at home, if it is not, no great matter. You sometimes complain that I never mention having received some of the letters which were sent to me. Since I have been here I do not think that any one of my letters have gone astray. If I do not get a letter every week keep your mind easy you will be sure to hear of it. There is one of my correspondents whom I must call a very bad one and unless I receive a letter from him very soon I must put my pen through his name both in my good and bad book, (viz) Dr Crockatt.

After a three-day bombardment (the sixth) by 775 British and French guns, a renewed assault was launched on the Malakov and Great Redan on 8th September.

My dear Father,

I intend writing you a very short letter this post which leaves early tomorrow morning as I believe there is to be an attack on the Malkoff tomorrow, we will be all engaged. Ever since the battle of Tchernaye we have been very much on our 'Ps' and 'Qs', expecting a grand attack from the Russians and about a week ago we have had two or three pleasant turn outs at 2am and had to stand under arms for about three hours. Each time we got the pleasure (?) of seeing the sun rise. Nothing took place and we were all sent to bed again, very well pleased to get to it, at the same time wishing the Russians were far enough off. We have a good many bombardments on a small scale and today we opened at noon with a tremendous fire on the Russian works. It has now (10pm) partially subsided but it will open again tomorrow morning and at about mid-day we will go at it. Everything has been kept very quiet this time and we have no idea that anything would happen until this afternoon when our HM sent to enquire if our hospital was in tip top trim and how many empty beds we had for wounded men as we had a good chance of getting them filled tomorrow. All the men who have gone to the trenches tonight have taken 48 hours provisions with them – cooked – in case they should require to stay there that time. I do not know where I may be tomorrow but I will take as great care of myself as of a barrel with the direction, 'Glass with Care, this side up'. I'll seem jolly and happy and the bands were playing 'Cheer, boys, cheer', tonight which is rather a rare tune here. Two nights ago we were gratified by a grand sight – viz, one of the Russian frigates in the harbour of Sebastapol on fire about 11pm. When all the rigging was on fire and the flames bursting out at the portholes it was a magnificent sight as I never saw before. The Russians seem to be burning all their shipping in the harbour, they have burned two since and one is burning now. They seem to be making preparations for leaving the place and all wish they would.

I received a letter from mother today dated 18th August and also three papers which were all very acceptable. I am glad to hear that the jams and jellies turned out well this year. It is a very satisfactory fact and if we make the Russians into jam and jellies tomorrow the fact will be equally acceptable at home I hope. I like to hear about all these things and although you laugh at mother for telling me she must not give it up. I was glad to hear you were all well. I am in prime condition just now and hope to remain so. The hot weather here is I think past now, the days are cool and bearable and the nights are decidedly cold. Everyone thinks we will have a bad winter but not such a wet one as last. You will know all about the attack before this will reach you but should it come off I will write you next post if all is well. Good bye Love to all etc. DG

PS. No word of the box yet but I have no doubt it will cast up yet. 'It canna be lost' as Flockhart used to say.

The Fall of Sebastopol: initially the attack on the Great Redan by the British forces failed, with heavy casualties. Estimates suggest 2,610 wounded, 550 dead including 29 officers. However, the French assault captured the strategic Malakov fortification, which led to the Russian hierarchy's decision to abandon the southern part of Sevastopol and, leaving their wounded behind, they blew up the fortifications and major buildings in the port before crossing the harbour to the northern suburb. The French suffered 7,567 casualties with 1,634 killed. Estimates of the Russian casualties suggested over 3,000 killed and a further 9,000 wounded.

The following day the allied forces were in complete command of the dockyards and the surrounding area and news soon spread that Sevastopol had fallen.

CAMP BEFORE SEBASTAPOL

10TH SEPTEMBER 1855

My dear Father,

Sebastapol is taken at last and I had the pleasure of being in at the death. You will of course know more of the particulars of this great event than I can at present tell you and you must excuse me if in this letter if I show myself a thorough egotist and only tell you what I saw and did. For any single individual who has been engaged in a battle to imagine he can describe it is very absurd, the truth is 'every man for himself and God for all'. I can only tell you what I saw and leave the special correspondent of the 'Times' to enlighten the folks at home on the affair as a whole. When I wrote my last letter the evening before the attack I knew I was to be down bur I did not like to make you uneasy by saying so as I had volunteered to be one of the party who should receive the wounded in rear of the attacking party.

The morning of the 8th September dawned cold and stormy. The cold got less about 10 o'clock and everyone felt in fighting condition. The dust was a great nuisance during the day and the men looked more like millers than anything else. We had a few drops of rain during the day but nothing of any consequence (so much for the meteorological part!). About 9am I had just finished a jolly breakfast and was sitting at the door of my hut as quietly as the roar of the cannon would allow, smoking the pipe of peace when our RMO came and gave me my final instructions and bade me be off and see if everything was right at the place where we were to be stationed. I took an hospital orderly with me and set off down the Morowzow Road where I found a marquee or large tent erected in a ravine behind the 21st battery. Everything was complete, lots of tea, hot and cold water sponges, lint etc. and two full surgeons beside myself from the 4th Division. The most terrible row was being carried on by the guns I ever heard before and every now and then a round of shot was bounding into the ravine or over where we by way of variety. Between 10 and 11 all the regiment from our Division marched past where I was. They were all in good humour but looking very determined and as dusty as possible. Many began chaffing me and wishing to know if it was a canteen I was in charge of. I told them they could learn on their way home what the tent was for and I was sorry to say many did so. A little before 12 the fire from our batteries was terrific, that gradually died away and was replaced by musketry which continued close to us for a short time. We then heard cheering both English and French, and the Malakoff was in the hands of the French, and the tricolour floating over the ramparts. The musketry and cannons began again on the left and I was told that the English had gone at the Kedan. All this time we had no wounded and were taking care of our heads. Immediately after the Malakoff was taken the wounded began to come in and all kinds of wounds were here, from smashed heads to smashed toes, and this continued all day. We had a plentiful supply of ambulance and mules and all we had to do was to render immediate assistance to such as required it and get them sent up to Camp on the easiest conveyance possible. As the wounded came in we learned all that was going on in front. At first we were in the Kedan then we were out of it, then in it, and again out of it. Time flew very fast that day and the evening came on before we knew where we were and the general impression was that we could not hold or even take the Kedan and some were beginning to think we were to have a repetition of the 18th June. Not so however. As it got dark the Russians began to leave the Kedan and blow up all their shells and magazines. During the night fires broke out in all parts of the town and the sight was something sublime. Every now and then a large quantity of shell would explode like a cart load of gigantic crackers and fly about in all directions. The best sight was when some of their largest magazines exploded. A bright flame would light up the sky for a moment, a large black pointed mass would shoot up into the sky, a terrific report would shake the whole ground and rattle along the hills in echo, while the smoke would extend for miles and miles. After the Russians had left the Kedan there was a tremendous lot of wounded brought to us, both English and Russian, and within about two or three hours I think I saw 2,000 patients. Immediately after the Russians left they crossed over by means of their bridge of boats to the other side of the harbour and left us in entire possession of the town. During the time the fight was going on I was not altogether out of danger although I was sheltered a little. Shot and shell were passing and bursting over us every now and then. The only shot which came near me was when I was placing a wounded man on a mule litter, it must have gone very near me for it passed between the mule's legs. Another shot struck the top of the hill and rolled into our tent. Another was more severe. I had placed a wounded man on a stretcher and he was being carried up to camp by four Turks. They had not gone far from me when a round shot took his head off. One young officer who had been found dead in the Kedan was brought to me by some Turks. He had been shot in the head and bayoneted in several places, he was lying in an easy position, his head thrown back and his beautiful black hair hanging over the stretcher. No one knew him. He had been rifled. His shoulder cords and even most of his buttons torn off. It even struck me that it was a melancholy sight. The Turks had found his body just as I saw it and brought it to me merely because they had not seen a ditch large enough to pitch it into. I saw by his buttons what regiment he belonged to and sent him to it where he was recognised as a young English Baronet. The Russians we saw were good enough looking fellows. I offered some of them brandy but they preferred biscuits and one fellow ate the hard biscuits as if he had not seen food for a very long time.

About 10 next morning I was relieved as all the wounded had been conveyed up to Camp so I thought as I had wrought hard enough for 24 hours I would now play myself and accordingly I went into the town with the other fellows. We first visited the batteries and the Kedan which were covered with dead. The batteries were well made and they had large guns some of which had been turned topsy turvy by the explosions but all seemed in good condition. There were a great number of huts where the men had lain in underground, they were shell proof. I expected to have found something in them but they had all been ransacked before. Lots of ammunition and pouches were lying in all directions but no such things as curiosities. I found a small hut which seemed to have been a Surgeon's hut and in it I found a few small bottles, two spoons, and a lot of Latin medical recipes and an old truss. The three former I carried off with me and will send home. Oh, what a place Sebastpol is, there was a cry of 'why did we spare the town?' You will know whether we did or not when I tell you there was not an entire building in the whole town, there is scarcely a tree entire. The town must have been a beautiful place before we came to it, the finest natural harbour I think I ever saw, the streets broad and handsome, and the houses with evergreens and vines in front of them. The houses were large and commodious as the 'Tickets to let' say, and all that had been worth anything were blazing when I saw them. The Russians had completely evacuated the place and were leaving in small boats when I was there. Their bridges had been broken and all their steamers and vessels of war were sunk or burned. Our men were not allowed to plunder but the French were going whole sale at it. There does not appear to be much left. I thought I was pretty early on the ground but every house had been entered before I got to it and anything of value carried off. The first place I got into was a kind of library, the books were all tumbled about the rooms and strewn on the streets, they were all Russian and a good many manuscripts. The French were carrying off the tables and chairs and all that was worth and what they did not want was broken or pitched out at the window. I got into a ship store at the arsenal a good many French and English were there and I never saw such a heterogeneous mass, butter, jackets, tar shirts, paint, trousers, and everything you could think of all mixed up forming a beautiful compound. I prowled about and entered a great many houses in all parts of the town, running my sword through all the bundles and ladies' bonnets I met in with. Some of the bonnets were very good and one grand white satin I took a savage delight in kicking along the street, and then tossed it into a burning house. Our sailors and the French Soaves were the boys, a lot had got a hold of some brandy and were very drunk, and one party had got hold of a piano and were hauling it along the streets on a wheel barrow, while others went alongside and struck the wires with their swords making the strangest music you ever heard. There was a Soave in the middle of a broad street dressed in a beautiful white muslin gown and red satin bonnet kicking up a great row, then an English sailor admiring himself in a large mirror and because he is not so good looking as he used to be he smashed it with his foot, in fact it puts one in mind of a fair and everyone as jolly as possible. The Russians seem to have bolted in a great hurry, they were prepared to defend the place to the last, and all the streets were barricaded and commanded by small field pieces but I suppose they saw it was no use and I am sure they were not far wrong. We have now some breathing time and I can scarcely tell you how odd I feel, the silence which reigns around, no guns firing now, and everyone saying 'How like Sunday at home'. What the taking of Sebastopol may do towards the finishing of the war I do not know. I hope it may do something but I rather fear we will have some more work to do soon again, and what is nearly as bad as trenches, heavy marching and fighting at the same time. However winter is coming and I hope they will allow us to be quiet until Spring. I think I have been a salamander long enough now and I should like a little rest, and if we only get till spring we will be able to have a go at Simpheropol and I hope it will not be an eleven month job like this. Well, thank goodness I have got on very well during the five months. I have assisted at the siege and I hope to get thro' all my 'sodgering' as well. We have (British) had 95 officers killed and wounded, 8 belonging to the 17th Regiment as you will see by the papers. Our Division has suffered very little this time as the Light and the Second were the fighting ones.

Now I shall bid you all a goodbye.

The enclosed leaves were plucked from the town.

My dear Anne,

I suppose you were all very glad to receive my last letter and it must have been good news to a great many besides you. Although I date my letter Camp Sebastopol we are still in the same old place before Sebastopol. All our camps are in the same situation and soldiers are sent down every day to the town and are engaged in putting it to rights, making roads etc. As for our wintering in it the very idea is all nonsense because the place is a mass of ruins and we are very comfortable and safe where we are.

Immediately after the town was taken there was a great talk of a move northwards or re-attack the Russians and I was very much frightened we would get the order, however we had a few wet and cold days and I suppose that put a stop to the idea of night bivouacking which I must say was not very pleasant. I have no doubt we will quietly remain where we are for the winter and as soon as the weather breaks up next Spring we will commence a splendid Summer campaign. I do not think we will be at all willing to commence another siege again but the great dodge will be to get the Russians in the open, and I think a good battle or two would bring them to their senses sooner than another siege. I do not think the camp was ever so dull since I came to it, there is no news of any kind whatsoever and everyone seems shut up for the season. We are all rejoicing, we have no more trenches and the men are being drilled and sharpened up every day. All thro' the camp you see squads going thro' their drill and performing goose steps the same as at home. There is a variety in our rides now, instead of riding through the camp as before we now take a ride to Sebastopol, the Kedan Zalakoff or Mamelon as the case may be. I have been thro' all the old Russian works now and well worth seeing they are. Were it not for the abominable smell from the thousands of bodies which are buried around them. The French have taken one part of the town and we another but still it is dangerous to be in the place as the Russians very often fire from the opposite side of the harbour into the town, very few men are in it and they do no damage. I have sent off a week ago a box with a lot of curiosities from Sebastopol. There is a list in the box which will explain the contents, the best thing in it is a coat which I am sure will astonish even Mr Mathewson's weak nerves. Whenever I fall in with anything curious I keep it beside me until I get a chance of sending it home, and then off it goes. I have wished very much to get hold of a gold cross or something of value but have never succeeded so you must just be content with small mercies and take what I can send you. Did you get a small medal which I sent you in one of my letters? I think it was the one I wrote about after the Battle of Tchernaya. The camp is very healthy just now and all the work we have to do just now is mere child's play. Only think our Regiment is about 800 strong and we have only about 30 in Hospital and that amongst a Surgeon and three assistants, cannot be killing work. Our new Assistant Mr Walker has now joined us, he is, I think I told you, a married man but he has left his wife at home. He is a very nice, jolly, easy going fellow and what is more surprising a very sensible fellow. I suspect he has been regularly taken in and done for. The other assistant who is with me is our Senior Assistant Dr Bone (Mrs Crockett and Pirie know him). He arrived from England the day before Sebastopol was taken – and of course comes in for the medal or whatever goes for the capture, while poor Mr Walker joined us the day after the capture and of course was a day too late for the fair! I have now before me a letter dated 27th August and another from Mother dated 1st September. I got one from Mr Pirie with an appendix from James Rodgers last post and I expect one from you tomorrow morning. I must get a letter every post from someone or I am miserable. Two posts ago I had a budget of Woolerian news. They are all very kind to me in that quarter and I often write them. Miss A. and I are always bantering each other even in our letters, when I say our letters I mean her father's and brother's. She sometimes ventures a PS but nothing more. Do you still write to her? You seem very indignant at me in your last and all because I hinted that you did not give me more news. All I can say is preserve me from a lady's tongue, it's decidedly worse than a regular bombardment, shot or shell is nothing to it. It is very pleasant to hear of all your visitors and my old friends. I only wish I had been in Dundee and could have gone to Montrose with them. Oh, wouldn't I have enjoyed myself. Just as I am writing I have received your letter dated 18th inst. I am surprised you do not yet know of the taking of Sebastopol, the news should have been home by that time, however you must know all about it now. Your letter has a different tone altogether from the former one and you all seem well pleased with my communications to the Editors of the P and J [*Press and Journal*] and CI. I am rather glad you saw it, as it was a general letter and intended for anybody. I really forget what I wrote but it has fulfilled its purpose and amused you. I knew the gun would be a real curiosity, it is a real Ruski and a very good one, it is a common 'Brown Bess', some of them are very fine rifles but I could not get one at the time. I may send one by and by when we have another smashing match. You may all talk to Jeems as you like but I can tell you he won't get married until he sees his way clearly. On a matter of that kind I must say Jeems is a very sensible fellow. I must say you give me a good deal of news. I am sorry father's apprentice has bolted so soon, I do not think he can be much worth and father is perhaps well rid of him. Joho Hutcheson's death is very melancholy and a loss which all who knew him will feel. ... I am sorry I can't tell you much about Dr Watson, all I know is that he went from Scutari home about three weeks ago and I hope he is all safe and well now. I am enjoying first rate health. We had some cold days last week but we have fine weather again and I suppose it will continue until it breaks up again and then we must expect cold weather and no mistake. I have written this letter in a careless style as I have a sore finger which a careless operator cut while amputating a leg yesterday, so must excuse me. Kind love to father etc., etc.

CHAPTER 6

Attack on Kinburn

On 7th October, Combined Forces sailed for the Dneiper River for an attack on Kinburn.

Partly to satisfy home government demands, an allied expedition was mounted to sail to the Dnieper River on the north-western shore of the Black Sea. Ten transports carrying 10,000 British and French troops set sail from Kamiesch protected by a naval flotilla of almost 40 ships. The immediate objectives were the Russian forts at Kinburn and Ochakov. The expedition anchored close to Kinburn on 14th October. Gunboats bombarded the beach, before an invasion force consisting of two British infantry brigades, supported by engineers, artillery and cavalry, landed to the right of the fort. French units established themselves to the left. Kinburn was bombarded, and on 17th October the Russian garrison of 700 surrendered with 80 guns. Next day the Russians blew up Orchakov and retreated northwards.

ON BOARD HMS ROYAL ALBERT, KAZATCH BAY
5TH OCTOBER 1855

My dear Father,

I have no doubt you will be very much surprised to hear that I am on board the great 'man of war' the Royal Albert, but such is the case and what is more no one knows where. When in Camp often and often have I wondered when we would leave it and what would be the cause of our leaving. My wondering was brought to a conclusion however on the 2nd inst. by the 1st Brigade of our Division receiving orders to hold itself in immediate readiness to march. None of us had the slightest idea of such a thing and of course we were very much taken aback. The most of the Officers in the Regt had erected huts like mine and mine was in beautiful condition, I had just got an armchair from Sebastopol in fact I am surprised the Commander in Chief did not take my hut into consideration, but it seems he did not and the 17th simply received orders to march. No one knew where we were to go to but all suspected that we were to go on board ship and so it was. Some supposed we were to go to Kertch, some Odessa, some Theodosic and some Nickalaoff, and I suspected the latter were right. The 2nd and 3rd (Tuesday and Wednesday) were very busy days, packing up and putting our luggage in store as we were only allowed to take as much as we could carry with us. On Thursday morning we were all up before daylight and commenced the march to this place at half 5am along with the 17th were the 57th, 20th, 21st and 63rd Regiments. The morning was very fine when we started but we had a good shower of rain to cool our ardour on the road. We arrived in safety at Kazatch about 11am and all the 17th Regiment was put on board the 'Royal Albert', the other regiments were put on other vessels. We have on board about 750 men and each of the other regiments average 500. Besides these I believe there are a great many French going and also the Marines. We are not certain where we are going but is thought it is to have a slap at the Russians some way to the north of the Crimea. I think to destroy Nickaloaff on the River Bong. We are sure to have some fighting and then I suppose we will return to our old camp again. However, some say we will not but I hope we will. I did not describe to you the 'Royal Albert'. I saw her at Scutari and I think I described her to you then. We are very comfortable on board except in the sleeping line. We have to sleep in hammocks or cots in the cock-pit the best way we can. Last night was my first in a hammock and I was frightened to go to sleep in case I should fall out. The noise and heat of the cock-pit is very disagreeable but that was not the worst of it, some of the midshipmen got loose amongst us and cut some of the hammock strings and the result was of course a row which continued for the greater part of the night and which was finished by a very wise conclusion that the boards were the safest. I was very fortunate and did not get cut down but some of my brother officers suffered.

We have beautiful weather at present. It is all very well on board ship but to bivouac on the South coast of Russia in the open will not be so pleasant. However we are all very jolly and expect great things. I suppose you know this is the flagship and we have Admiral E. Lyons on board. I sometimes see him walking on the poop. He is a good looking old fellow and that is all I know about him. None of us have our horses on board and I had to leave mine in camp under the tender mercies of a commissariat officer who is to take charge of and live in my establishment while I am away. In the last letter I had from Mother she mentioned how glad you all were when you saw that none of the 17th were in the list of wounded published in the newspapers. I have often told you all never to believe anything you see in the papers except births, marriages and deaths, and even these you may doubt, and here you have another proof. We had three officers and eighteen men wounded. Certainly not many but still quite enough to show that we were under fire. This is a most disagreeable place for writing and I must conclude. We expect to sail with the whole fleet on Sunday 7th and I will drop you a note as soon as possible.

My dear Father,

When I wrote last I was on board the 'Royal Albert' in Kazatch Bay expecting to sail on Sunday and so it was. Great preparations were going on around us, frigates, gun boats, floating latrines, transports and lines of battleships all congregated around us and being on board the Admiral's flagship I had a very good opportunity of seeing all that went on. On Sunday morning at 11am the whole fleet set sail and passed along the coast of the Crimea in front of the harbour of Sebastopol. It was a most beautiful Sabbath morning and I enjoyed myself very much, in fact all were in high spirits. I do not know what the inhabitants of Sebastopol or rather the Russians on the north of Sebastopol thought of our fleet as we sailed along the coast but their feelings must have been very different to ours, and it was quite evident we were not going on an errand of peace even altho' it was a Sabbath morning. We moved along very slowly and had time to enjoy the scene. The ships were mostly all screw steamers and the manner in which they sailed along was very pretty. All the large vessels in lines on the outside and the small ones in the centre between them. Our large vessel always kept about the centre and every now and then had to go slow and bring up some lazy hulk. Then she would scud forward to learn what the vanguard vessels were doing, in fact we were here, there and everywhere. We had six small gunboats with us and they kept following the Royal Albert like so many chickens, everyone trying to see who could keep next to her. They are very smart looking little boats and look like private yachts. At night the sight was equally interesting there was no moon and the Black Sea looked doubly black while all around us we had lights of all colours denoting the various vessels. In the morning we had to stop for a little and get the fleet collected and then went on again as before. Life on board a large man of war is in some respects very nice but in general I would not care much for it. We had good feeding that was one thing and nothing to do was another, but beyond these I do not know but what I would have preferred the camp. When we first came on board we all considered it a great hardship in not being allowed to smoke when we liked but the Admiral taking into account how free we had been before removed the restrictions. When on deck sailors seldom or never sit down and I think it annoyed them to see us sitting. We were always in the way. If we sat down on a box or coil of rope the box or coil of rope was sure to be needed. The sleeping accommodation is bad on board a man of war, our men occupied the 2nd or 3rd decks (I do not know their nautical name) the sailors the 4th deck and we were all in the cock-pit in cots or hammocks. As you may well imagine there is not much comfort in such a place, it is hot and close and the very lights which burn there never look bright. I think I told you that the midshipmen are given to practical joking at night and altho' it is quite harmless still it is very annoying and at the same time amusing to those who do not suffer and I am happy to say I have never suffered. The first night some of our fellows had their hammocks unstrung but it was in the middle of the night and the most of us lost the fun. Every night since none of us have got to sleep before 12 o'clock as there was always some fun going on. One of our young Ensigns has I must say been rather victimised. He neglected to get a cot for himself and had a trick of turning into the first he came to – of course the owner always turned him out and the other night he did get a hammock for himself. This was something unusual and attracted attention. He was allowed to get into bed with a good deal of difficulty and we were all laughing at him. As soon as he was comfortable a fellow pulled the tape at his feet which was in a slip knot and down he came with a thump on the floor and of course threw us all into convulsions of laughter, this took place four times and then he was allowed to sleep. Monday 8th October was as beautiful a day as the preceding one and about 2pm we came in sight of the Russian coast and about three hours afterwards we anchored in front of Odessa along with the whole fleet. Odessa seems a very nice town and the buildings are not in the state which I expected to see them after the bombardment. They seem entire and when we look at them from where we are no one could tell that the town had been bombarded. No batteries are to be seen but no doubt there are batteries there. Although we have come to Odessa I do not think we are to hurt the town but this is merely a ruse to deceive the Russians and I hear it is intended to attack a fort at the mouth of the River Bong called Kinburn and then perhaps go up the river to Meolaon. However I do not know at present. Time will show.

Tuesday 9th October. We are still at anchor off Odessa the fleet forming at it were a semi circle round it. The morning was dull but we had a good view of the town. Towards afternoon it became very thick and quite obscured the rest of the fleet. The day passed over heavily and we were all very anxious to know what was to be done. Wednesday the 10th, morning very dull and misty, has been raining during the night. It is now given out openly that we are to go to Kinburn, land there and take the fort. Towards afternoon the fog cleared off and I had a nice sail thro' the fleet as I was taking two sick to an hospital ship. I must say my old enemy nearly spoiled the pleasure. I mean seasickness and as the boat pitched along I thought on Broughty Ferry when I used to say 'Oh, there's another big wave coming', however this was in the Black Sea and by a great resolution I managed my excursion without getting sick.

Thursday 11th. All is now settled and we leave this place tomorrow morning. There is a great commotion on board the fleet, ships are being put into fighting trim, their top gallant masts are all hauled down, the rigging is thinned and cleared, and the splinter nettings are being put up. It is a most beautiful morning and Odessa is seen to great advantage. We are putting ourselves in fighting trim here as if we were to attack this place, while in reality we are up to go 80 miles eastwards and then disembark. We can see the people in great commotion in Odessa and a great many troops in the street. Admirals, captains etc are on board getting their final orders and boats of all sorts and sizes are at our sides. I do not think Kilburn will be well marked in the maps and so I send you a chart of the place which will explain it all. It is a very curious place. It is at the mouth of the River Bong and on the right hand side as you approach the mouth of the river. There is a massive tongue of land which forms a kind of breakwater or harbour and on this the Russians have a strong fort mounting 64 guns and two earth batteries. This place is called Kinburn Spit and the fort Kinburn Fort, it guards the entrance to the river and therefore is a guard to Meolaor which is a great building place for the Russian Black Sea fleet. This spit of land is therefore an important place and this is what we are to take. You will see there are three or four small lakes and a small hamlet below them, well it is proposed to land the English at this hamlet to prevent the Russian reinforcements coming into the fort while the French will be landed above the lakes and prevent the retreat of those in the fort and prevent them attacking us in the rear. While we are doing this the ships are to do their best to destroy the fort. We expect tough work but I should say there is every chance of success. However we must not be too sanguine for we must remember the Scotch saying of 'mice and men'. Many a poor fellow I have no doubt will be knocked over and everyone hopes the lot will not fall upon himself. We are just going to take our last dinner on board and a jolly one we will make it. The soldier's motto is 'never mind the morrow' and so we must all be jolly today. The greatest row is going on on board and it is no easy joke writing so I must draw to a close, and wish you all health, strength and happiness, and ourselves good luck for tomorrow. Kindest love to Mother etc. etc. as I cannot find time to write to any of my Edinburgh friends please send a sight of this to Jeems Rodgers. I will write next post but when that will be I do not know. Kinburn for ever!!

17th October 1855. Capture of Kinburn on the Dneiper River

CAMP KINBURN
19TH OCTOBER 1855

My dear Father,

In the last letter which I wrote to you from on board the 'Royal Albert' I think I gave you an account of my wanderings up to the 10th inst. (Thursday) and at that time we were lying off Odessa. We were kept by contrary winds here until Sunday morning the 14th. Nothing particular occurred during that time with the exception of my dinner with Admiral Sir Edmund Lyons on the 11th. He is a jolly old fellow and gave us a first rate dinner which you know goes a far way in getting a good opinion of anyone. The dinner was a first rate one, and dining with us we had some of his chief officers and the General and some of his. All the officers in the Regt. Were asked in rotation and my turn came off on Friday. On Sabbath morning about 4.30am I was awoke by an awful noise, roaring of voices, rattling of chains, and the tune of 'Pop goes the Weasel' played in furious style by a violin and fife. I found we were weighing anchor so I got up. I was a beautiful calm morning and the fleet were soon under weigh, and we bade adieu to Odessa. We sailed along the coast in an easterly direction. The shore was very beautiful, generally precipitous, and every here and there we saw neat, small villages at the seaside and all the people looking at us as we passed along, what their thoughts must have been I do not know. The day was hot, still comfortable from the sea breeze, and we enjoyed it very much examining all the land with glasses and always discovering something worth looking at. About one and a half pm, we came in sight of Kinburn fort and anchored about five miles off it. It seemed a very strong place but no shots were fired that day as we were out of reach, but some were fired by our gunboats which were sounding during the night. We were all as merry as possible although we knew we would have tough work on the morrow. We had a small jollification and went to bed at 9 o'clock in order to be up in time on the morrow and land as soon as possible in boats.

15th October – Monday

We were all roused this morning at 4am. And such a row at an early hour you never heard. The men had a hurried breakfast and so had we. I could not drink my tea I was in such an excited state, so I made a claret breakfast and relished it. All the regiment was paraded and marched into a small steam boat with six small boats behind them. We got all settled down in our places and the sun was just rising out of the Black Sea when the band struck up 'Cheer Boys Cheer'; and with three cheers from the sailors who manned the rigging which we returned with three times three we pushed off from the 'Royal Albert' very much satisfied with the treatment we had experienced on board. The morning was somewhat chilly but we went along merrily. As we approached the low sandy beach we saw some Cossacks riding along and who took themselves off as soon as possible. One however, stayed awhile behind and when we were close in shore he threw his lance, sword and pistols from him and galloped off as fast as he could.

We landed without opposition in boats about 8am on a sandy shore very like the sands at Broughty Ferry (in fact you could not get a better resemblance) close to the small salt lakes, all the ground was covered with *bent* just like Broughty. The boats as they were full of soldiers could not get near the shore and it was quite amusing to see the fellows wading on shore. Some with bare legs, others with trousers and boots on just as they were, every now and then you would see a fellow go head and ears in the water, ammunition, musket and all he had on. As soon as they got on shore they formed into companies and went out skirmishing.

The British were the first to land and the first boat which touched the Russian coast had a 'Union Jack' on board which was immediately planted on a small sandy hillock and three British cheers rent the air. The 17th Regiment was the first to land and their colours were the first regimental colours on shore. I had off my shoes and stockings but a sailor would not let me wet my feet but carried me from the boat to the shore on his back. As for my luggage I had very little to trouble myself about, a knapsack, a blanket and a water keg was my whole equipment. After we had all got landed we all squatted down on the top of a sand hillock and each taking a biscuit and a lump of pork from our haversacks we made a hearty meal and finished off with a glass of grog. Our haversacks are canvass bags in which every man carries his provisions and on this occasion we had three days grub to carry and all agreed that it was far easier to carry it in the stomach than on his back. While we were all at our repast we were startled by a shot proceeding from a body of skirmishers which we had sent out. We all rushed to see what was the matter and found the officer commanding the party had shot a calf, of which more hereafter. There were 4 or 5 small houses close by but we were not allowed to go to them, some sailors landed however in a boat, above our sentries and carried off a whole boat full of poultry which was certainly robbing us of our dues. Dr Ward (our surgeon) and myself passed our sentries and went on to the houses and found that the place was a Cossack station. It consisted of five small cottages, a large stable, and outhouses. The cottages were small neat and clean and consisted of a cooking place and one small room. The inmates had evidently left in a great hurry and a great many things were lying about in all directions. I picked up a few. They were of very little worth. Our grand object was something to eat, and having discovered a poor unfortunate hen we set off in pursuit of her assisted by one of our sergeants and an officer of the Marines. It was quite a farce to see three officers and sergeant pursuing a hen with drawn swords all round the houses. At last she took refuge in one and I caught her. I had never killed a hen in my life before and I certainly made a mess of this one. I wish Aunt Pirie had been here, she used to be good at it. However I managed it and carried it off in triumph. Soon after this our Regiment was moved more inland where we had to remain for the night. We soon had the hen cooked and with a piece of the calf and some fried pork we made a splendid dinner. I must say it was a romantic sight to see us all sitting around our bivouac fires pitching into our grub with an appetite which few folks at home ever experience. There it was that you heard the soldier's bivouac song and the tales of battle and bloodshed. One thought of the kind faces at home and wondered what they were about, and if all was well. It was a curious moment and at the same time a dangerous one for had a mass of Cossacks come upon us we would have had a different tale to tell. However no one disturbed us, and rolling ourselves in our blankets, with our packs for our pillows and one's feet to the dying embers of the fire, I fell asleep under the clear blue sky, the shining stars and last, though not least, a heavy dew falling.

Next morning (Tuesday) we were roused at bugle call and certainly we felt stiff but nothing more. We washed ourselves with a very small allowance of water, breakfasted again on the calf and pork (the said calf seems to have served the Regiment at least the officers for two days with luxurious feeding). Nothing particular was done on this day and I amused myself examining our position. The soldiers, French and English, were throwing up entrenchments to protect us from an attack either from the mainland or the Fort which we hear contained 12,000 Russians, and either we or they are in one awful trap. The wind was blowing strong inshore so the fleet could do nothing safely that day. In the afternoon tents arrived for the Regiment and were soon up. The Surgeon and I agreed to stick to one another so we got a very nice tent between us, which is a great blessing. He is my chum at present and we mess and forage together along with another young fellow who is adjutant in the Regiment and who will be a baronet some fine day when his father dies. This night was more comfortable than the last, in fact I may say we are very jolly, but still frightened for an attack.

Veal cutlets again for dinner. Blessings on the calf. Next morning (Wednesday) was turned out in a great hurry by our servants informing us that the Regiment had marched off. Of course we got up in great haste and got the Hospital panniers put on a pony and just as we were about to start we saw the Regiment come back again. It had only gone a short distance with the 57th which had gone out on a reconnaissance up the country. It was a nasty, cold raw morning, so we had the pleasure of turning into our blankets again. The wind was blowing off shore today and the fleet commenced to bombard the fort at about 10am and the fort returned their fire with vigour for some time. We could not very well see what the fort was about as the Russians had set fire to the village between us and the fort the day before and the smoke obscured the view. We were about four miles from it and we saw the movements of the shipping to great advantage. A bombardment from the fleet is far worse than any of ours from the trenches. At first they fired slowly but it soon became worse and worse until broadsides after broadsides poured into the place and also over it. I could not see the effect on the fort but saw all the shot which went over it and fall into the water on the other side and when a broadside chanced to be fired rather high by the rolling of the ship for example, the round shot fell into the water like a shower of hail. It soon became very evident that it must be a very strong place indeed to resist such treatment. When a broadside was first fired you thought the whole vessel had blown up, it was something so very grand, and we were all collected in groups watching it and keeping the garrison in. About noon the Russians thought they had had enough and ceased firing. A boat was sent off to the fort and I do not know how many hundreds were taken prisoner of war and everything fell into the hands of the Allies. We were all very well pleased, it put us in a better position than we were in before when we had Russians on each side of us. When I came to my tent after seeing the bombardment I was very well pleased to find that the post had come in and that I had received a letter from Anne dated 22nd September. It contained an ivy leaf plucked I dare-say from the front of the Burnhead house and had a dreadful smell of musk. I had also a letter from Dr Ewing and another from Jeems. In the afternoon all the prisoners were marched out of the fort with all the honour of war. Each man was allowed to carry off whatever he liked and the officers were allowed to wear their swords. They were all very fine looking men and I believe had only arrived at the fort a few days before. It seems to have been a second Bomersound. All the prisoners were sent on board 'The Vulcan' the next day. On Thursday morning we were all roused by a tremendous explosion and on looking out of my tent I found the Russians had blown up Fort Ochakov. Why they did so I cannot imagine. I would have gone to the fort today but being on duty I could not get away. I went down to the seaside however and had a bathe in the Black Sea. It is the first bathe I have had since I was at Portobello and I enjoyed it very much. It was a beautiful warm day and so like bathing on the sands at Broughty Ferry. As I was prowling about I fell in with some pumpkins and resolved to have pumpkin soup for dinner as I had heard such a thing could be made. Accordingly the pumpkin was duly sliced and along with a lump of pork (pork is an essential element in all dishes here) we set the pot a boiling. The soup looked very like greasy water, and we puzzled our brains how to thicken it and as we had a packet of groats which we did not know what to do with it was agreed to thicken the soup with them. The result was not so successful as might have been expected for our splendid soup was just like a thin paste and lumps of boiled turnip floating in it, no pepper and very little salt. However we swallowed it and we will long remember the pumpkin soup. We were in luck today for Ward caught a young pig and won't we have a stew tomorrow.

Friday
Letters are going off at mid-day so I must draw to a close. We are to march into or near the fort this afternoon and I believe some of the Regiment is going to the Crimea again. There is a rumour that the 17th and another regiment is to remain here all winter and that Kinburn Fort will be a depot for stores etc. for a Spring campaign in the south

of Russia. Oh, Gemini. What a place to remain in. Patmos or the Bass Rock is quite a joke compared to it. However some must remain and as well the 17th as any other. I forgot to mention one thing and that was that we had Lieutenant Geneste of Hango celebrity with us in the Royal Albert. It will be quite impossible to write to any of my friends until I am somewhat settled but I will write them as soon as I can so you will perhaps send a look of this to some of my Edinburgh friends.

PS Address as usual 17th Regiment. Mr Struthers would perhaps like to see this. J R will send it to him and he can send it home to you again. DG

My dear Father,

After sending away our letters at midday on Friday the 19th inst. our camp was struck and we marched bag and baggage on to the village near the fort. It was dusk when we arrived and our ground was no sooner pointed out to us then all our tents were up in double quick time. I employed myself in picking up drift wood on the sea shore, and within an hour after our arrival we were sitting in our tents quietly enjoying roast pig. Our camp was pitched close to the sea shore and mine was within 20 yds of the water. I slept very well and at six next morning got up, rolled my blanket round me, ran to the sea, threw it off my shoulders, and had such a delightful dip. After we had breakfasted we marched with our haversacks filled with four days provisions – pork and biscuits or course. The day was warm and I can assure you I felt my pork heavy. We had no tents with us. We marched on through a very uninteresting country, sand, sand, everywhere with a few trees and a little salt lake every now and then. About 4 in the afternoon we came to a mill and soon afterwards to the village of Petrouski. Petrouski if village it can be called, consists of about two dozen cottages scattered over a wide extent of low sandy marshy country. To each cottage was attached a garden in which grew potatoes, cabbage, tomatoes, and stramonium, the latter in large quantities. Some French had gone over the country before us we got very little plunder. We had no sooner halted than I bolted up to a cottage, I found it plundered and broken to pieces, so I turned to the garden. Already our fellows were in hacking away at the cabbages with their swords. I did the same and filling my handkerchief with potatoes and tomatoes, I went in search of my servant. We had all the same and got a beautiful vegetable dinner, pork of course as an accompaniment. Out camp was close to a small wood and we chose our resting places for the night under two trees. I collected some hay and rolling ourselves in our blankets we went off to sleep. I lay next to the Adjutant and the only thing that disturbed me was his spurs which came one or twice rather close to me. We had a shower or two during the night but that was not much, but towards morning I must say it was dreadfully cold.

Sunday 21st October

I was awoken up to examine two men who were to be tried by court martial for getting drunk. This morning was very cold and after breakfast I had to see them flogged (50 each). The Brigade was paraded and went through some evolutions. We all thought we were to march but did not. When we landed at the mill yesterday we got some meal of a very coarse kind. This morning I made a dish of porridge. But as I was making them our PMO [Principal Medical Officer] rode past and enquired what I was after, and he being a Scotchman he joined me and we had a splendid dish, rather a curiosity on Russian soil. The afternoon was spent in making a kind of hut with boughs cut from the wood close by, and we managed to construct a very nice little place under the trees, and at the same time highly romantic with our blazing bivouac fire in front of it. On Monday morning we were all paraded at 9.30am and marched out 7 or 8 miles further inland to destroy a Cossack village. The marching was very heavy through the sands and there was nothing worth mentioning occurred on our march. The 59th, 63rd and part of the marines were with us. About 1 o'clock we came in sight of the village and as the Regiments were moving rather slowly some of us surgeons and assistants marched on ahead to the village. Some of our Cavalry were there before us and all the inhabitants had fled. There were lots of poultry and pigs however and we had splendid fun amongst them. Each of us had a stick and getting into a flock of geese I began right and left and soon had a few lying round me. One of our fellows fired at a pig but missing it the pig got into a great fright and rushing past me, I had just time to draw my sword and make a thrust at him and transfixed him on the spot. This unfortunate pig was the first thing my sword had ever killed. I went into a good many of the houses, they were very clean and whitewashed outside. Very little was to be found in them except pumpkins and broken furniture. I picked up a lady's thimble which I will send home; if it will fit any of you, you are welcome to it. I had the honour of taking a Russian prisoner and I must tell you about it. As I was rambling through one of the houses I looked behind one of the peculiar stone places (which all the Russian houses have) in search of pipes and I can assure you I was very much taken aback when I discovered a pair of Russian boots with legs in them. I do not know why but I retreated to the door as fast as I could. I called a big dragoon and told him what I had seen. He took out one of his pistols and I drew my sword and marching into the house again we called upon the fellow to give himself up. He did not move but when I touched him with my sword point he showed animation enough and came out. He was an old man and had been left in the village because he could not walk off. I brought him out and was marching him off when a drove of pigs rushed past me, so handing him over to the Dragoon, I bolted after the pigs and heard no more of my prisoner. I was slashing away amongst the pigs in grant style when an Aide-de-Camp galloped up and informed us that the General was in a great rage at the conduct of the medical men and ordered us to our regiments immediately. It was great fun with the pigs and when the soldiers were allowed into the village they made good use of the bayonette, and a first rate pig striker it is. About 3 o'clock in the afternoon the men were all withdrawn and the village was set on fire and in less than an hour, what the day before was a beautiful, neat, quiet village, was nothing but a smoking ruin, although I enjoyed the day's expedition very much still I was very worried to see such a melancholy sight as the blazing hay ricks and the total destruction of a whole village. Yet it was quite necessary so that no Cossacks could find shelter or harbour in any way near the fort as to disturb us during the winter. The pigs and geese were put into a cart and we returned to our spot under the trees tired enough from our long march. Next morning we all started for Kinburn again destroying and laying waste the country as we passed along. The men had followed the example of their officers and erected bough huts, the little wood beside which we were encamped was completely cut down, and as for the houses and cabbage gardens you would never have known that such had existed. Nothing particular took place on our way back with the exception that I killed two snakes as we marched through the grass. In marching back to Kinburn I had the feeling as if I were marching home and when I got to my tent and felt I had somewhere to put my head I felt content. After dinner and a forum of rum punch I got my clothes off for the first time for four days and tumbled into the blankets, the ground was hard enough but I slept soundly and enjoyed it.

It is a curious thing that while on the march and living in the open, sweating perhaps after a heavy march, I would swallow my dinner and lay down on the ground just as I was, get up in the morning and march again, and yet I never enjoyed better health all my life, and as for colds or coughs no one had such a thing in the Regiment. I suppose if anyone tried such a thing at home even in July, he would be looked upon as mad.

Wednesday, the day after I got back to Kinburn, was spent in resting our wearied limbs, in fact was what we might call a camp washing day.

All our shirts and stockings were scrubbed in the sea. I commenced bathing regularly every morning and what is more have kept it up. The water is cold but it is very refreshing. The Black Sea at Kinburn is, as you might suppose not very salt, and when we have a scrub with the sand and a roll about in the water we feel quite new beings. To one who has been accustomed all his life to see ebb and flow of the tide, an inland sea is rather a curiosity, the water is always at the same level, sometimes it rises a foot or two but never more, and one great advantage is you can bathe at any time. Yesterday (Thursday) I visited all the forts on the Spit and went to the very end of it. The village in front of the great fort which you will see marked in the plan I sent, is no great thing, it consists of about 4 dozen small houses each with a small attached garden. The houses are very small but have a clean look about them, being whitewashed, in fact the village is very like Callander. There were some respectable houses but they were all burned the first day we landed. Kinburn or the great fort as I have called it, is a very old place, I believe it was first built by the Turks when they had the south of Russia and that is a long time ago. It looks just like a small town surrounded by walls and the walls are somewhat of the form I put down on the plan, whilst the houses are in the centre. The place has been very much improved of late and about four feet of turf and sand has been put on the top of the thick walls. These are casemated batteries, the most of the guns were seaward, some were on the top of the walls but they were very old ones. By our bombardment the place was very knocked about and all the interior was in ruins, so much so, that our men are employed at present in making it habitable. The second or centre fort is a beautifully made one and of quite recent construction. It is made of large logs of wood dovetailed into each other and then several feet of turf and sand on the outside and over the solid wood framework. In the centre of this fort there was a bomb proof house made of logs and supported by numerous wooden pillars of great thickness and on the top of this house was several feet of turf, altogether it was beautifully made, The one at the end of the spit was of a horseshoe shape and more care was bestowed on this one, the large logs were firmer and more carefully joined together, and each of the guns were in a casemate. A battery is said to be casemated when there is a shell or shot proof covering over the gun so that men can work there in comparative safety just like on the decks of a man of war. The casemate at this battery was the only building and some of our shot had struck it and from what I saw I think a few broadsides from one of our line of battle ships would soon have knocked it to smithereens. In the centre of all the batteries were large furnaces for making shot red hot so that it is quite evident the Russians intended to give us a warm reception. Some of our gunboats went up the river to within 10 miles of Nicolaif and only encountered one small battery. It was thought at one time that we would be sent up there too, but no, the season is too far advanced and I believe we are all going back to the Crimea in a few days leaving the French to take up the fort during the winter, a thing we are all very glad of. During this expedition we have very good weather, it is somewhat cold however, we do not mind that much as long as it keeps dry. The next letter which I send to you will in all likelihood be from the Crimea and then I will give you an account of our voyage back again. Hoping you are all well. I am sure I must be in all your good graces for writing so often.

I am, my dear father, your affectionate son, David Greig

PS. I have received various newspapers since I came here and also a letter from mother dated 29th September in which she tells me you had got my letter of 10th September. What a lot of marriages are taking place, in fact, I am beginning to think with D. Ewing that from the marriages and giving in marriage, wars and rumours of wars, the world must be coming to an end. But, whether or not, that is no reason why we should not enjoy ourselves when we can and if father would not let Anne [go] to Edinburgh to attend her friends' marriages I must say it was a hard case. Of course it is all over now and I suppose it will be the same a hundred years hence and Anne need not grieve about it.

Father's word to all at home will be I suppose something like the Income Tax to me, it is sometimes hard but everyone must agree there is no getting out of it.

My dear Mother,

In my last from Kinburn I think I told you we were all going back to the Crimea and to leave the Fort in possession of the French.

Our last three days at Kinburn were very uninteresting. There was nothing doing at all and the only way we had to amuse ourselves was wandering along the seashore picking up shells, digging holes and building forts with the sand, in fact the warriors of Great Britain might be seen amusing themselves like children. Before we left the Fort was put into something like order and a good many guns mounted so that there is no fear that the Russians will take it again. On the 29th October we were all very glad to learn that we were to embark for the Crimea, so next morning we were all roused up between 4 and 5, our traps packed, and our camp struck. It was a disagreeable dark cold morning, we had to march about half a mile to the place of embarkation and then the Regiment was divided into two divisions, one was on board the 'Terrible' and the other on board the 'Odin'. I was on board the former vessel, I did not like it so well as the 'Royal Albert' but still it is a fine vessel, 21 large guns and about 1,000 horsepower. What I object to is she does pitch and no mistake. I have not been sick but very near it. In the forenoon of the 30th we got safely into Kazatch Bay where we came to anchor just in time to allow me a good dinner. We were first in the bay but could not land as orders were to remain on board until all the troops had come up. This morning a good stiff breeze sprang up and our Hospital Ship, the 'Orient' having broken loose the 'Terrible' was sent in search of her. I very soon was obliged to give up writing and in order to keep my stomach in at all good tune I had to go on deck and walk as if my very life depended on it.

7th November

I have postponed and postponed finishing this until I am quite ashamed of myself. Oh, how lazy a fellow is when he is on board ship, eating, drinking, lying on deck, and doing nothing. I am still on board the 'Terrible' however and will continue my narrative. I felt off, because my stomach could not agree. Well, we continued our hunt after the runaway hospital and a very curious event I must say it was. We steered in the direction of Eupatorium and overtook the hospital very near that place, and we brought it into Kazatch Bay that night, and having taken up a position for ourselves in the Bay we have been here ever since.

Immediately on our return from Kinburn I thought we would be sent to camp but we were not, and there was talk of the fleet with the troops on board being sent on to Kaffa or Arrabat. We spent the first day waiting for the arrival of the Admiral, the next I believe a council of war was held at which the generals and admirals could not agree and they had to send home for instructions etc etc. and so they have kept us on board for a week and we have no idea what they are to do with us yet, but I suppose the Kaffa business will be put off till Spring. I must say it is very late in the season now but still the weather is most beautiful and the few days we have been lying at anchor at this beautiful bay have been just like July days at home. Every day on board ship is so much alike that I am quite at a loss what to tell you in the shape of news, however I suppose I must.

Since writing home last I have received a letter from Anne (6th October) enclosing one from Stewart Lithgow. I would send it to you but there is really nothing of importance in it. He describes his voyage from Cork to the Cape of Good Hope and seems to have enjoyed it very much and he is now doing duty with a party of the 73rd regiment at Fort Fordyce. He regrets that that he did not wait for his degree before he joined the Army and seems to be very angry at not being sent to the Crimea instead of the Cape. Oh, he is a very nice fellow and I must write him soon. One part of his letter amused me very much, he says 'that if a Kaffer war should break out what a nuisance it would be to be frightened to go to bed'. I wonder how he would like to sleep in his clothes for a week and have his sword and everything that he has with him put in such a position that you can seize what you want in the dark and be ready in a moment should the bugle sound 'Stand to Arms'. Here we are always glad to get to bed frightened or not. Your kind letter of 18th October I received today. I do not know where it had been but I think it must have been at Kinburn and back. So Anne has got to Edinburgh and enjoyed herself very much at the marriages of her two friends, but I will expect to hear all the news from herself in a day or two.

You ask me if there is anything I would like sent out in the shape of clothing, boots, etc. No. I am much obliged to you but I can get almost everything I need here and before I would bother myself again about another box or even about the one which is on a cruise of its own as yet, I'd rather take my chance with the clothing which the soldiers get served out to them.

At the same time I may mention we are not so badly off for luxuries as most people at home think. As for going to Scutari and looking for the box myself I might as well ask for liberty to go and look for it on the moon. Pray, do not trouble your mind in the least about it; if it casts up I will get a feed of marmalade and if it does not I can get the same here for a few shillings. The best news I have heard for a long time is the pleasing account of your uncle's restored health, you may send him my congratulations and hopes that he may never be in such a state again for from what I saw of him I felt very much for him. I do not know what all my friends will be thinking of me for I have never written to anyone since I left the Crimea – five weeks ago. But I hope they will excuse me when they know how miserable I am always on board ship and it was what I would call corresponding under difficulties when I had no table and when I did write home the letters were written on a knapsack lying on the sand. When I get comfortably settled in Campaign I will remember them all. I hope father, and aunt etc. are all well. Aunt will remember how frightened she used to be when I slept with the window open. 'Certain to get my death of cold' she would say and of course I was 'a positive fellow' etc. How changed times are now. I hope you will excuse this non-news-ical letter and I will give you a better one next.

My dear Anne,

Since writing home on the 10th I have received a letter from you giving an account of Miss Flockhart's marriage, and another from mother dated 27th October. You seem to have enjoyed yourself in grand style in Edinburgh and I hope you did so in reality. I have not yet received an account of Miss McD's but I suppose it went off with the usual eclat. She was kind enough to send me cards which I can assure you are something out of the common here and to which I returned a congratulatory note on the great event. I suppose you will have settled quietly down again into the quiet home routine but still you will not be altogether quiet for I suppose the festive season will be commencing again with its usual number of hop-parties and tea-fights. I am afraid my tea-fights will be very few this season as they were last year, however we must hope for the best. You will see from the date of this letter that I am once more 'before Sebastopol' and very glad I am that we were not left at Kinburn. That now celebrated place was all good enough in its way but blow me if I would have liked to spend the winter there. Oh, no, I am far more comfortable in my hut here. I enjoyed myself on HMS Terrible very well. We all landed at Kazatch on Sunday morning (11th). I do not know why we always do everything on Sunday but such is the fact, I suppose it is on the principle that 'There is no rest for the wicked'. Be that as it may we all bundled on shore and marched up to our old camp. Nothing of any importance occurred until we drew near the camp when all the men of all the other regiments came out to meet us and gave us their congratulations on a safe return, and what was best of all the 48th sent their band to play us home, and we all marched thro' the Division to the tune of 'Auld Lang Syne' – everyone was happy to see us back in safety again.

My hut I was happy to find much in the same state as when I left it and I immediately took possession of it again but it will be a while before I get it into such order as it was before. My stock of brandy, port etc. I put into the store but as bad luck would have it the store was broken into and my drinkables went the way of all living things and I am now under the necessity of foraging for more. I had sold all my horses except one and when I came back I found my favourite 'Bombardier' (for so the brute was christened from having been in the artillery) had got a sore back. My saddle and bridle I had entrusted to a friend in the 4th Dragoons, they were ordered a few days after I left off to Eupatoria and of course took my horse gear with him, so much for a few tit-bits in the campaigning line. These are my misfortunes but some of our own fellows are worse off than I am. The camp life here is just the same as before and the men are still employed making roads. We are glad of anything in the way of excitement so a few days ago we had a blow up by way of a change. I suppose you have heard of it. I was working outside my hut in the afternoon when my attention was attracted by a flash and when I looked up I saw a cloud of smoke and a shower of live shell flying all over the camp. The explosion took place in a French magazine close to our Light Division and set fire to our artillery park there exploding some of our ammunition stores. We did not lose much but the French must have. The explosion was terrific and a great many men were killed. The magazine which exploded is about three quarters of a mile from my hut but some of the fragments of shell passed over it. The Sebastopol coat seems to have amused you all. I am not the least surprised that you have not found a person whom it will fit. Oh, I should like to see Dr Pirie and Crockatt in it. I am sure I would have such a laugh. I was sorry I could not get epaulettes for it but I got a pair at Kinburn which will do although they belong to the 10th Regiment and the coat and buttons are, I think, the 26th. However it will complete the thing and I will send them when I can. Mother shows as much curiosity as ever in wishing to know where I found it. Tell her I found it in 'Prince Tortchakows' and I am sure she will believe it, and after she has swallowed the big name you can tell her quietly that I found it kicking about a marine store. I am surprised you have never received my letters from Kinburn. I wrote you two or three from 'that there locality' and I hope they have reached you by this time and they will give you a slight idea of campaigning in the open. Many thanks to Dr Luckie for his compliments. I hope he is not going to get married in Wick or I fear there will be a heart to let in Montrose. I have never heard of Dr Ramsay since his letter to Dr Pirie but I often hear about his ship, and I think the less said about the Hornet the better after the beautiful mess she has got into by letting the Russian fleet escape from Castres Bay. I see by the papers which I receive very regularly that you are likely to have a severe winter and that some snow had appeared already. From all appearances at present it appears we are to have a very mild one. The weather is beautiful, just like autumn at home. It is very cold in the mornings but no rain, and as for snow there are no symptoms of it as yet. Huts are being erected in all directions and the whole aspect of the camp is very much changed from what it was before I left Kinburn, in fact so much so that I would scarcely know some parts again.

From all accounts the 'scarlet fever' seems to be raging violently at home. Mrs J M Baxter calls her boy Colin Campbell and Miss Pirie lines her cloak with red of which I duly received a specimen, in return for which I thought of sending her my old jacket which I got spoilt at Kinburn, and which she would find was made of stronger stuff than she sent me. Not knowing how that might be received I enclose a flower for her and another for Agnes, both of which were plucked in 'Holy Russia' near Kinburn. I am sorry I cannot send them presents of more value. I was very much surprised yesterday when I learned that D J L Erskine of the 4th (Kings Own Regt) had gone home sick. I had not seen him for about seven weeks and he was quite well then. I hope he will be himself again by the time he reaches home, where I am sure he will be no end of a swell.

I hope father, mother etc. are well. Remember me to aunt and Uncle Pirie etc. etc. Write again soon and hoping you are none the worse for your Edinburgh excesses.

My dear Father,

What I am to write about this time do not know and I suppose I must use the common dispatched phrase 'Nothing new in the Crimea since last report'. The weather is now very much changed and winter is regularly commenced. We have snow, hail and rain, and when we do not have frost we have mud up to our knees, and I suppose you know Crimea mud is no joke. However I am very snug in my hut and when I have a blazing log fire at night and hear the rain beating on the tarpauline roof I often think I have no reason to complain of my lot. The day is very short and closes about 4pm and I must say I enjoy the evenings very much. My friend Walker and I sit and smoke our pipes each reading a newspaper or book, but that does not long continue we rather prefer chatting about home, and all our friends there, this generally ends in me chaffing him about the wife and how the little 'un would pull his beard if he was only at home. He chaffs me in return and so on while our laughing by the patients in hospital might be heard. In fact we spend a very merry time of it. My hut is nice and dry which is a great thing here and the only fault I have is with the chimney, but as I have the same fault myself you will say I have no right to grumble. It smokes. I am to improve it however when I can get some bricks from Sebastopol. You see we are not particular what kind of work we do here. In my last letter which I had from mother she mentions that she and Anne have sat for their portraits. I hope the artist was successful and if so there is nothing I would like more than a copy and I hope one will be sent me.

I am a great swell now for I received my Crimean medal the other day. I suppose you know what like it is. We are all very well pleased with the medal and also with the ribbon when it is new. It soon loses its colour and then looks very seedy indeed. I enclose a small piece of the ribbon which may get a place in Anne's album, and will show what it is like.

In a paper which you sent me a few days ago there was a mark opposite a paragraph by G. Fenwick. I read all the letters from 'our new correspondent' and I must say they amuse me, more especially about his being the first in the Redan. I must say I never read such a cram in all my life. If the folks at home can swallow it, which I am sure they can easily do, it will do them no harm. I was sorry to see that Lieut. Fenwick's trumpeter had been shot at the taking of the Redan and that he was under the painful necessity of blowing his own horn. What a grand thing humbug is and how clever people are who can use it well. I have not seen Fenwick for a long time now, his regt. is about 7 or 8 miles from ours beyond the village of Camara near the valley of Kiadar where the Highland Division are encamped. It is an out of the way sort of place and visits are seldom exchanged.

I suppose Erskine will be home by this time and I hope he is well now, he will in all likelihood call upon you, and I have no doubt spin very long yarns about the trenches etc. I am much obliged to you for the two extracts which you sent me but still I confess I would much rather have preferred a letter. The one from the 'Family Herald' – 'Where are we to go when we are ill?' – is to say the least of it a bombastic piece of nonsense, written by some mad mesmerist who of course strikes out right and left at the medical profession. It is very amusing and ought to have appeared in the 'Morningside Mirror'. I have packed another parcel of relics of Sebastopol and Kinburn and will send it whenever I get an opportunity. I do not know if you care for the stuff I send home these things are not much thought of here, but I suppose they are curiosities at home. I am sorry I could not get a Russian rifle before now, but the next engagement we have I will try to get one.

How odd it seems to me to be reading a newspaper from home. Town Council elections, Harbour Boards etc all I suppose very important with you but quite a scrawler book to me. I am sure Dundee must be changed very much since I left, yet it cannot have changed like what we have here. It is now nearly fourteen months since I left England in company with sixteen others, and it is very curious to think what has become of them all, four are dead, four in the Crimea, and the rest gone home, chiefly from sickness. In a former letter from mother she asked me what books I read, not medical books I can say, I read everything I can get a hold of 'Light Infantry Manual', 'Gibb on The Attack of Outposts', 'Essays on Fortification', 'Wellington's Dispatches', 'Waverley Novels', 'Allison's History' and 'Guthrie's Military Surgery'. So I am sure you will say I have variety and there is always a large supply in the possession of the Chaplain for the use of the Division. Reading is a difficult matter here. One becomes lazy and never likes to sit still, must always be roaming about and as for study that is an impossibility. I enjoy first rate health which is a great thing, and although I stay for two years I hope still to be as able for private practice as ever and perhaps in a better position to do so than if I had never been out here.

I received a letter from Dr Pirie the other day which had been about a month on its passage, which I will answer in a few days and then perhaps will have more news than I can give at present.

I hope the rheumatism is better and that you are otherwise well and also I hope you will write me. Postage stamps are all very good but you might have given me a word or two along with them.

CAMP SEBASTOPOL
7TH DECEMBER 1855

My dear Anne,

The letter to Father dated the 4th inst. I intended to have sent off that day but by bad luck I lost the post and then when I received your letter dated 17th November I thought I might as well write to you too. And so Dr Crear has been humbugging you by saying that I was coming home in the summer? It may be true and I may have said so to him, but to tell you the truth I do not know myself when I will be home. I wrote to Dr Simpson some time ago asking him what he would advise me to do, and, as to the time of coming home that will all depend upon his and Mr Struther's advice. I like the army and were it not for my friends at home I should remain in it altogether. Now I have told you as much about my coming home as I know myself and if you wish more particulars you must suppose them. Dr Crear was very kind in offering to bring out a box for me but I fear it will be too much trouble for him, not that he would think so, for he and I are great friends, and when he was sick I saw him safely on board ship and have written to him since. So do not make a large box or a heavy one. The only thing which I require are two pairs of boots lacing up at the front and some half dozen pairs of socks. Everything else I require I can get here and I could even get these were I hard pressed for them. Let the boots be strong, thick soled, and one pair with nails in the soles – they should be like navvy's boots – and they will please me. These would make a small parcel so you can fill up the box with a bun and eatables. I am sure to get my former box yet. It is in the store at Scutari and I have no doubt but I will get it by and bye. The weather is still beastly and the whole camp a sea of mud several inches in depth, to go about in the daytime is difficult but at night quite impossible, so I am quite a home bird – sit in my hut, by the fire at night and feel as happy as a prince. I am very much disappointed about the portraits and all I can say is that mother and you must sit again. I won't attempt to send you a picture of my hut until I receive them. There is nothing whatever new here at present except that we are all preparing for Christmas. I have a goose tied up by the foot at my door and which we are feeding up for that great day. We are also to get some raisins and currants and if possible start plum pudding. We will all lend a helping hand and as my servant is a good cook I have no doubt will spend Xmas in grand style. My last Xmas was not a pleasant one. Dr Struthers had just taken ill and Dr Mason and I had to eat our dinner very quietly together. I hope this one may be somewhat better. I do not know if I told you that Dr Mason's things were all sold and the proceeds were in the hands of the Assistant Adjutant General at Scutari. If mother was writing to Mrs Mason she should tell her to enquire at Messrs. McGrigor, Army Agent, they are the people thro' whom to get the money and all particulars. Altho' this is a short letter to you, you cannot expect a very long one both to you and father. I leave the kind of socks to Aunt, I am sure she knows what will suit.

My dear Father,

Last night I received a letter from Anne dated 31st Nov. Other two mails are due but owing to the severe storms they have not arrived and it is rumoured that one is lost but I hope not. I was glad to hear that you were all well and everything going on at home as much as usual. Since I am in camp and nothing whatever doing in the fighting line you must not expect to hear so often from me as you have done, and I must fall back upon my old plan of writing once a fortnight which is often enough, although I must have an alternate letter from mother and Anne every week. I am quite surprised at the news about Dr Fleming and I am, I must say, very sorry he is giving up the profession for I liked him very much, if his practice likes to wait until the end of next summer then I will perhaps think of it. I doubt much if he had been getting on as well as people thought, however I hope he will succeed as a merchant. I am sure I do not know what to think of the kindness of the Wooler folks and if I do not know what to think I am sure you must be puzzled. I have not heard from any of them for some time now but I am quite convinced they have not forgotten me altogether and any box if it comes all right is very good, we shall see however. I had a visitor here for two days this week and very happy days they were. He was an old school fellow from Dundee. ... his name is James Millar, he used to live in Newport and has one or two sisters married in Dundee. I met him on board the Sutley at Balaclava Harbour and invited him up to camp. He had never slept a night in camp before and seemed to enjoy himself very much. He does not belong to the army but is acting as super cargo on board the Sutley. We had such long talks about Dundee and all our old school fellows that we completely took all the conversation, and my friend Walker could not get in one word.

I have not had such a talk about Dundee since I left it. I am sorry he had no better weather for it snowed all the time. There is another parcel on its way to you and you may expect it as soon as this letter. The things are all described and you will easily understand them. They are taken home by a Dr Dair of Edinburgh and when Mr Millar goes home I will try and send another with him. We have had very stormy weather for the last fortnight, snow, snow and frost that would astonish you at home. Although we have a fire in the hut we often have the floor covered with snow and it never thinks of melting. We jump into bed and cover ourselves up with all the blankets and coats we can. It is a somewhat difficult matter, everything is ice and no water, our drinking water, vinegar, pickles beer and everything frozen, nothing fluid except the brandy. Again when walking about more especially against the wind the breath gets frozen on the beard and moustache and forms icicles, and your mouth is quite closed. No laughing aloud or loud talking. I have seen icicles 3 or 4 inches in length hanging from each moustache. I am sure you will doubt it but it is quite true and you can have no idea how cold the men look. The whole army is very healthy at present. We had a few cases of cholera about ten days ago but it is all gone now, and in its place we have frostbites, which although painful are much to be preferred.

I suppose you will be surprised when I tell you I have got a new appointment (viz) that of Pathologist. A pathological board is established at Scutari, Balaclava and in camp and I am of the one in camp. Our board consists of a first class Staff Surgeon, an Assistant Surgeon in the 39th Regt. and myself. We have appeared in general orders but will not commence duty until about the new year. Our duty will be to perform all post mortem examinations in camp, make out reports on them, and prepare specimens and preparations for the Chatham Museum. I do not know how I will like it but I think very much as it is just to my taste and more especially as I was approached by the Director General and asked if I would take it. The letter I received from Dr Hall our Inspector General here I enclose to show it to you and I think it is a very kind letter indeed. I think I got the appointment through a Dr Guthrie, a retired great swell for whom I made a few preparations and wrote a paper on 'gunshot fractures of the femur'. I am to have no regimental duty whatever but I am still to remain in my hut with the 17th Regt. which is a good thing. I do not know if I will get more pay for this but Hall said he thought there would be but he could not be sure, however the honour is a great thing of itself, although a little more pay would not be a bad thing. By the time you receive this it will be AD 1856 and I hope you will all be well, and that 1856 will be as good a year for us all as '55 has been, however we must hope for the best, and this I promise I will be in Dundee if it is at all possible before the New Year is finished. Christmas will be here now in four days and we intend having a dinner in my hut on that day, and the goose is already fattening for the occasion. I will give mother the first letter in the New Year and give her an idea of Xmas and New Year in the camp. The post goes off now at night instead of morning, so I have been forced to write this in haste, so you must excuse.

Please return Dr Hall's letter.

My dear Mother,

In my last letter to father I promised to write you soon after the New Year and give you an account of how it and Xmas day was spent in the Crimea. These days this season were very different compared with last. We had fine hard frost weather for about a week before Xmas. There was snow on the ground but it was quite firm and crisp. On Christmas morning I was awakened at daybreak by 'the reveille' followed by a great many tunes among which was the most prominent 'Home Sweet Home' and such like so that if we did not know what day it was one might easily guess it was something out of the common. We had arranged to have a dinner in my hut and had been feeding a goose for three weeks before Mr Walker and I were busy all day superintending the cooking. We had got a sheep's head and a leg of mutton coaxed out of the commissariat and plums or rather raisins bought a few days before. I am sure you would have been amused to have seen us cooking the goose and heard the various remarks on how it should be done and on cooking in general. However we got it done very well. To make a plum pudding was rather a feat, and one which Mr Walker and myself did not feel we were able to perform. So rather than make a mess of the materials we handed them over to my servant and he turned out a stunner. Our party consisted of three Scotchmen, and three Irishmen, all Asst Surgeons and of course we sat down to dinner in uniform. You will be wondering how we managed with regard to plates, spoons, etc. Although it was a swell dinner it was a case of bring your own plates but to do the thing in genteel style we had collected all we required during the day. We had such a Christmas fire burning and what was more a beautiful white tablecloth, which cloth, had it come to have been carefully examined, would have been found to be an Hospital sheet borrowed for the occasion. The dinner consisted of sheep's head broth, boiled mutton and giblet pie, roast goose, plum pudding and fruit, and of course plenty of drinkables to wash all down. The broth was very good, the mutton superb, the goose was beautiful and as for the pudding it made one blush to look at it in the face. We were all hungry and did great execution on everything, so that I am inclined to believe if we got a better dinner than usual our servants got a worse. We spent the evening in as good style as circumstances would permit, that is to say we were very jolly, but we had no mistletoe, no dancing and only a few headaches next morning which we all agreed was the result of the sheep's head broth.

On the last day of the year I was very much surprised and pleased to find that six letters had arrived by the post for me. This was a trick of James Rodgers who had made all my friends in Edinburgh promise to write to me by that post so that I might have something to cheer me on New Year's day. They were very acceptable I can assure you and I do not mind how often they repeat the trick. I brought in the New Year at a small party in our camp, it was a nice quiet part (of course) but I must say I did not relish it so well as I would have done at home. We had no clocks striking twelve and there was none of that excitement of waiting for the exact moment. We sat and smoked, first one fellow would remark 'that it was surely twelve now' so after arguing the question for about an hour we at least came to the unanimous conclusion that it must be past twelve and that it was the New Year's day begun, so we all shook hands round and went to bed. New Year's Day seems to be taken very little notice of in the Army, all the fun and jollity takes place on Christmas the same I believe in England. Since New Year's Day nothing new has taken place here except that Mr Walker has 'hooked it' to camp where he now resides and I am all alone beside the Hospital. I expect Gibaut out very soon again as his leave expires today, but I doubt much if he will come here as the Hospital is to be changed over to camp and I think he will go there while I remain in my hut. I am going on with my new work but can scarcely say it is fairly begun yet. I will be struck off all regimental duty but expect still to remain with the regiment as before, as long as I choose however. I am still working away in our Hospital as before. We have now got a theatre started here and I must say it is a great treat, it has only performed once and of course I went. The pieces performed were two little comic pieces entitled 'To Paris and back for £5', 'Box and Cox', 'Married and Settled'. They went off very well and of course we had a first rate band. The greatest amusement of the evening was the ladies, who were acted by some of our beardless subalterns. The dresses had been gotten from the French at Kameish, and some of them I must say made very pretty handsome girls. Some of them imitated the voice well, others did well as long as they did not speak but whenever they began to talk their voices betrayed them and on looking close at them you might have seen small whiskers peeping from under their cap strings. The whole wound up by the Royal Anthem and a dance by the actors and actresses. You enquire how my dog 'Viki' is flourishing. I am sorry to say I had to kill him soon after coming back from Kinburn. He went mad and I was glad to get rid of him and so knocked him on the head with a stick. When you mention it I think I did receive a letter from Dr Crockatt just as I was starting for Kinburn but in the bustle I almost forgot all about it and had an idea that I had answered it. It appears however that I have not but you may tell him I will do soon. When we were at Dryburgh Abbey I thought Mr Roberts was engaged to one of the Misses Sime, but it seems not. I think some of them would have liked him and it will serve as a lesson to them in future if the war comes to a close there will be lots of Crimean heroes to be picked up, perhaps they are waiting for them.

All the folks at home seem to be very much amused at the dissipation which goes on in camp but it is all the fault of the Government giving the soldiers too much money. They get a sixpence a day extra pay and very often have working pay which is by far too much and the result is they spend all this at the canteen. There is not nearly so much drunkenness now for the men are never flogged, at least very seldom. The hard labour confinement principles are adapted with a white stripe round their caps, their hair cut quite close, have all the dirty work to do, are roused by three times a night in all weathers, and are not allowed to smoke. The men are frightened at this treatment and my man would rather take 50 lashes than have his hair cut close. When the siege was going on we could not punish a man this way because we could not want him, therefore the more expeditious mode of flogging was always done. In my last I think I wished you all a Merry Christmas and a Happy New Year, and now I hope that you have enjoyed both and that this will find you all well.

Just give Father a hint to drop me a note now and then.

My dear Anne,

I have now before me a letter from you dated 17th December, and another from Mother dated 22nd, besides various newspapers and Punches Almanacs. Punch was a great treat and I think it was the best I have seen for a long time. I have cut out all the pictures and they now adorn my hut.

So Dr Erskine has cast up in Dundee and told you all about me, and that I have grown very stout. It may be true, and I am sure I can't say I am very lean, but I think I am much the same as when I left Dundee and am what would be termed in robust health. If Mother as you say has taken a liking to medicine I have not for I have never tasted it since I had fever. I was sorry to hear that Aunt had been complaining, by this time I hope her eye is all right again. Mr Rodgers is I fear too kind to you all and if the young man continues sending my letters home I fear I must be more careful in what I write to him. Mother says in her letter that it is quite exhilarating to hear me talked of. Nothing seems to go wrong with me. In truth nothing does. I always take things as they come and am contented and I hope they will continue so until next September or October when if I do not get home I am sure you will hear me grumbling. Since I have commenced by new duties I can assure you I have had no time to grumble for I may say I am very busy. My duties now are something like a country practitioner only we have no humbugging old wives to chatter to. I get on my pony and trot away to whatever regiment requires me to visit it, finish my work there and then go to another and so on, then in the afternoon I have to write out all my cases and enter them in a great big book that would frighten you. I like the work very well, barring the writing which is a great bore and which I am very often like to grumble at. I have now left the 'Royal Tigers' after having been attached to them for nine months but although I have nothing to do with it I still hail from it and all my letters are to be addressed to it still. The Commanding Officer was very kind and has allowed me to keep my servant still from the Regt. In fact I liked it very much, and if I mistake not the officers liked me, which is everything of course towards making a regiment pleasant. I do not like to talk much about being liked in the Regt or you may accuse me of egotism, but when one of our officers was wounded at the taking of Sebastopol he would scarcely allow another

Asst. Surgeon to dress him and insisted on being taken to me. However I was out of the way and could not be found and he had to submit. How long I may be employed as I am at present I do not know, it will depend altogether on how the things go on.

You seem to have great difficulty in sending out a box to me. There are regular agents in London for these things and the one who sends most parcels is the firm of Hayton and Howard. I think they call themselves Army Packers but I am not sure … I saw Fenwick the other day. He called on me one afternoon and was looking very well and promised to come and spend a night with me soon. I am very much obliged to Mother for the portraits and looking at them I think I could almost speak to you, they are on the whole pretty good but you have studied attitudes too much, and have been too anxious to please and when mother tries it again she must put a smile on and look just as usual. I am sure I just once saw her look so doleful and that was when her servant (Lindsay) went to church in her boots and split them up the sides. If I was only beside her I would make her look cheerful. You look quite stunning but I do not think you have shown your bonnet to the best advantage if that was what you kept it on for. It looks like a cap with a large border to it. However I prize them both very much and will keep them carefully in my desk. Father is in a great hurry to get the papers I mentioned to Dr Pirie. I am not sure if he will get them as No. 2 will not be published before next month. I will be sure to get a copy and if you can't get them at home I will send it to you.

After sending off my last letter to Mother we had a very heavy fall of snow which remained a long time on the ground. A thaw took place a few days ago and we are now as usual up to the knees in mud. The weather is very mild and it has been a heavy rain all day, which however will not improve the roads, but of course with boots to one's knees we always manage to move along somehow. There are little or no news to give you from this quarter, everything is quite, only a shot now and then from the north side of Sebastopol. Merely to keep us in mind where we are.

Of course you will be head and ears in parties and tea-fights at present. All our jollification ceased after the New Year and everything is as usual again. The theatre in the division is still going on and affords some amusement and something to talk about, I was at it three nights ago and it was very good. Of course the pieces are all short, one-scened affairs, but we have two a night and that makes up for it. It is all comedy – no tragedy. Comedy is what we require here. Of tragedy we had enough last summer. The two pieces I saw were 'A phenomena in a smock frock' and Major Lord A. Russel (brother to the ex-premier) being the phenomena and 'The moustache movement'. There were about half a dozen females acting and of course created great amusement. General Garrett late of the 40th Regt the 'non me recordo' of Windsor notoriety is the great patron and is always present. What I like most is the rifle band which is always there and plays waltzes, polkas, etc., without number. I hope you enjoyed New Year's day at Liff as usual and I suppose some of my Edinbr friends were over and joined you. On New Year's night I was sitting quietly in my tent thinking of all the parties that would be going on at home, so I brewed a tumbler and drank all your healths thinking at the same time you would not be forgetting me in your merrymaking. I wish Father to send me out a book to assist me in my present work and the title of it I enclose. It can be sent by post. The margins can be shown and no writing inside. I wish you would also send me an Army list for February as soon as they are published for that month. An Army list is a very useful thing out here as much use as an Almanack at Home. It tells one where one's friends are and a great many useful particulars which you could not appreciate. Now I must bid you Good bye. Remember me to Father, Mother, Aunt, and also my cousins. If George has not written a dispatch from the Garrison of Liff by the time you receive this tell him I'll have him tried by Court Martial and flogged.

Kind comps to Mr and Mrs Sandeman and family, and hoping they are all well, and hoping this will find you as well as I could wish you.

PS. I will write to Father about the end of the month or the beginning of next. On second thoughts you need not mind the books as I have written to Mr Rodgers for them and he will send the account of Father who will please pay him. DG

My dear Father,

Since writing you last I have received three letters from home, two from Anne and one from Mother. You all seemed to have enjoyed New Year's day at Liff very much not to mention the beautiful weather you had in the evening. Messrs Rodgers and Lindsay seem always to be turning up and come to Dundee every time they can and I have no doubt are a great acquisition to the parties which are going on just now. Mother tells me that you have come to the conclusion 'that I am as well off here as trudging through the dirty streets at home'. I am sure you are not far wrong for if I was at home I would be always grumbling and discontented and here I am as busy as a bee and as happy as a prince. In the last Gazette which arrived here I see I have got a commission and that I am now as it were regularly enlisted as a 'sodger'. As regards to leaving the Army it does not matter much as I can resign when I like, in the meantime it gives me a higher standing in the Army. It is a permanent appointment if I like. Should I get wounded or be sick and unable for duty I get a pension and should I be shot my widow gets one which I must say is a great thing to look forward to in my case. On the whole although I do lose 2/6 per day by the transaction I am very well pleased with it, especially as I get my commission antidated to the time I entered as an Asst. Surgeon on the 27th October 1854. All the pros and cons of this question I cannot give you on paper but a permanent appointment is I think better than a temporary one and so I am sure you will have no objections. I suppose the Director General thought he must give me something for this pathological business and gave me a commission '*n'importe*' be content and don't grumble.

...

The 'Sutley' has gone to Eupatoria and where she is going next I do not know. Before she left I put a parcel on board knowing that when she does arrive at home, thought that should be year hence, the things will be all safe which would not have been the case had they remained with me. The parcel is of no great importance but when I had a chance I thought I might as well send something. I enclose a list which you can keep and which will explain everything when you get it. I see you are still at your old tricks buying books and getting Anne to smuggle them into the House. I have a very curious volume beside me which I got out

of Sebastopol some time ago, viz – a French marine dictionary with a
great many old pictures in it of old ships, shipbuilding, etc. It is about 200
years old and is rather a curiosity. I must try and send it home. I am sure
you would like it. I had a letter from Dr Crerrar the other day. He is at
Chatham just now. He is still far from well and it is a very great chance
if he comes out here again. So you need not expect to send a parcel out
with him.

Mother mentions that Smith the student who is in the Turkish
contingent had not written home for two months. As I have not the
most remote idea where the Turkish contingent is, I am sorry I can tell
you nothing whatever about him but I have no doubt 'he canna be lost'.
I am very much obliged to Miss Mary Baxter for her beautiful present,
it has been admired by all who have seen it and you must return her my
very best thanks for it. In my last I think I told you that Mr Walker had
gone over to camp to live there, but the young man was never content,
he sent in his resignation and bolted home to his wife three days ago.
What he is to do at home I do not know. He is not sure whether he
will go in a Militia Regiment or commence practice. Dr Gibaut made
his appearance here about ten days ago. He is now quite well and seems
to have enjoyed himself very much at home. But he is changed since
he came back. He looks very eagerly for the post and is often engaged
in writing long letters, talks sentimental and various other little things,
which clearly indicate that the young man has been and got engaged. He
no sooner came to the hut than he commenced making improvements,
stopping up rat holes, doing the best he could to cure a smoky chimney,
repairing everything that was broken down, etc., etc. In fact he is something like James Rodgers, rather a useful man to have about a house.
We had some very wet weather when he came out and the wet found its
way into our hut and we were nearly swamped. To cure this one of the
boards which forms the floor was raised and a hole dug which had to be
emptied about six times a day. The water does not come in so fast now
but the hole has now turned into a beautiful well of clear spring water of
which we always have a large supply on hand, and may be obtained by
raising a trap door about six feet from the fireplace and instead of being
annoyed we are rather well pleased at having things so handy within
the small compass of our little hut. During the latter part of last month
we had very bad weather, it rained continually. Some days were very
beautiful and warm, the beginning of this month is very different, for we
have hard frost and snow. We are all very comfortable – lots to eat and

drink – and plenty of fuel. Gibaut has still ideas of England and comfort about him, keeps a very jolly fire always going, he has brought hams and jams out and I may say we are living luxuriously at present. He has still a great love for the old but and altho' the Hospital is to be changed to beside the regiment he is still to remain beside me at which I am very well pleased. Nothing new is going on whatever. There are strong rumors of peace, some believe them and some do not. No one has any objections how soon it comes. I was looking at the Russian camps on the hills over Inkerman today with a glass. I saw some Ruskis moving about but the place where their camp is must be very cold and I doubt very much if they are as comfortable as we are. I had a letter from Dr Pirie the other day. I was glad to hear from him, everything seems to be going swimmingly at Liff not to mention the Manse and the parson's daughters who seem to have a great respect for 'the doctor'. Happy may … Every dog has his day, and I suppose mine will come sometime. As it is at present I think I would subside into my boots if I saw a lady, and if she spoke to me I am sure I would tremble like a criminal. Talking of criminals I was at a general Court Martial the other day, giving evidence in a case where a private in the 77th a patient in hospital, had given another patient a chip on the head with an iron bar and he died the same night. The man was found guilty of willful murder I believe but I do not know what is to be done to him yet. Miss Pirie wishes me to send her a small Turkish coin as an ornament to her watch chain. I am sorry I have none beside me just now but have no chance of getting one but the first I get I will send to her. I think we have now got the worst of the winter over and am looking forward to the stewing summer again, all its beauties. If the War continues we will in all likelihood be in Asia Minor and if it does not – why – that is too much of a good thing to look forward to. I am as usual in health, strength, and spirits.

My dear Father,

Enclosed is a letter from Stewart Lithgow which I would like you to hand to his brother as I do not know his address. There is nothing new here. I am quite well and hope you are all well. I received a letter from Mother three days ago. By next post I will send you home a bill for some money, please write and tell me if you receive it and if you get these bills cashed easily.

My dear Anne,

Sometimes when the day for writing comes round I am at a loss what to write about and just now I am in that happy state. 'What must be must' and since it is again the middle of the month I suppose I must say something for myself. There is one great thing in answering the letters however which I receive every week, I always manage a good beginning and then fill up the rest of the pages with the few news which we have in camp. I have now before me a letter from Mother dated 23rd January and another from you dated 30th. So you have sent me off another box via the 'Royal Exchange' of Montrose which I will keep a look for three months after this, when I suppose it will arrive at Balaclava. As for your opinion that it is perfect laziness that prevents me getting my first one I am sorry to say I cannot agree with you. I have asked and bothered so many people about it that I often wish that the confounded thing had never been sent me at all but at the same time to keep your mind at ease I am sure 'it canna be lost' and when it does cast up I shall be most happy to receive it just to show you there is no ill feeling. As for the whisky M sent I will not return thanks until I receive it. Mother's question about Mr Robert's marriage I refuse answering except 'viva voci'. It wouldn't do on paper. And so you have seen Dr Watson RU and thought a great deal of him, of course you could not do less of any Crimean hero. I am very glad you saw him and I think with you he is a very nice fellow, but I am feared you bored him too much about camp, Kulalie, Therapia, etc. You say he explained the pathetic part of Miss Stanley's letter. I do not understand what you mean but I suppose you refer to the time when

I was seeing all sorts of funny things, and talking all sorts of nonsense. Dr W never liked Miss Stanley much and I can't say I did either. Mrs Tice I thought a great deal more of, but Dr W. did not think much of her either. I do now know why. Dr Erskine has been so long in Dundee he ought to have been out here ten days ago but I suppose he liked home during winter better than the camp. You seemed to have had a grand party a Liff and what is more enjoyed yourself well. What extraordinary fellows Lindsay and Stockhart are. I would not be the least surprised to see them pop in upon me some fine evening, just to show there was no ill feeling. Enclosed in your last was a letter from the Cape from Stewart Lithgow, he is well and is still at Fort Fordyce. He has not much to do and seems enjoying himself but he is still grumbling at things in general and his bad luck which sent him to the Cape and not the Crimea. He has taken to bird stuffing and collecting all sorts of curious things which he can lay his hands upon. He is wishing very much to get a permanent appointment and grumbles at Sharp having got one before him, but I have no doubt he will get one by and by. Sharp is in the 33rd Regt and is now in India. There has been little or nothing going on here during the past fortnight, with all the rumours of peace the guns are still roaring across Sebastopol harbour and the French and English have been blowing up all the docks and destroying the forts which are in our possession. The weather has been mild during the day and cold at night. The snow has all disappeared and the grass is making hard attempts to appear once more. The roads are as hard as ever and the well in my hut is full of clear beautiful water. My friend Gibaut has been very busy hammering away as usual. He has re-erected the stable, made an armchair and invented a rat trap into which rat trap the rats won't go, and are therefore not to be caught. Enclosed is a theatre playbill of last night's performance in our theatre which has been changed since I wrote you last. The former theatre was too small but now we have got a larger hut beautifully fitted up which holds upwards of 200 officers. There are regular seats rising towards the back gradually so that all may see, the first seat is stuffed and kept for generals and staff swells. In front of this is the orchestra and a splendid one it is with a leader who waves his stick in grand style. The stage is very neatly got up; on each side is the picture of a Turk and a Sardinian in full uniform and above the stage are the Royal Arms and the numbers of the regiments in the 4th Division surrounding them. This is all painted on calico and then lights are placed behind which give it a beautiful effect. The Royal Arms over the stage were very much admired and were arranged so you must excuse the drawing, the lion and unicorn look rather tipsy I must say but it will answer what I wish to give you an idea of. The acting was the same as usual (very good) and of course comic. In the last play 'going to the Derby' there was actually a cart drawn by a live horse on the stage and I must say the horse behaved itself very well. With regard to light of course we have no gas but there is always a great number of candles and it does very well. I am sure you will suppose we enjoy ourselves very well and I can tell you it is one of the greatest pleasures we have here, we always have so much laughing, for more than a visit to a theatre at home would cause.

News – I have none to give. Rumours of peace here are still as strong as they were fortnight ago and from all accounts I think it very likely that we will get it but it will only be for a short time. Russia is not bit humbled, and why she wishes peace now is very strange to say the least of it. I hear that the position and condition of the medical department of the Army is to be much improved very soon, and some of the parts of the new warrants are Asst. Surgeons on entering 10/- a day and after a certain time to be made Surgeon Major at 25/- per day, and leave to retire after 20 years' service on a pension, and a greater pension after 25 years, and still greater after 30, promotion rapid etc., etc., in fact too many good changes to be true. However we are promised some changes. The Col of the 17th has come back again to his regiment and one of the first things he did was to write for me to be gazetted to the regiment but as I am required at my present duty his request was not granted. I did not mind much what was done to me but as my present work is to my taste and will do me good hereafter I am very well pleased as I am. When I tell you how I am getting on I do not wish anyone to be telling tales and boasting about me which I fear Father is too fond of doing, if I may judge from his conversation with Dr Bell. And now dearest Anne I must bid you Good Night.

On 29th January 1856 Russian guns in Sevastopol's northern suburb opened fire with a vast canonade against the allied forces. The French forces responded by destroying Fort Nicholas. These were perhaps the last acts of attrition in the Crimean war and hostilities ceased soon afterwards. A peace conference met in Paris on 25th February and after three days an armistice was signed, to last until 31st March.

My dear Father,

Here I am again in receipt of a letter from Mother dated 6th and another from Anne dated 12th February. It is quite useless telling you that I was glad to hear you were all well as you must always take that for granted when I have anything else to tell you, but this time as I have no news of any importance to communicate it will serve to fill up a line or two. Well on the whole I consider that a very good beginning and I must see what I have got to say for myself. Mother asks me if the large silver coin which was in the parcel I sent by Dr Fair is Russian or Turkish dollar valued at 4/2 English money. At home you all seem anxious for peace, with us here I must say it looks very much like it. There was a meeting of the 'Chiefs of the Staff' English, French, Sardinian, and Russian two days ago at Frontier Bridge. An armistice was concluded so far that there is to be no firing at one another. The Russian General was accompanied by about 15 Cossacks and our General (Wyndham) had a few of the 11th Hussars with him. They were very friendly together but I can't say who stood the brandy and water, since then there has been great fraternising across the Tchernaya but none are allowed to cross the river. The Russians have got medals for Sebastopol as well as me and this affords a great source of bantering. I have never been down yet but intend going in a day or two if the weather is good. Talking of thimbles and the contents of the helmet, Anne asks me how I get on with my mending, very well I can assure you. I can stick on buttons and torn coats very well, but darning stockings is I must confess a sad trial of patience. Latterly I have given up the attempt altogether and handed over the duty to my servant who does it in a kind of way. I can't say his darning pleases me nor does it last long. In fact when a hole appears I concluded they are of little use to me. You seem interested in Dr Aitken who was out here. I thought his situation was kept open for him in Glasgow but from what Anne says I fear not. He will need to 'put his shoulder to the wheel' now. He is too old to enter the Army altogether and as you know 7/6 would be rather indigestible after £2 – 2/- per diem. Alla el Alla Allahem!!! My long lost box has turned up at last after 18 months knocking about. I have just now received it. I can tell you it took all Gibaut's mechanical powers to open it – nails seem to be cheap in Dundee. Everything is in good condition, the gingerbread splendid, the boots splendid – in fact – everything 'Buono', there are only a few pipes broken. I have to finish this before I can get the things examined to be in time for the post. So hoping you will excuse this hasty scroll. I will write Mother a very long letter next time and send her the drawing of the hut at the same time. I am so anxious to examine everything that I must give up.

PS. 'Gib' is beside me pitching into the sweeties and says they are first rate.

CHAPTER 7

Cholera Again

In the early months of 1856 typhus and cholera broke out once again, especially amongst the French who suffered over 50,000 cases, of which over 10,000 men died.

CAMP SEBASTOPOL
14TH MARCH 1856

My dear Mother,

The last letter which I sent home to Father was a very short one and I suppose I must make up for it this time and give you one longer than the generality of my letters. When I was writing to Father I had just received the box and as it took some time to open it and some time to talk about the contents, and some time to look over the contents, as you may easily suppose, I had very little time to write as the mail left the same evening and I did not wish you to lose the regular fortnightly letter. Hence the shortness. In the first place the box was fastened in the most extraordinary manner as if it was never intended that it should be opened. However 'Gib' and I managed to get into the inside after a good deal of hard work. The pea jacket is a very nice one and rather good for the Crimea. It will be quite a swell affair to wear during the summer. I have a large sailor's jacket just now which is a better winter dress. The same I have said of the jacket applies to the boots, they are too fine for Crimean winter but will make beautiful summer riding boots if I can get them on which is rather doubtful at present. The boots being rather tight or my foot has got changed since I left home. The leather leggings are very good. The waterproof leggings are not good. The woolen leggings are first rate but it is rather late in the season for such warm things. The mits, I do not know who made them but 'Gib' and I are both highly pleased with them, he has got one pair. The comforters I am sorry to say are quite useless, as I never wear a neckerchief I am never likely to put on a comforter. The two knives are a great boon and 'Gib' has got one. The knife and fork ditto. The pipes are quite a luxurious donation to all in the Regt who smoke. The pipe from 'Jeems' is beautiful. The 'Etna' will be a useful thing for hot grog in the evening. Sodgers' cooking apparatus I am at a loss what to say about it. It may come into use yet, but I have no use for it just now. The lavender water, wax vestas, and soap are luxuries out here. The confections make us all laugh, they are a thing never seen here. The song book – ah, yes – I did not expect it was a song book of that kind. Still I am glad you have sent it. The newspapers as you might suppose all rather old. The gingerbread was in first rate condition, in fact you could not have wished it better, it was not too soft and not too hard. I have seen a cake of gingerbread not improved by a journey to Edinburgh but much to my astonishment this one seems to have improved by being left to its own resources for 18 months. Happy contented gingerbread. I feel a great inclination to moralise over you. The pots of marmalade did not (I am sorry to say) behave so well, they seem to have been disgusted with their treatment and I suppose were longing to bask in the sun once more in a shop window. They did all they could to force out the bangs, but it was 'no go', so they fermented and threw out their ill humour in the shape of syrup which made a beautiful mess of the newspapers. Thinking, I suppose, that this was a way to make their grievances and imprisonment known to the public. So this was the box and this was the state of the contents when it arrived here, all very welcome, all very nice, but all rather late. I hope that you are pleased that my word has come true 'keep your mind easy it will turn up and canna be lost', and that you will cease to accuse me of carelessness inactivity, want of energy, etc., etc., too many and beautiful epithets it would make even me blush to mention. So with this will make my bow and hope I may never be troubled nor my nocturnal rest broken, not to mention my ravings in fever about a lost box.

In my last letter I think I told you that all firing had now ceased and that we have an armistice at present. The armistice is a great boon and we can now ride all round our outposts with safety and wander through Sebastopol as we like. We had a severe snowstorm which lasted from the 3rd to the 9th. I think it is the severest we have had since the winter began. The snow was at times about two feet deep and the thermometer seventeen degrees below freezing point. The snow has all cleared away and after undergoing the pleasure of a Crimean thaw we have once more beautiful weather although still rather cold at night. The rides we have in Sebastopol and down by the ruins at Inkerman are so delightful that

I often wish I had you all down here with me. Last Sunday afternoon I took a walk over the field of Inkerman and then along the South bank of the Tchernaya towards Sebastopol. The ground was hard with frost and just in walking condition, the air was clear and everything was quiet and like a Sabbath at home. 'Not a gun was heard' except an occasional pop from a Frenchman shooting sparrows, an annoying amusement to which the French are rather addicted. We walked all over the field under the guidance of Dr Ward our Surgeon who was at the battle. There is nothing to be seen on the field now except a stray shot or a broken piece of shell. On the slope of the hills as they lead down to the Tchernaya, and the top of the harbour of Sebastopol, there were a great many clothed skeletons still remaining as sad mementos of the Battle of Inkerman. When one was kicked or struck it all went to smash and if a boot was picked up it was found filled with bones, and the remains of a stocking. These bodies had not been buried at the time of the battle and it was quite impossible to get at them after that. They were all Russians. The small river Tchnernaya is the boundary between the two armies, and here and there groups of Russian and English soldiers chaffing and laughing at one another throwing money across the water to each other. All seem happy. The Russians seem strong but miserable kind of animals. Their officers were seen riding about on the opposite side of the water examining us with equal curiosity. The town of Sebastopol is completely destroyed now. I scarcely think you could get an entire plank of wood in the whole town, every house is gutted from roof to cellar and now nothing remains but heaps of ruins and crumbling solitary, blackened, smashed walls. The place has a desolate melancholy look about it which I can't describe. If I may give an opinion I should think that when the landed proprietors of Sebastopol are allowed to return to their possessions they must feel rather disgusted with the aspect of things in general. The Russian batteries which protected the town are now dismantled but even now on visiting them one stands lost in amazement at their strength, battery above battery and ditch behind ditch. The flagstaff battery, central bastion, quarantine battery, Redan, Malckoff, etc., etc., can still be seen but much changed and all the guns gone. As for Fort Alexander at the south side of the entrance of the harbour and Fort Nicholas a little way further up, they are nothing more than a mass of stones and rubbish. As for the docks I can say nothing about them not having seen them now for more than a month, but I believe they are amongst the things which were. The caves at Inkerman and also the aqueduct are well worth seeing. The caves are on the Russian side of the Tchernaya and we can't get to them as yet, but we have a very good view of them, they are cut out of the rock which is quite soft and white like the camstone at the new Infirmary in Dundee. A temple with an ornamental front cut into the rock is the most striking object. The aqueduct is on our side of the water and at one point it passes through a hill by means of a tunnel about a quarter of a mile in length cut through the rock. This I believe is to be blown up, in fact, everything which will destroy is to be destroyed, so that in the long run Sebastopol will not be worth rebuilding. As for the far famed Russian Black Sea fleet it is quietly at rest at the bottom of its favorite harbour. The army is so healthy at present that I must say I have very little to do. Since the good weather has come I feel I am not so much inclined to remain in my hut writing cases but rather prefer to get some excuse for riding or walking about. In the front here where we (the pathological board) have 27,000 men under our supervision we had only 22 cases of death during last month, and as far as we have gone this month it promises to be less still, in fact no one could wish the British Army to be in a better condition. The French are however very sickly and I would be almost afraid to say how many sick they have, but they have more deaths in one day than we have in a month. I was sorry to hear that Lieut. Fenwick had been sick. I have not seen him for a long time now but I suppose he will be better again. If he had been very ill he would have been sent home. Dr Erskine called on me the other day, unfortunately I was out so I have not as yet got the latest news from Dundee. I hear he is looking very well. It is now a long time since I promised to send you a sketch of 'the house I live in' here it is at last and I hope it will please you. It was done by my friend 'Gib' as I was too lazy to do it myself. The sketch on the whole is very good and will give you a good idea of the place, it looks rather grand and romantic on paper and so clean that you may well wonder what use I can have for knee boots. However, it is intended to represent a beautiful day after a fortnight of dry weather. I leave you to imagine what like it looks after a fortnight of wet weather. Well, you see the hut in the centre with the smoke coming out at the chimney with such apparent good will that you would at once conclude it always did so. Oh, no, it is merely going well at present in order to make a good impression on the friends at home, so don't believe it. The porch looks rather 'knobby' does it not? Quite in the tea garden style. 'Tea and shrimps for 10d.' Rhubarb tarts with cream – 'in season' etc., etc., There is a figure in front of the hut that is supposed to be Dr Walter Moses Gibaut of Her Majesty's 17th Regt. He has got 17 on his cap in front, only you can't see it at present as his back is towards you. On the extreme left you have the stables and on the right the servants tents. Beyond the hut on the other side of the road you see a number of huts these are the Commissariat stores of the 4th Division, the old rum casks being made into a kind of wall around the place. This then is a description of the picture and I hope you may understand it. I repeat again that it is very like the place, but decidedly more elegant, cleaner, and neater than the place ever was or ever will be. Since my last I have received as usual two letters, one from Mother and another from Anne. I was very sorry to hear of Mrs Boyd's illness, and still more so of David Maxwell's death. With regard to Mrs Botch's request about a monument to her son all I can say is that I will be most happy to do all I can to get it erected. I will not be able to write to her until I hear from Scutari about it, in the meantime if you are writing her you may tell her what I have said. I think she ought to write to Mrs McGregor and counter-order what she told them before. I have very little doubt I can get it done but I cannot say for certain yet.

Anne in her letter to me encloses verses entitled 'A Balaclava Reverie'. Tell her I am much obliged to her and that there are lots of reveries and no realities in the market here. I am not at all pleased at she and you attempting to do me out of a letter should any of you ever carry out your base intention, do not imagine that postal irregularities will at all screen you. I must have a letter every week or woe betide you. Miss Alexander seems a most extraordinary girl if she calls me 'a brick from Sebastopol'. I will call her a 'blue stocking' she is so smart and clever that she quite frightens me. She can do everything from writing in magazines to making pills. When Anne writes to her next she must not tell her I am frightened at her or she would think it a great triumph. She can ask her if she remembers our discussion about cooking and making soup and that she had better not try me on that department now. They all are very kind at Wooler and seem determined to have Anne there by and by. I hope I may be there at the same time. Anne asks me a very difficult question, whether I am an Episcopalian Catholic, or Presbyterian? In fact I cannot tell her for I do not know, still I may safely say I am a Catholic but not a Roman Catholic. She asks me what a Sunday in the Crimea is like? It is just like any other day only we have service in the forenoon on the top of Catheart's hill and lots of music marching to and from that place. As for myself I usually sit in my hut and read, then have a walk in the afternoon. Were it not for the bands playing the 'Merry Church Bells' in the morning I would not know it was Sunday. I think this long letter will make up for my short one last time and I hope you in return will write me a very long one. Remember me to Father, Aunt, Anne, cousins, Mr & Mrs S and family, Mr McIntosh etc., and hoping you are all well.

PS. I would (of course) have written a much longer letter than this but you must excuse me this time as there is nothing doing in camp. In the last Gazette which came out here yesterday I was very glad to see that my friend Stewart Lithgow had got his permanent appointment. He is now Asst. Surgeon 75th Regt. His regiment has been two or three years in India and will be 5 or 7 more. Stewart will in all likelihood go on and join it in India. He may meet his friend W. Sharp who is in India with his Regt the 53rd. I think they will both like the country. I have received the two books which I asked Mr Rodgers to send me and I hope he has sent Father the a/c.

My dear Anne,

I wrote Mother on the 15th of last month and enclosed a sketch of my hut. By this time I hope you have received the letter in safety and have now a very good idea of my abode after having had a fortnight to discuss the subject. Before I begin I may as well tell you that I expect this will be a very short letter as our last mail which brings your weekly letter has not made its appearance yet owing I suppose to the rough weather. Why we should have rough weather at this time when we are all so anxious to hear about peace I do not know but such is the fact. To make up for the want of your letter I am happy to say that I received one from Father. It was short but most welcome. He says that he sends me all the newspapers and that I cannot expect news from him. Even in the newspapers I discover his sentiments by some tit-bits which he marks off for my perusal. I generally like them very much but one which he marked in the last 'Advertiser' which I received I am sorry to say I did not enjoy and I cannot imagine why he should. It was a leading article written I suppose by some penny-a-liner-black-guarding Lord Kinnaird. I did not like it and you must tell Father it does now show a good spirit to enjoy these sort of low squibs written against a man who did all he could to forward my views out here and who I am sure has never done Father any harm. From Mother's letter of the 4th ult. I learn that concerts and all sorts of fine things are going on in Dundee at present. From what Dr Erskine says that seems not to have been the case when he was there for he seems to have found it quite painful to be in Dundee even for a short time and he has given me such a bad account of the dull town that I am quite frightened at the idea of coming home. Jack is looking well and as strong as ever. He gave me all the news and that was not much. I am not a bit surprised at the smash Rob Cochrane has made again, there are a great many people in this world who, let them have ever so good prospects will never get on, and I fear that he and his worthy brother are a couple belonging to that class. I pity his wife very much. What a fool she was to marry such a scamp. Mother asks me 'if I am personally acquainted with the correspondent of the Morning Herald'? How on earth, excuse me, can she ask me when she knows I hate the very name of the tribe. I was very glad to hear Mrs Boyd was progressing so favourably after the operation. I hope by this time she is now well. If it will please her at all you may tell her I was asking after her and sorry to hear she had suffered so much. From all Dr Erskine tells me Dundee will be very much changed by the time I visit it again. New buildings, new streets, new faces, and most of all a great many old faces gone. Even the meeting house as you say will be very much changed but still there will be something the same as ever, and amongst the rest Mrs Maxwell (poor body) coming into the meetings about five minutes before it separates. I hope you will all excuse me saying this, it came into my head and I could not help putting it down. Odd remembrances do sometimes turn up in my brain, more especially in this place when one has so little think about. I suppose Father will be busy with his flowers now and the windows will be looking quite gay. Our crocuses and snowdrops have made three or four attempts to get above ground but they have always been nipped by the frost, even this morning we had a shower of snow. It was not much but still it shows that winter is not yet over. However I am sure this will be the last and that before the end of the month we will be roasting with heat. So soon as the flowers are out I shall begin to collect some from Sebastopol, Inkerman, etc., for you, for I suppose they are rather curiosities at home. I do now know what is worth picking up and what is not, certainly there is not such to be got now but anything in the way of flowers collected from any remarkable place I can easily send you if you let me know. Very little has been going on here since I wrote Mother. We have had races and steeple chases near Fraktir Bridge which were very good and would have done credit to England. General Codrington sent an invitation to Luders the Russian General to be present at the races but he declined the honour and said that as peace was not yet signed he would not do himself that honour. I think he was quite right. The river Tehernaya is still the boundary between the two armies and no one is allowed to cross it. One day last week I was at Kamara seeing the Highland Games which had been got up by the Highland Division. The games took place in a small valley surrounded by high hills. It was a most picturesque spot and brought Scotland so much to one's mind. I saw a good many there I knew and amongst the rest Lt. Fenwick. I was not near enough to speak to him but he was looking as well as ever, i.e., very fat. The games consisted of the usual amusements, putting the stone, throwing the hammer, tossing the caber, foot hailing etc. All went off very well. I enjoyed one race very much, that was a race in 'heavy marching order.' As you are not much of a soldier I must tell you what that is. A man is in 'heavy marching order' when he is in full dress and all he possesses on his back, including blanket and fifty rounds of ammunition with musket and bayonet. Now it is not very easy work racing in all this and more especially when a Highland feather bonnet is on the head. There was one fellow of the 'Royals' who had on the trews and shako and it was thought he had the advantage but no, a big Highlander ran far better than he did. I and two other friends dined in the Highland camp with an old Edinburgh friend who was there and in the evening we met three French doctors who dropped in to have something to drink. They were very jolly fellows and we spent a very pleasant night with all sorts of French songs going. I must say I talked very little but that did not matter much. The night was rather dark and the ride home rather long but we arrived at our respective huts in perfect safety. The French have all got on Crimean medals on their breasts. They are far prouder of it than we are ourselves, they wear the side which has the Queen's bust on it always shown, which we never do as it looks so like 5/-. Last week I received a letter from James R. and another from J. K. Lindsay they had no news to tell me. James as usual grumbling at Income Tax and wishes the war to go on, in fact he seems not to know very well what he would like. As it is term time he is busy and has not much time to think about his grievances.

My home establishment is much the same as usual with the addition of a kitten, which is a great amusement to us and keeps the mice away. We can get no milk for the little beast. It has to make the best it can of the tough salt junk. It catches a mouse occasionally however by way of variety. The army still continues very healthy and of course I have very little to do. I amuse myself the best way I can, riding, reading novels, etc., and having got hold of a very old French Grammar I am going over it again. Our theatre is still going on but the plays are becoming less and less frequent. I fear the time is not far distant when it will die a natural death. By way of variety the men of 'The rifles' acted one night and did very well. I have been enquiring after the Something (I forget the name) of Montrose at Balaclava, but I don't think she has come in yet. This is a very rambling letter but when I have very little to tell you must excuse such.

My dear Father,

Although this is not exactly my day for writing home still as the mail leaves to-night and as it would be four days more before I would get another, I do not mind much if I give you this letter a little before the proper time, provided the female portion of the family will promise not to go into hysterics, should I not write before the proper time the next time. Since writing to Anne I have as usual received two letters. In the first one Mother gives me such a blowing up for not writing and fears that all that is bad has happened to me. It is needless to say how I received the letter. It was with the air of an injured man and I leave her own feelings to return the blowing up. The next letter from Anne in which she makes the thing worse by telling me that this letter had arrived all safe and that it was the fault of the mail. Had the letter been lost I would have excused your anxiety but you must not be disappointed should any of my letters be a day or two behind hand. However, much as the blowing up does stick in my throat, let bygones be bygones, if Mother writes me a very long letter by way of punishment I shall say no more about it. Anne's letter is rather a rambling one. She tells me a great many things and amongst the rest that 'she has now got property'. She does not finish her story and I have doubts if she has clear ideas what she is talking about. At any rate I can make neither head nor tail of her story, and have come to the conclusion that she must have been dreaming.

I was sorry to hear you had been so much annoyed with your apprentices. I hope you have now got a good steady lad and one who knows something of the business so as to allow you to have some relaxation. I have not get Box No. 2 yet. I have no doubt it will turn up very soon. If it is not landed I suppose the ship will take it back to Montrose again. If it should be so I would be rather pleased for since we have peace we will be moving very soon and the less I have with me the better. What makes me doubt if the ship will come into Balaclava is that the Harbour is being cleared out for transport to take troops on board. Since peace has been concluded the ship may not come to Balaclava at all. The kind folks at Wooler are determined not to be behind and I have received notice that a box is on its way to me and what is more that it will be in Balaclava in a few days. I do not know what to think of their great kindness. I send you a list of the contents to show you how careful they are of my creature comforts, for as Mr Alexander remarks that food for the body in the Crimea is of greater moment than books or food for the mind. I am sure you will say it is very kind of them.

CHAPTER 8

Peace

The Treaty of Paris was signed on 30th March 1856, formally bringing the Crimean War to a close. Before peace was concluded, 4,273 British officers and 107,040 men had fought in the Crimea; 2,755 were killed in action and 2,019 died of wounds received in battle. In the theatre of war, 21,097 officially died, meaning 16,223 succumbed to cholera, typhus and other diseases. The French sent over 300,000 men. French estimates give 10,240 killed in action and approximately a further 20,000 who died of their wounds. A further 75,000 were lost to disease. Sardinia committed 15,000 men suffering over 2,500 dead from all causes. Turkey sent 35,000 men but their casualty figures have never been made clear. Total Allied losses were calculated at 140,000. The Russians suffered a minimum of 110,000 dead.

We have Peace at last.

On Easter Sunday the dull quietude of the armistice was broken by a salvo of 101 guns for the Birthday of the young Emperor of France and on the 2nd of April 101 guns again thundered for the Peace over the world. Since then 'not a gun is heard' and everyone is looking forward to the time when we shall once more step upon British soil. After the news of Peace came we were restricted for some days to our old boundaries, but now all line of demarcation is gone and all can mingle together.

The Russians first made their appearance in our camps and were received by the men with great good will, which of course ended in a great many getting very drunk. They are a set of fine looking men and appear not a bit inferior to our own. Their Officers are young and seem intelligent fellows. Some talk French and English very well. The railway interested them very much and more so as the wagons were employed carrying off their captured guns and shot from Sebastopol. The sight was a bitter one to them I have no doubt but it was something they must swallow. I got a slight taste of their feelings the other day and therefore sympathise with them. I was over on the North side riding about some of their works. I came upon two English 12 pounders. Of course, I was astonished and could scarcely believe my eyesight but there was no mistake. In all probability these were the guns which were captured from the Turks at the battle of Balaclava. The mud forts on the North side I found not to be so strong as they seem, some had no guns in them, and in others which had very few were in position and of course useless.

The greater part of the Russian Army is encamped on the Belbic and as yet I have only visited their advanced camp. For the most part they all live in mud hovels. Cleanliness which is of so much importance in a camp for the preservation of health of the troops is not much attended to. One officer very politely invited me into his hut but the place looked so beastly that I politely declined his offer. The greatest goodwill and harmony prevails amongst us and everyone is more polite than another. Some nights ago the theatre in our Division was honoured with the presence of General Luder's staff. The General did not come himself but about eight of his Officers came. They were very much pleased and after the acting was over they wished to see the actresses as they could not be persuaded that they were only young officers. The actresses however acted their part to the last and appearing as bashful and modest as possible refused to come forward. At the conclusion the band played the Russian 'God save the Emperor' followed by 'Partant pour la Syrie' and last of all 'God save the Queen'. It was a very good night. I enclose the bill. We have not as yet heard the terms of peace. We have no idea when we will learn this but I should think very soon from all appearances. In anticipation of a move I repacked Box No. 1, with a variety of odds and ends which I did not require and wished out of my way, so as to lessen the bulk of my kit. I have sent the box to Balaclava and may reach home 'per' some ship or other, at least it is consigned to the care of a Mr J. W. Deal, Custom House Agents, 80 South High Street, Southampton. He will forward it to you after getting it through the Custom House and charge you something for doing so which you will place to my account.

The box as usual contains a few stupid curiosities which will speak for themselves. There is a large fur coat which may be useful at home but it is too heavy to wear here even in Winter. As it is rather bulky I thought it best to get rid of it. I have also sent home my blue uniform coat and seales epaulets?. Soon after I got it the uniform was changed and I have worn it very little. It can be easily changed to the new uniform (which is a double breasted coat and no seales). I wish you to keep it until I get home. I can get it changed so as to do for the Army or private life. There are a pair of old jacket shoulder cords and a set of buttons in the seale case. Keep them too they are old trench friends. I think you will understand all that the box contains. What you do not, keep till I am home. We have now beautiful weather here and a great many parties are being got up for visiting that part of the Crimea near us. Some have gone to Baktshi-serai, Yalta, Alam, etc., I intend to take a trip some of these days to the Alma and go over the road the Army marched when they came to this place. The Army is very healthy at present and I have very little to do. However I spend my days very pleasantly rambling amongst the romantic ravines of Sebastopol and riding as far as my horse can carry me. You will naturally be asking since Peace is concluded when are you coming home? Dinna ken, but I should think in two or three months now. I will remain as I am now until the Army breaks up, then as my services as Pathologist will be no longer required here I suppose I shall be sent home. Well, supposing I am sent to England I shall then try to get leave for a month or two. Supposing I get that you may then suppose that the supposition of seeing me will not be a supposition but a real reality. Yesterday (Sunday) I had a long walk with Dr Erskine. He is quite well and is like every other person in camp here, wondering where his regiment is to be sent to. It has very little chance of being sent home as it has completed its home service already. We were proposing to get up a party in the beginning of next week to visit Baktchi-serai and Sympheropol, taking Alma on our way home. If we can take this journey it will furnish a letter when I come back, as yet it is doubtful.

I think I may now draw to a close, and wishing you all health and happiness.

My dear Father,

You may tell all my correspondents not to send me any more letters until further orders. The camp will begin to break up next week and I may be sent out of this very soon now. The 17th are ordered to Canada and will embark it is expected in about a week. Still send me a 'Scotsman' every week and address it to the Post Office, Balaclava, so that should I not leave this so soon as I expect I may still hear that you are well and that I will know by your sending the envelope with red wax. The newspapers will be no great loss although I do not get them but I would not like my letters to go astray. I am well and hope you are all the same.

My dear Anne,

From Mother's letter dated 1st April it would seem that all the inhabitants of Dundee were taking advantage of the news of Peace, including that grave and important body 'the town council' were making fools of themselves and no mistake. I hope they enjoyed their cake and wine. It is not often they have such an event to celebrate. I was very glad to hear that you were all so well and that Father had got such a good shop boy which must be a great comfort to him. Mother's request re the lace collars etc., I will do my best to fulfill. I have also received your letter of the 30th inst. I was very glad to hear of Tom Maxwell's marriage with Miss Luckie. It is an old topic and I am sure it will be good for all parties. James Rodgers will be sure to be there as 'best man'. I would not be at all surprised if Jack Lindsay should turn up in their diggings along with him. From your last letter it seems as if you are enjoying yourself as much as ever, in fact I may say you are very gay, notwithstanding the absence of your brother which you bemoan so much. I have been rather gay also since I wrote home last. I have had a jaunt to Sympheropol and enjoyed myself very much. I suppose it is no use trying to escape giving you a full, true, particular account. I must just tax your patience and tell you all, at least I will try to do so.

Our original party for this trip would have consisted of six, including Dr Erskine but through some mistake he could not get away, and another of our party dropped off from the same cause. We had still a party of four including Gib and myself and after a good many committee meetings in the shape of evening parties for the purpose of arranging matters it was concluded that we were ready to start on our journey. Each of us were mounted and we carried with us some [provisions] for ourselves and horses. We left camp one fine day and crossed the Russian lines at Traktir bridge about mid-day. We rode slowly along and ascended the Mackenzie heights from which we had a beautiful view of the valley of the Tchernaya. When the Army came from the Alma they came down the heights to their present position. The Russians have had possession of them every since and as we passed up we saw a great many of their guns still in position, it would have been a very difficult matter to have ascended those heights while the war was going on. I suppose you have heard a great deal about Mackenzie's heights or farm, it is situated on these heights and here the Russian advanced camp was situated. Mackenzie's farm takes its name from a MacKenzie who was an Admiral in the Russian Service and who got a grant of land for his services. There is no farm but there was still the ruins of a farmhouse standing, while the country all around was covered with brushwood and stumps of trees. It was at this place that Dr Mackenzie of Edinburgh died of cholera but the country is now so much changed that no one can find out his grave. The Russians are not encamped in tents but in small underground mud huts which are covered with boughs and on the whole look very neat. The road is very hilly until you arrive at the valley of the Belbec, which stream is crossed by a wooden bridge, here another part of the Russian Army is encamped. The country beyond this is rather flat and it may be said to be the commencement of the Steppes. We crossed another small stream the Katcha, without meeting with anything extraordinary, we arrived rather tired at Baktchi-serai about 7 in the evening.

We had great difficulty in finding out an Inn but at last we succeeded in finding out a kind of an eating house with a courtyard in which we tied our horses. Baktchi-serai is a very good specimen of an Oriental town, the streets are narrow and covered with mud. As you stumble along the main street, which is nearly a mile in length, you see the tailors, shoemakers, etc., sitting and selling their goods in little open booths in true Eastern style. This little town was at one time the capital of the Crimea when it belonged to the Tartars. The Palace of the grand Khans is still to be seen although now partly converted into a Hospital for Russian troops. The palace itself must have been splendid in its day but I must confess my taste for Oriental architecture does not carry me so far as to say that I thought very much of it. We had dinner at the Inn, such as it was, and then we went out for a stroll. We returned about 10 o'clock and were informed by the landlord that a soldier from the Commandant had been seeking us. We were rather alarmed at this and views of Siberia began to float through our minds. We were very much relieved however to find that it was a civil invitation to sleep at his house. The soldier returned in about half an hour and off we went with him. He took us a short way out of the town and then handed us over to a dirty half Turk, half-Tartar, who seemed to be waiting for us at the door of a large empty house. Our friend the Tartar took us to a large room and by means of signs explained to us that two of us were to sleep on a sofa, which, with a few chairs, was the only furniture in the room and for the other two he made a shake-down on the floor. It was altogether a very ludicrous proceeding but we slept well and next morning when the old Tartar appeared he cleaned our boots, gave us coffee and sent us on our way rejoicing. After giving our horses breakfast and having the same for ourselves we started for Sympheropol much pleased with our treatment in Baktchi-serai. The food we got to eat was very good, greasy soup and fish seemed to predominate but substantial roast beef and cutlets were not rare, and what was the greatest treat of all plenty of milk. The drinkables were few and in general dear. 'London Porter' 10/- per bottle and foreign wines much the same price. The wine we usually drank was the wine of the country. 'Crimean Wine', it is very like the 'vin ordinaire' of the French. People at home would think very little of it indeed but after a time you like it very much. The road from Baktchi-serai to Sympheropol is very uninteresting and is nothing but a succession of plains stretching out on either side of the road. The whole country looks very barren, save in the valleys of the Alma and Bulgarnac there are no trees to be seen. The part of the Alma when we crossed was about ten miles further up than where the battle was fought. The river flows through a beautiful fertile valley, its banks are covered with vines and orchards. At the spot we crossed there was a large hotel with I believe 'good accommodation for man and beast'; we did not go in however. Here and there was to be seen a deserted farm house, no sign of civilised life was to be seen, the country seemed to be wholly taken possession of by soldiers. We met a great many carts loaded with provisions making their way to the front escorted by bands of Cossacks with their long lances, other carts were bringing sick from the front to Sympheropol. They all looked miserable enough, the most of them were suffering from Typhus fever, and I am sure they must have suffered greatly in these little wooden springless carts. The most of the troops we saw were militia. I believe the regular troops are between Sympheropol and Pericop. They seem strong men but did not look either well clothed nor well fed. We reached Sympheropol about 4pm and had some difficulty in finding a hotel. We at last succeeded in establishing ourselves in a very nice one. As for beds there was not use asking for such a thing. We were promised part of a sofa on the floor, which we considered 'Superior accommodation'.

After dinner we went out and had a stroll about the town, looked at the shops, etc. The inhabitants seemed quite amused with us and looked as if they had never seen English before. We found a few Russian officers who spoke English and almost the whole spoke French fluently. The

Russian officer is very like the English he is generally of good family, and has a great deal of true politeness about him which contrasts strongly with the French officer. They were very kind to us, showed us all they could and told us all they knew. I asked one fellow who was with us, 'how he liked the Allies?' His answer was, 'We don't like the English much, we hate the French, we despise the Turks, as for the Sardinians we have not seen much of them but we believe they are very good.' When we question them about the battles they will not admit that they have been beaten and rather snub us with the question 'What have the Allies done?' Sympheropol is, considering the place, a very nice town. It has a large market place, good broad streets, good shops, fine churches, and I believe a good theatre, which however was not going on when we were there as it was Lent. After wandering about the town until we were tired we returned to the Inn and meeting a new party of Russian officers we of course fraternised and soon became very happy. Another party of English who were in the room joined us and in all were a party of 16 or 18. We wished to be content with coffee and cigars but they ordered champagne and when we saw that we were fairly in for it we accommodated ourselves to circumstances and of course a jolly night ensued. The health of the Queen was drunk about twenty times each with three cheers and the smashing of glasses, the health of the Emperor Alexander ditto. Toast and sentiment followed with so much rapidity that after singing 'For we are jolly good fellows' (which by the way amused the Russians very much) it was discovered that our Ruski friends had got very drunk and as for the British a great many had headaches next morning. We wished to pay for this or at least a share, but the Russians would not hear of such a thing. I think their hospitality must have cost them something like £10 or £15. Not bad fellows, who would have shot any of us with great pleasure a month before. Next morning to my surprise I discovered a large swelling on my horse's back having been caused by a beautiful saddle which I had borrowed for the trip. It was at once evident that my humanity could never allow me to put the saddle on his back for two or three days. Of course here was a fix. How was I to get back? Fortunately my horse had kicked one of my companion's horses so of course he was lame, we after consoling him the best way I could we agreed to coach it to Baktchi-serai and let our horses run behind. When the said coach turned up at the Inn door it proved to be a four wheeled covered cart drawn by four ponies abreast. We rather grumbled at this turn-out but it was no use so in we got and after a most extraordinary smashing, crashing, shaking kind of ride we landed in safety at our old quarters in Baktchi-serai. This night the Commandant, much to our disgust, forgot his illustrious visitors and we had to content ourselves with a 'soft plank' for a bed. I slept very well however and next morning when I was roused to allow an old woman to sweep the floor I could scarcely believe I had been asleep. Next day it was coach again and after travelling over a road still rougher than that of yesterday I was very glad to find myself once more safe in my hut in the evening, having enjoyed myself for four days in glorious style, but still resolved not to travel in the Crimea any more until I take a trip to Balaclava to be followed by a trip across the Black Sea. Now I must draw to a close. I hope you are all as well as I am and I am sure I could not wish better health. Please do not write any more to me until I tell you as we may be moving soon. Remember me to all my friends, Mother, Aunt, etc. Thank Dr Pirie for his letter. I shall write him soon.

My dear Father,

As the mail did not go off yesterday I could not keep my usual time
of writing but as I am not far behind it I hope you will not be uneasy
and will forgive my apparent neglect. I fear you will be imagining that by
this time I am on my way home but it is not so, I am still in the old hut.
I know you will all be very anxious to know when I am to leave this. In
this letter I propose to tell you all my ideas on the subject. The 17th Regt
or as I may say my 'old regiment' expected to have started for Canada
about the end of last month. The Colonel in order to do a sharp thing
wrote to Constantinople to have all the letters for the Regiment stopped
there and the result has been that I have never got a newspaper or letter
for the last three weeks. However that can't be helped and as I am not
inclined to imagine all sorts of evils have happened to you at home – as
Mother does if one of my letters is a little behind time. I must believe,
that no news is good news, that you are all well and that my letters
'canna be lost' and will cast up by and by. All the Canadian regiments
have left now and the 17th embarked on the 8th inst. They all seemed
very glad that they were going to such a nice station. I must say I almost
felt sorry I was not going with them. Since they went one regiment (3rd
Buffs) have gone to Corfu. And two or three more are going off in a
few days for Corfu or Malta. (40th, 68th, and 14th.) Since the 17th left
I have been rather busy and have not missed them much. I am still in
my hut all alone. If I did not see others going off I would never think of
leaving myself. I tried very hard to get the Pathological Board broken
up at the end of last month and at one time I thought I would be on
my way to England by this time but as am not my own master, here I
am still. One of our members belonged to the 89th Regt and when it
embarked for Canada he had to go with it, leaving only Dr Home (the
president) and myself to do the work. We thought of course this was
the first step to a dissolution followed by being ordered to England,
and Dr Home proposed this to Sir John Hall who had no objections
whatever to offer. We wound up the affairs of the concern and in fact I
was begun to pack up when we were informed that the Board was not to
be broken up yet and that we were still to go on as usual. All I could say
was 'Well I'm blowed, what a sell.' And began work again with as good
a grace as I could. It was I must say rather provoking but it was no use

grumbling. I am very busy and as happy as I could wish to be. I do not intend however to let the subject drop. At the end of the month again I shall call on Sir John Hall KCB, and if he still says that he cannot let me go I have a very good mind to put in for 'urgent private affairs' such as 'coming of age,' or 'having fallen heir to an estate' (I wish I had). The 'sick dodge' would be 'no go' for I am in such rude health it would be quite an absurdity to attempt such a thing. Well what's the odds? A month or two in the Crimea does not matter much so it would be useless to vex myself about getting away. I am sorry to inform you that the 'Royal Exchange of Montrose' has never appeared yet in Balaclava Harbour, and in consequence I have not got my boots. No great matter I have received the box from Wooler which was a great treat, full of eatables, the most of them in a good state of preservation. If I did not spoil my stomach with them it's a pity that's all, but I won't tell you definitely whether I did nor not in case you should call me a baby instead of a 'Crimean Hero' which would be rather a down-come. Since writing you last we have had beautiful weather. I have enjoyed a great many beautiful rides and boating excursions in the Harbour of Sebastopol, visiting Fort Constantine, etc., etc., fraternising with the Russians who still keep their character of being very jolly sort of fellows and always lots to drink beside them. Isn't it romantic, only think of a spree in Fort Constantine. The Sardinians have very nearly all embarked now and the French are embarking as fast as they can. The English with their large Transport Fleet seem to be embarking very slowly. We expect to be all out of this before another two months are over. When an English regiment does embark it does so very quickly, the men march down to Balaclava in the morning, they are all on board ship and the ship may be out of Balaclava harbour in less than half an hour. Although there is every prospect of me moving very soon I shall not promise to write oftener than I used to do, so you must not be disappointed. I received a letter from Dr Pirie a week or two ago and shall write him next week so you will hear if I expect any change before the end of the month. In my last I mentioned that I would not expect a letter from home after this but as I have had a slight taste of that sort of thing just now you must tell my two faithful correspondents to begin again, in case I should be moved, to write me only once a fortnight and address to Staff Asst. Surgeon Balaclava PO. Should I have left I will leave word with the Postmaster to send off after me. I wish it to be kept in mind that these fortnightly letters must be very long ones, ten pages at the very least. I am sorry I have no news to give you this time and I fear I must draw to a close. I won't forget the Maltese lace should I call at that port, so Mother and Anne may keep their minds easy. I wish very much to know what Aunt would like me to bring home to her and I hope I will hear in the next letter. I hope you are all well. Remember me to Mother, Aunt, Anne, cousins and other friends too numerous to mention. Hoping to have my letters soon not to mention newspapers. Only think of being these weeks behind the world in news.

My dear Anne,

Here I am again all alive and kicking, still in the Crimea, day of
writing come round again and blow me if I know what to write about.
Since writing last I have received a letter from Mother dated 15th April.
It was rather long on its way as it was addressed to the 17th Regt. I
suspect it had been kept at Constantinople, then gone on to Malta,
and from thence found its way up here. As for the rest of my letters I
think I may expect to get them in about six months for I feel sure they
have all gone to Canada. One letter from home in about six weeks is,
I must say, rather slow work, still I must not grumble, it could not be
helped. I must just fancy you are all well and rejoice over this letter I
have got. I was very glad to hear that Mr Millar had turned up at last
and that you had got the bear skin. It is no great thing but I hope you
are pleased with it. I do not remember what was in the parcel besides
the skin but I suppose you understood all. If you did not you must wait
till I come home. So you thought Miss Alexander wished to pay you a
visit. I cannot say whether she did nor not but I fully agree with Mother
that a visit from my Wooler friends would be best when I was at home,
whenever that may be. They are kind beyond measure still I think you
would find it difficult to cause visitors whom you had never seen. I am
quite amused with Mother her servants seem always to come to grief
in some way or other. I hope the thumb is better now and Abigail able
for her work. Mother asks me what I think of Miss Luckie's marriage?
I think she will find all my opinion in another letter. I think it is a lucky
match for both parties. I was very glad to hear that Father had such an
easy time of it in the shop, as actually propose to visit me. With regard
to fishing and what bait would be most suitable I am at a loss to answer.
Very few of our people ever try such a thing. The French are always busy
in the Tehernaya and in the harbour of Sebastopol. The fish caught are
very small and chiefly of the mullet kind, very little pleases a Frenchman.
It is quite amusing to see his eyes sparkling as he hooks up a minnow
or stickleback, as well pleased as if it were a 20lb fish. There is a saying
and a very true one 'A Frenchman can live luxuriously where a darkey
would starve.' I do not think Father would like this kind of fishing. He
must just wait till I come home when I will enjoy a day's fishing very
much. As I talk about 'when I come home' you will naturally ask when

is that? I cannot tell you yet. I may as well tell you all I know. At present I am busy with the report of last month and taking things easy it will not be finished before ten days. Well if at that time Sir John Hall says that as the Army is now broken up we can go to England – good – we go – if he tells us to continue on still, we may stay all this month. I do not think there is any probability of remaining on here beyond the first week of July. I am quite indifferent about it, determined to take things as they come and in fact a week or two does not make much odds in the long run. If I got my choice I would prefer hearing this on the first week of July. I will tell you why. Part of our pay out here we get in the shape of field allowance, being about £11 per quarter, paid on the 1st July. If I am in the Crimea on that day I get £11, should I leave the day before I lose it – d'ye see? I doubt if you do. Since my last letter I have changed my place of abode and have left my old hut for good and all. I was very unwilling to do so but the rats compelled me to do so whether I would or not. For a long time before Gibaut went away the rats used to run about outside the hut but were too polite to come in, latterly however all their sense of politeness wore off and besides making large burrows into and under the hut they became very impudent and used to have large evening parties and committee meetings under the tables after I had gone to bed. I could not sleep and often I had to rise and clear the place. I used to strike out right and left with a large stick, killed some and wounded others. The killed were all right enough but the wounded in order to have their revenge crept into all sorts of out of the way corners and died. When a mouse gets shut into a drawer or chest and dies you know the smell it makes, just imagine six rats about the size of small cats rapidly undergoing decomposition. When the weather is very hot and often 86 degrees in the shade, you can image the cause of my leaving my hut. The hut I have removed to is a very nice comfortable small one which was built by the Surgeon of the 57th and his Regt went off to Malta a week ago I took possession and am very well pleased with the change. It is more solidly built than mine was, is nice and cool for summer and not a single rat near it. Huts are not worth much more now and are to be had in all directions simply for the taking, in fact all that are not occupied are being pulled down and as whole camps are disappearing and men becoming fewer and fewer the place has a very desolate look now. All the regiments for the Mediterranean stations have gone off now, and regiments for England will begin to embark I believe this week. The Guards go first then the Rifles followed by the 7th Fusiliers,

23rd ditto, rest of Light Division, Highlanders, and it is difficult to say but we may be all out of this before another month is over. Dr Erskine's regiment (the 4th) has left the front and is now stationed at Balaclava where I believe his is in a very good hut. All the store keepers and army followers are beginning to consider their trade gone and are now taking themselves off. Balaclava and Kamish are busy places and things are now selling very cheap – cheap from a Crimean point of view. Beer 1/- per bottle and such like. When the 57th left I fell heir to a lot of cocks and hens, which are a great amusement to me and supply me with no end of pancakes and egg-flips. The latter when cold are very acceptable in this weather. What a curious country this is, thermometer below zero in the winter and something near the boiling point in summer. In my hut I have a nice large window which I always keep open and which looks down upon something like green grass, it is so pleasant to sit as I am doing now in a hot stewing day, almost in a state of nudity, fortunately there are no ladies passing so no one's feelings can be shocked. Oh isn't it jolly when you can dress and do as you like? I think I have now talked enough nonsense for a fortnight so I shall draw to a close. Hoping this will find you all well. With kindest love to Father, Mother, Aunt etc. Remember my health at supper on the 16th inst.

My dear Father,

Since writing to Anne a fortnight ago very little indeed has taken place here. I have received no letters from home which I can assure you is a great blank to me indeed, it is true I have received two or three newspapers but even the red sealing wax did not make up for the want of a letter. Had the mail come in today I expect I would have got a letter but that event has not come to pass as yet so I must just live in hope till to-morrow. Within the last fortnight a great number of regiments have left for England. The first Division including the Guards is gone and the Light Division also. The remains of the second will be off tomorrow, the fourth is extinct, and all that remains now of the 'old British Camp before Sebastopol' is the 18th (Royal Irish) and one or two battalions of the land transport corps. The camps of the Regts that are gone look very desolate, a few of the best wooden huts were taken down and sent to Malta, by far the greater number were left. As all our fellows left with a very strong impression that they would never require their huts in the Crimea again everyone tried to destroy everything as much as he could, smashing windows and unroofing huts during the day and having large bonfires during the night. The night before last I counted no less than 10 large fires blazing all over the camp, last night although it was Sunday a large fire was blazing in the light division all night. Since all the Regts have gone you will naturally think I can have nothing to do and I can with safety say that such is the case. I have only had one case this month and it is very improbable that I can have another.

I have not been altogether idle for I have been very busy writing and finishing off all our reports, they will be all finished tomorrow and then I will have nothing to do whatever but wait with patience until I am ordered home, which I strongly suspect will be before the end of the month. While I am writing Dr Home has gone over to headquarters to ask Sir John Hall what we are to do now or if we are to be sent home immediately. I shall not finish my letter until he comes back and then I shall put in a PS, to tell you what the old fellow has got to say for himself or for us. In the meantime I can tell you that we have at present as broiling hot weather as an Indian with a moderate development of covetousness could wish for. The result is is that the heat of the day is spent very listlessly indeed. In the cool of the evening we have long walks or rides.

We spend the time the best way we can and as things are at present that is not at all difficult to do pleasantly. You will, I am sure, say I am fond of changes when I again tell you I have again changed my habitation. I am now in a beautiful cool wooden hut close to Dr Home's. It is not at all excavated like my former ones and is therefore much cooler. In this hut I intend to remain until I get my final orders to quit which I could easily do any day at half an hour's notice. My kit is not a very large one now, the most of the things which I shall take with me shall be on my back, and then for an outfit in London or wherever I land. By the way I wish you would tell mother and Aunt to be getting some of my white shirts and socks ready so that they can be sent to London whenever I tell them to do so. At present I have not a single white shirt. I suppose these things are still worn in civilised society. I must once more take to 'stiff fronts' and 'stick ups', cut throat collars. This last expression puts me in mind of a very serious case which occurred here about ten days ago. Do you remember me mentioning the name of Dr O'Connor when I went first to Kulalie? He was PMO before Dr Tice came to take charge. He had been up here some four months, had very little to do I fancy. I suppose to amuse himself in the long evenings he had taken to drinking rum and water, rather more of the former than the latter, took the DTs, and cut his throat with one of his own instruments, leaving a wife and three children to the care of the government. Rather a poor way to go out of the world. Although a simple, good natured Irishman he was not a man one could admire.

I suppose you see by the date of this letter what an important day of the year it is. I have no doubt you will all be drinking my very good health at home tonight and I hope I may soon be with you all once more. How time flies. It appears that it is about time I was beginning to think seriously what I intend to do. I do not consider that the last two years have been altogether lost to me. I feel that I would not have missed seeing what I have seen for any sum of money and only regret that I was not with the Army from the very first. Oh, how splendid it would have been to have shared in the victories at Alma and Inkerman, but it could not be helped. I have no doubt it was all for the best. I am sure it will be a very difficult matter for me to do. When I do once more come under petticoat government I hope they will not be too severe upon me but will deal gently at first. Since I cannot learn that you are all well I must just hope that you are and adopt as my motto that no news are good news. As you wished for roots of plants I have made a small collection such as they are and will bring them home with me, you need not be telling anyone about them for they are no great things, after all, and, if I mistake not, I have seen them all as natives either wild or cultivated in Scotland. Now I fear I must bid you goodbye. I am sure you cannot expect either a long or an interesting letter when I have nothing new to talk about. You will be anxious to know when I am moved so I will promise to give you a note every week. Dr Home has come home but no news. Kindest love to Mother, Aunt and Anne.

CHAPTER 9

Home to Britain

———

My dear Father,

In my last letter I think I told you that I intended to remain in my new hut until I was ordered home but the camp got quite deserted, as a matter of safety we were ordered down here where we are stationed on a most beautiful spot overlooking Kordikoi (?) and Balaclava. We came down yesterday and had just got our tents set right when we received notice that we are to appear in orders today and start for England in two or three days. I do not intend this for a letter but will perhaps write you next mail again. Dr Erskine's regiment left for England yesterday or leaves today. I think I will be sent home by the 'Foyle' or the Resistance. What kind of vessels they are I do not know.

Saturday morning.

HMS RESISTANCE, CONSTANTINOPLE
MONDAY 7TH JULY 1856

My dear Father,

You see at last I am on my way home. I embarked on board the Resistance at Sebastopol on Wednesday last, we sailed to Kasatchi. On Friday evening we left the Crimea and arrived at this place yesterday morning after a most beautiful quiet, smooth passage across the Black Sea. I am happy to say I enjoyed it very much and was not at all seasick. I have not time to give you a long story just now. I merely drop this note to tell you I am on my way. We are to proceed on our voyage this afternoon. I shall write from Malta where we are to spend two or three days. Hoping you are all well.

My dear Father,

I arrived here last night after a very slow but very fine passage from
Constantinople. We had two or three days of very rough weather off
Cape Matapan when I must say I felt decidedly squeamish and had to
keep my bed as the only comfortable place I could find. At this I was
not in the least surprised but was rather disappointed I was so very ill
on this voyage. After rounding Cape Matapan we had something like
a dead calm for a week. The sea was like a lake. I commenced to write
a long letter a few days ago and intended giving you a long account of
the voyage but the good intentions I am sorry to say broke down, you
must now have patience until I get home when I shall spin you a yarn.
To write on board is no easy joke, there is always a noise and row going
on together with considerable motion and a feeling as if your head
was undergoing a process of churning. In this condition it is not very
pleasant to sit down to a long letter so you must excuse me. I expect we
will be here for two days as we have some cargo to board during which
time I shall have an opportunity of seeing all that is to be seen. We could
have had a far quicker passage in a steam vessel and in that case I might
have been able to say when I would land in England, in the present state
of things I am unable to say. Our journey is divided into three parts of
nearly equal lengths. We have only completed one now and have taken
three weeks to do so. If we get home at the same rate that we have
been going you may expect to hear from me in England in about six
weeks from this date. We expect however to drop into Gibraltar. If so
I shall write from that place. We are not very sure where we shall land
in England, at present our orders are for Portsmouth. I enclose a list of
all the things which I might wish to send me to London where I may
get it when I arrive. I shall put up at the New Opera Hotel, Bow Street,
Covent Garden. Please prepay the carriage and mark on it 'to be left till
called for'. I have of course no news and excuse a long [letter] and be
content with a simple intimation that I am quite well and hope you are
all the same.

My dear Father,

After being again 18 days at sea here we are at the far famed rock of Gibraltar and I am happy to say we have got over the longest two thirds of our voyage. The voyage from Malta to this place was a very nice one and we had light winds and a calm sea the whole way. It is true we have been going at a snail's pace but still I would rather take that than suffer from seasickness and always in fear of the next big wave coming, as you will remember was the case when fishing at Broughty Ferry Castle. I am in robust health and as jolly as you could wish me to be and only wish I could be assured you were all the same. It is a long time now since I heard from home. As for a description of Gibraltar and the other places which I have seen during my Mediterranean voyage you must have patience until you see me when I guess I shall spin you a yarn for I consider myself a bit of a sailor barring a little seasickness now and then. When you receive this I wish you all to write a long epistle and tell me all the home news for the last three months. Please address to the care of my agents (Messrs McGregor). I shall be sure to call them first. It will be so jolly to hear from home. I am still very comfortable aboard and when we land at Portsmouth I intend to pop up to London and see if I can get leave which I expect to do immediately and then home for Dundee. Do not be too sure however I may not get leave so soon as I expect. However look on the bright side of the picture at present and you may expect to see me and my little Ruski dog cast up at Burnhead House some fine evening asking for lodgings and good treatment which I have no doubt we shall both get. I have nothing new to tell you, have merely sent this to show you where I am. So good bye.

PS. We sail again in the afternoon.

My dear Father,

After a voyage of 19 days from Gibraltar here I am once more on English soil and expect to be home very soon now. I have not reported myself yet and of course can tell you nothing about leave or when you may expect us home. I shall drop you a note from London as soon as I know. The voyage from the Crimea although it has been a very long one (63 days) has been I must say a very jolly one and I have never been what you would call regularly seasick. The Bay of Biscay is rather a rough and tumble kind of place and the old tub did roll furiously but I was not sick. I am wishing very much to hear from home and expect to find letters waiting for me in London. I hope you are all well. I have landed from the vessel at Ventnor in the Isle of Wight and am in Portsmouth.

My dear Father,

Burns says something about 'the plans of mice and men'; certainly my plans at present have gone 'aglee'. Here I am stuck in Portsmouth doing duty at the Marrison Hospital. Isn't it an awful sell? However it can't be helped and in order to make myself jolly under the circumstances I propose to tell you in this note how this happened and in my next letter when I have more time I shall give you a long screed about the voyage and things in general. When I arrived here as I was in medical charge of the troops I had to go and report my arrival to a Dr Bell who is the PMO here. He is an old Scotsman and a very civil old fellow to boot. He comes from Edinburgh and we soon got into a long talk. I told him I was so very anxious to get home that I would do anything to attain my object. He told me that as for leave just now it was no use asking for it as there are great changes taking place and a lot being put on half pay. The Director General is in no good frame of mind and if I asked for it he might put me on half pay or give me a flat refusal, in all probability the latter, and the best thing to do at the present time was to quietly remain with him and he would do what he could for me. As the getting leave is highly problematical he has promised to put me in charge of the depot of the 21st Regiment which has every chance of being sent to Scotland soon when I shall go with it, or if I do not get to Scotland on duty that way he is to try and get me exchanged for an Assistant Surgeon in Glasgow, in fact he was such a jolly old fellow I took his advice and here I am a gentleman at large, in respectable lodgings, with a front door and brass knocker. I must say I am disappointed but I suppose it can't be helped. When I only get some letters from home I shall be quite contented, I have sent for my box in London, I shall write you in a day or two again. Love to all.

My dear Father,

A soldier's life is a very curious one. Here I am again changed. When you write me you must address me 'Fort Pitt, Chatham', there I am to proceed tomorrow. I was very much surprised when I was at Hospital this morning to get an order from the Director General to proceed immediately to Chatham for duty there and of course I must go. I intend to start tomorrow for London and spend Sunday with my friend John Alexander and report myself at Fort Pitt on Monday morning. As good luck would have it Dr Taylor (who is the PMO at Chatham) and I are great friends and I shall see what he can do for me in the way of getting leave. I must say I am very much disgusted not having been able to come to Scotland but still I look upon it as a thing that can't be helped. So I must just make the best of it, be happy under the circumstances and hope it is all for the best. As for resigning my commission and coming home immediately I do not wish to do so until I have time to look about me. If I did so without thinking well over it I might take a step which I might repent all my life. At any rate we must have a little patience and be as jolly as possible in the meantime. I shall write to you in Chatham and tell you how I get on.

Oh I was so glad this morning when I received from my agent in London three letters he had for me, two from Mother and one from Anne, one of Mother's is a very old one dated April 28th, the other two dated August 23rd and were enclosed in one envelope. It is useless saying how glad I was to hear that you were all well. As for Anne's toothache I am sorry to say I can sympathise with her, for two of my teeth have been a great annoyance to me since I left the Crimea. I am so unsettled at present that to give you an account of the voyage would be a great task to me, however I have notes of all my proceedings and I shall tell you all some day. I am sure I am much obliged to the Misses Sime and all the rest of my kind friends who are asking for me, it would be a great pleasure for me to see them as it would be for them to see me. I have got poor little 'Ruski' beside me but how I am to get to Scotland is rather a puzzle. I suppose that can be done some way or other by and by. Living on shore and in civilised society seems very curious to me but I am becoming accustomed to the soft beds and pillows which at first I could not put up with, it was with the greatest difficulty I could sleep at all the first three nights. Portsmouth is a very curious place and seems to be composed of fortifications, drawbridges and ditches. I have not seen much of it but still quite enough. The Isle of Wight is I think the most beautiful place I ever was in. I am not at all surprised the Queen having a palace there. The letters which I write now you must think careless ones but really I am in such an unsettled state to write a few lines to tell you where I am is about all I can do, so you must excuse me and I will promise to be a good boy when I settle down somewhere. I am of course very well and in high spirits, in fact I never let these go down.

Kind love to Mother etc.

I am YMAS [Your Most Affectionate Son] DG

PS. Many thanks to Mother and Anne for their very kind letters, as for my absence they must just make up their minds to it as a good thing for if I come home direct from the Crimea I might fall in love and get married and so make an awful fool of myself.

My dear Father,

On Friday last I wrote you from Portsmouth that I had been ordered to this place and here I am at last. I left Portsmouth on Saturday morning and arrived in safety in London where I found my friend John Alexander waiting for me. I went to his lodgings and remained with him till this morning and then came down here. He was very glad to see me in fact he did not know what to make of me he was so kind. As the little Ruski dog was rather a bother to me while I was being changed about from place to place I left him with Mr Alexander who has kindly volunteered to see him safe on board the steamer for Dundee and you may expect to see him very soon. I am not put on duty here yet but I shall begin tomorrow, not at Fort Pitt as I expected but at the Garrison Hospital which is near Brompton Barracks. I suppose that is all Hebrew to you. I saw the Principal Medical Officer immediately on coming down here. I am sorry to say there is not the least chance of me getting leave at present, not for a month at least. Such being the case what would you advise me to do? I like the Army well enough but I know you wish me to come home and settle and if I am to do so there is no time like the present, because just now I have the éclat of the war which in six months or a year might wear off and it would not tell us much then. If I am to settle how would Dundee answer and how would Burnhead House do for practitioner's dwellings? I have asked you these questions because I have not the slightest idea how things stand in Dundee. You may have ideas on the subject which may settle my wavering mind. Do not of course mention this beyond the family circle but I feel at present that whatever you advise me to do I shall do it. Perhaps you would advise me to remain in the Army, or would you advise me to wait until I get leave and then look about me and see how things stand. As I am going out to drive with a friend here I have no time to write more. Get Mother to write me a long letter with all the pros and cons of the questions.

My dear Mother,

I have just had a long chat with my old friend Mrs Tice, she was of course asking kindly for you all and wondering very much why I had not been home on leave yet. She is quite well and so is her husband who is stationed here at present. I received your very kind enigmatical letter yesterday and acting on your advice to try and get home as soon as I could I went to see Dr Taylor the Principal Medical Officer in Chatham and acting on the 'urgent private affair' matter, I succeeded in getting him to promise to send my application to the Director General if Dr McLern – who is the PMO at the Garrison Hospital – would recommend it. When I made my request to Dr McLern he seemed to have the greatest difficulty in understanding why I would wish for leave as he had been 28 years in the service and had never asked for leave. I stuck to my point however and after threatening to resign my commission he signed my leave this morning. Dr Taylor will sign it today, the Commandant here will sign it, then the Director General, then the Adjutant General at the House Guards, and then I expect to get it in four or five days. If all these swells sign it you may expect to see me next week some time.

I have put in for two months but I do not know if I shall get so long. Do not at the same time be too sanguine for I may fail after all. However I hope not.

Chatham I still consider a dull place, although races are going on here they do not amuse me a bit – not being a racing man.

I expect to hear from Anne some time some of these days and I hope her letter will contain a lot of news. I think I have said my say and must now shut up, so with kind love to all.

At this point the letters from Dr David Greig ceased. The following two letters confirm that Greig resigned his commission on 25th November 1856 and returned home to Dundee, Scotland.

Sir,

*Your great exertions as a member of the Pathological Board in the
Crimea having been represented to the Secretary of State for War, I have the
gratification to inform you, by the desire of Doctor Smit, that his Lordship has
been pleased to sanction the issue of £50 to you as a gratuity on account of these
services, and Sir John Kirkland has been authorised to pay the same.*
I am
Sir
Your Obedient servant
D Dumbreck
Dept 7, Inspector General.

TO DR D GREIG, LATE STAFF ASSISTANT SURGEON ETC,
HIGH STREET DUNDEE
NB

Hospital Staff.
Assistant Staff Surgeon
*David Greig MD has been permitted to resign his commission dated 21st
November 1856.*

ARMY MEDICAL DEPARTMENT
25TH NOVEMBER 1856
Sir,

*I have to inform you that the memorandum named above appeared in the
Gazette of the 21st instant.*
I have the honor to be, Sir,
Your Most obedient humble servant
A Smith,
Director General.

CHAPTER 10

Return to Scutari, 1890

Dr David Greig returned to Dundee where he became a distinguished surgeon at the Dundee Royal Infirmary whilst also maintaining his military connections with the Forfar Rifles for many years. The census of 1881 shows that he married in 1858 and had seven children: two daughters and five sons. His son, also called David, followed in his father's footsteps to become a surgeon in Dundee. In March 1890 Greig returned to the Crimea, Scutari and Constantinople, writing home one final time. This last letter in the collection is a wonderful postscript to the story of Greig's journey and fascinating experiences in the Crimea. He died the following year, 1891, aged just 58.

CONSTANTINOPLE REVISITED
MARCH 1890

Within the last thirty years I may say the place and people have changed very much. The City is improved but still bears the palm for filth, dogs and bad streets, while the people have become much less Oriental both in dress and habits. Even the women have changed in wearing the veil, you see very few wearing the veil, as of old when nothing was seen but the two eyes, now many expose the entire face and even the most rigid seem to cover it only with thin transparent gauze generally with a flowered pattern on it.

Thirty years ago every man you met was smoking the long Chibouk pipe, this visit I never saw a pipe of this kind, all were smoking the modern cigarette. I mention these as striking incidents of how manners have changed in old Constantinople.

We paid, to me, a most interesting and impressive visit to the grave-yard at Scutari, like everything else it too had changed. Formally it was a rough bit of ground on a small headland overlooking the sea at Marmara, now it is transformed into a beautiful garden cemetery having in its centre a very noble granite monument erected by 'Queen Victoria and her people' to the memory of those who died at Scutari Hospital during the Crimean War. At each angle of the monument stands an angel with a palm branch in one hand and a laurel wreath in the other. The calm celestial look of these figures, the quiet of the place and the sad memories of the place thirty-five years ago made a deep impression on me and I felt I would have liked to have been alone with my own thoughts for a quiet half hour. Dr Alexander Struther's tomb is half hidden by a large cypress tree whose branches I had to hold aside till I could read the inscription on it. Dr Watson's was more exposed, some pretty flowers were growing round it and on it were two wreathes of flowers (metal) sent by someone at home as a token of silent sorrow for one they loved. As I stood by the grave I could not but remember the last time I was on that spot when having buried the last of my two friends and the few mourners had left the grave, I stood alone and looked across the Sea of Marmara and with a very, very full heart thought of home. I remember too I felt ill and likely to break down, for although I did not know it the fever was already on me. I gathered some cypress twigs and flowers as memorials of my visit and left the cemetery very much impressed and yet very pleased with my visit. On Thursday forenoon we had a sail up the Bosphorus to the Black Sea and back. It was a fine forenoon but as the wind was from the north it was rather cold. We had to wait an hour at Belo so we took a *caique* and were rowed across to Kulalie to see my old quarters there. Kulalie was changed also. The whole barrack building had been lately white, or rather yellow washed, giving it the appearance as if it was a new building and not the old place. It is occupied by Turkish soldiers. I was anxious to see the room in which I lay between life and death for a week, but, as the Commanding Officer was not in the Barracks, no one would take the responsibility of allowing a foreigner into the building, so I had to be content with a look up at the window. We visited the graveyard where many of my former patients, both Russian and English, sleep quietly side by side. It is a desolate place and I must say I am thankful I am not lying there as I had at one time every prospect of doing. There are about 600 graves but only three of these are marked by any memorial whatever. A Dr Thomson, a Sergeant Douglas of the Rifle Brigade, and a nurse. All the others are already unknown graves.

We left Constantinople on Thursday evening about 7.30, arriving on Sunday morning at Budapest – Hungary, 30th March 1890.

David Greig

Chronology of the Crimean War

1853

8 June	British fleet leaves Malta for eastern Mediterranean.
2 July	Russian army crosses Pruth River to invade Moldavia and Wallachia.
14 October	British and French fleets anchor in Dardanelles.
23 October	Turkey declares war on Russia.
30 November	Massacre at Sinope; Turkish flotilla sunk.
24 December	Sir James Graham(first Lord of the Admiralty) calls for destruction of Sevastopol.

1854

3 January	British and French fleets enter Black Sea.
11 January	Russia warned that warships in Black Sea must return to Sevastopol.
13 February	Cabinet approves Lord Raglan's appointment as Commander in Chief of British Expeditionary Force.
22 February	First troops leave Great Britain.
26 March	First French troops leave for Turkey.
27 March	France declares war on Russia.
28 March	Britain declares war on Russia.
8 April	British and French troops in Gallipoli.
22 April	Naval bombardment of Odessa.
29 April	Raglan arrives in Constantinople.
11 May	Siege of Silistria commences.
29 May	British troops sail for Varna.
22 June	British Navy blockades the White Sea.
23 June	Siege of Silistria raised.
2 July	Russian troops leave Moldovia and Wallachia.
16 July	Raglan receives Cabinet orders to invade Crimea.
10 August	Major fire at Varna and outbreak of cholera delays invasion.

24 August	Bad weather further delays invasion.
31 August	British and French naval force attacks Petropavlosk.
9 September	After reconnaissance of Crimean coast Raglan decides on Calamita Bay for landings.
13 September	Eupatoria surrenders.
14 September	Allied landings commence at Calamita Bay.
20 September	Battle of Alma.
23 September	Advance continues southwards – Russian warships sunk to block Sevastopol Harbour entrance.
27 September	Siege of Sevastopol commences.
17 October	First bombardment of Sevastopol commences.
25 October	Battle of Balaclava – Charge of the Light Brigade
26 October	Skirmish at Little Inkerman.
4 November	Florence Nightingale and Doctor David Greig reach Scutari.
5 November	Battle of Inkerman.
14 November	The Great Storm.

1855

5 January	Omar Pasha lands in Crimea with Turkish reinforcements.
25 January	Lord Aberdeen's government resigns.
5 February	Lord Palmerston appointed Prime Minister.
17 February	Russian attack on Eupatoria.
24 February	More Russian ships sunk in Sevastopol harbour.
4 April	Second Baltic fleet leaves Britain.
9 April	Second bombardment of Sevastopol.
22 May	Kertch expedition.
6 June	Third bombardment of Sevastopol.
7 June	Capture of the Quarries and the Mamelon.
17 June	Fourth bombardment of Sevastopol.
18 June	Failed attacks on the Great Redan and Malakov.
28 June	Death of Raglan, who is succeeded by Sir James Simpson.
16 August	Battle of Tchernya.
17 August	Fifth bombardment of Sevastopol.
5 September	Sixth bombardment Sevastopol.
8 September	French Capture Malakov – British fail at the Great Redan.

9 September	Allies occupy southern Sevastopol.
7 October	Combined forces sail for the Dnieper River.
17 October	Capture of Kinburn.
15 November	Massive ammunition explosion in French lines.
25 November	Surrender of Kars.
16 December	Peace plan submitted to St Petersburg.

1856

16 January	Tsar Alexander II accepts peace proposal terms.
29 January	Last major Russian bombardment across Sevastopol Bay from the north.
28 February	Opposing officers meet in Crimea.
30 March	Treaty of Paris signed.
27 April	Treaty of Paris ratified.
12 July	Last British troops leave Crimea.
1 September	Dr Greig arrives in Portsmouth.

Florence Nightingale and Dr David Greig

Although Florence Nightingale will forever be remembered as 'The Lady with the Lamp' it would appear that her presence aboard the *Vectis* was not even worthy of comment in Dr Greig's early letters home. As stories of her achievements at the hospital in Scutari grew, only then did Greig give her brief mentions in his letters, no doubt prompted by correspondence he was receiving from his family. It is worth extracting the relevant sections from Greig's early letters and comparing them with the well documented, and controversial, comments that Florence Nightingale was making at the time.

Mary Stanley, who had become a close friend of Florence Nightingale through their common interest in nursing and hospitals, assisted in the recruitment for the hospital at Scutari, writing: 'All London we scoured for ['nurses'] ... We felt ashamed to have in the house such women as came. One alone expressed a wish to go from a good motive. Money was the only inducement.' Mary Stanley was herself to play a major part in developments at Scutari with Florence Nightingale, and in Dr Greig's time at the hospital.

Thirty-eight 'nurses' were recruited. Miss Nightingale later wrote, 'As to that stuff about "enthusiasm" of the nursing in the Crimean Campaign – that is all bosh, we had, unfortunately for us, scarcely one woman sent out who was even up to the level of a head nurse.'

On 28 October the recruited 'nurses' sailed from Marseilles aboard the *Vectis*, together with Dr Greig and his colleagues. The *Vectis* was a notoriously uncomfortable ship, infested with cockroaches and used mainly for carrying mail to Malta and Constantinople.

Dr Greig, Marseilles, 26 October 1854:

> This town is one of the best we have seen in France it is somewhat like Dundee, but larger, has splendid docks, and of course strongly fortified. We hired a boat and went out to the 'Vectis' this forenoon. She is a splendid steamer belonging to the Peninsular and Oriental Co. and carries the mails from this to Malta, Constantinople and Egypt. We sail tomorrow at 2 o'clock, will call for about six hours

at Malta, and then go direct to Constantinople … and besides we have about two dozen nurses, or rather Sisters of Mercy, from London, going out with us to Scutari.

Miss Nightingale and Dr Greig were both, by their own admission, bad sailors and as luck would have it the ship ran into severe gales the second day out from port.

Miss Nightingale was too ill to even disembark at Malta and wrote of the *Vectis* 'blustering, storming, shrieking' on its way to the Bosphorus.

Dr Greig:

> What a cargo we have, it consists of 18 doctors, from Inspectors downwards to Assist. Surgeons, 48 nurses, – black and white nuns included, Protestants, Episcopalians, and Catholics, Sisters of Mercy, Nurses from the London hospital, etc. I do pity them during the voyage, they are all so sick. When they do get to Scutari or wherever they go, some ladies who are amongst them – even ladies of fortune and title – will, I am sure, very soon tire of their good works.

The *Vectis* anchored off Seraglio Point and on seeing the massive structure of the Barrack Hospital in Scutari, and the appalling condition of the wounded being landed there Miss Nightingale's first impression led her to remark, 'The strongest will be wanted at the wash tub.' Wounded were expected at any time from the Battle of Balaclava fought on 28 October, and the nurses and doctors were ferried across to Scutari in *caiques*, gondola-like rowing boats. They entered the hospital through a large imposing gateway which Miss Nightingale remarked 'should have had a sign above "Abandon hope all ye who enter here".'

Dr Greig:

> What a sight we met when we landed here, a steamer had just arrived from the Crimea with 150 wounded and they were trans-
> porting them from the ship to the hospital on stretchers, carried by four men each. You cannot conceive the feeling I had, the sight of man after man being carried on shore and the same continuing for hours as if it would never cease. This is the work day after day and is performed by convalescents. Talk of large hospitals, I wish our friends in Dundee only saw this one here. It is a large square, as large as the High Street, three flats, and as far as I saw quite

full. The rest of the wounded are in the Barracks which are about a quarter of a mile from the hospital. Oh, what a sight it is, upwards of 2,000 men sick and wounded, I cannot give you the least idea of it and will not try.

Lord Stratford wrote to the Duke of Newcastle that evening saying, 'Miss Nightingale and her brigade of nurses are actually established at Scutari under the same roof with the gallant and suffering objects of their compassion.'

The hospital had severe sanitary problems, was overcrowded and lacking in basic amenities. Many of the soldiers who died there died not of their wounds or the illnesses they arrived with but from diseases contracted in the hospital. Shocking statistics disclosed after the war revealed that sick and wounded men treated in makeshift field hospitals had a better chance of survival than those transferred to the hospital in Scutari. From January to February 1855 it was estimated that the average number of patients at any one time was 2,349; in the same period 2,315 men died, and even this was probably an underestimate.

When the Barrack Hospital became overflowing with cholera cases, and large numbers of new cases with more wounded from the Battle of Alma expected to arrive in a few days, the Turkish Barracks in Scutari were taken over by the army to be used as a hospital facility. However, there was no hospital equipment in the barracks, which were also filthy and in need of extensive repair. Orders were issued to procure all the necessary equipment: bedding, clothing, surgical supplies, etc. Red tape and army procedural failures added to the miserable conditions. One officer would order equipment and as far as he was concerned he had done his duty. The fact the army stores recorded that they had 'none of the items in store' all too often became the end of the process and no further action was instigated. 'Their heads', wrote Miss Nightingale, 'are so flattened between the boards of Army discipline that they remain old children all their lives.'

Miss Nightingale demanded clean bedding, soup, hospital clothing and other basic items which the medical authorities treated with disdain, suggesting that they would 'spoil the brutes'. Even the doctors in Scutari received the news of Miss Nightingale's appointment and demands with outrage. They had suffered the shocking conditions for several months and deeply resented having this society lady and her pack of nurses foisted upon them. On 14 November Miss Nightingale wrote of the doctors, 'Two of them are brutes and four are angels – for this is work which makes angels or devils of men… and as for the assistants, they are all cubs and will while a man is breathing his last under the knife, lament the annoyance of being called up from their dinners by such a fresh influx of wounded.'

Dr Greig's opinion suggests an altogether different picture:

> I have only been once or twice at the General Hospital, all my work is confined to the Barracks and enough I have to do. We go at 9 am to visit our patients, dress the sores, wounds, etc., and work away till about 1pm then we have lunch, at work again till 3, we have dinner at 5, tea at 7, evening visit at 8 and generally go to bed about 11, this is our plan, but we seldom get it carried out, something or other always comes in the way. The work is most pleasant and interesting. The wounds we see here are things we can never see at home; today for instance we had three operations, amputations at the thigh, excision of the shoulder, and amputation of an arm.

On 14 November one of the worst storms in living memory struck Sevastopol resulting in the sinking in the harbour of 21 ships, including several laden with medical supplies for the hospitals, another stunning blow for the hard-pressed medical staff.

Miss Nightingale had access to a large source of funds, obtained from government support and other sponsors and well-wishers. 'I am a kind of General Dealer,' she wrote to Sir Sydney Herbert on 4 January 1855, 'in socks, shirts, knives and forks, wooden spoons, tin baths, tables and forms, cabbages and carrots, operating tables, towels and soap, small tooth combs, precipitate for destroying lice, scissors, bed pans and stump pillows.' As more wounded arrived, she purchased more and more supplies for the hospital wards and the 'Nightingale Power', which initially met with indignation in some military quarters, soon changed to respect as it became known that her actions were fully supported by the War Department.

Dr Greig, now aware of Miss Nightingale's growing reputation, writes:

> By the by if you look in the 'Illustrated London News' for 16th December you will see a view of a part of Scutari Hospital, it is one of the passages and the view is taken from the door of Miss Nightingale's quarters, just where I live. The picture is not good but will give you some idea of the place. The passage is not nearly so high nor so broad, in the centre between the two rows of beds we have only two or three feet, while in the picture you would think

it was eight or ten. You see the first arch crossing over the passage, well, on the right hand side you see a fellow entering or about to enter a door, you may say that is me for he is going into my quarters. The beds are placed close to our doors and of course all the moaning of the patients at nights is heard to the best advantage while we are in bed, in general however, I sleep so sound that that never disturbs me in the least.

Later he writes:

You asked me by the by about Miss Nightingale – when on board the 'Vectis' I did not know who or what she was, but since then we all know her very well. She is a very kind lady and what is more has £8,000 a year which we all joke about here. The nurses are all under her charge, sometimes we get a visit from her in the wards and if a nurse is required for a patient she sends one. At some parts of the hospital they attend every day and dress the patients, but to do that at all the hospitals would require 50 times the number. She keeps strict watch over them and they work very well, but I think just the same could be done by the orderlies which we have always in our wards (soldiers who act as nurses). I had a farce with Miss Nightingale today, she was visiting some of my patients who were very bad and was asking one poor fellow who had got his leg shot off and who was complaining of thirst, if he would like rice water or barley water to drink. He thought for a little and then said, he would prefer brandy and water if it was all the same to her!

Maintaining discipline within the wards was a major part of Miss Nightingale's responsibilities and she was often thought to be callous and self-serving. The situation came to a head when an experienced nurse, Sister Elizabeth, complained that the patients' diet was inadequate. Miss Nightingale refused to change the diet until a senior doctor had visited the wards and recommended increased rations. Sister Elizabeth wrote home detailing the terrible conditions in the hospital accusing the doctors of callousness and inhumanity. The letter subsequently appeared in *The Times* as a letter from a 'heroic nurse' and caused great problems for Miss Nightingale, finally leading to an investigation. However, Miss Nightingale was eventually vindicated and Sister Elizabeth was asked to resign. (Dr Greig too had reason to regret expressing his innermost thoughts in writing to his family when some of his letters appeared in the local and Scottish press at a later date. Even in one of his early letters he wrote: 'Some good folks may be wishing to make extracts from this but I would rather not, more especially anything about the hospital as I might get into trouble about it, so use your discretion.')

Miss Nightingale again felt her position was being undermined when she heard that Miss Stanley was due to arrive in Scutari with a support party of 46 nurses. She wrote a scathing letter to Sir Sydney Herbert. After much hand wringing and political manoeuvring, compromises were reached and Mary Stanley and some of her party were eventually located at Therapia, then the hospital at Kulahli. As fate would have it, a few months later Dr Greig became seriously ill and near to death. He was sent to Therapia where Mary Stanley cared for him, even writing a letter home to his family (letter dated 12 March 1855).